New Theories of Welfare

New Theories of Welfare

Tony Fitzpatrick

Consultant Editor: Jo Campling

© Tony Fitzpatrick 2005

HN
28
F56

First published 2005 by
PALGRAVE MACMILLAN
Houndmills, Basingstoke, Hampshire RG21 6XS and
175 Fifth Avenue, New York, N.Y. 10010
Companies and representatives throughout the world

PALGRAVE MACMILLAN is the global academic imprint of the
Palgrave Macmillan division of St. Martin's Press, LLC and of
Palgrave Macmillan Ltd. Macmillan® is a registered trademark in the
United States, United Kingdom and other countries. Palgrave is a
registered trademark in the European Union and other countries.

ISBN-13: 978 1-4039-0151-4   hardback
ISBN-10: 1-4039-0151-1   hardback
ISBN-13: 978 1-4039-0152-1   paperback
ISBN-10: 1-4039-0152-X   paperback

This book is printed on paper suitable for recycling and
made from fully managed and sustained forest sources.

A catalogue record for this book is available from the British Library.

A catalog record for this book is available from the Library of Congress.

10   9   8   7   6   5   4   3   2   1
14   13 12 11 10 09 08 07 06 05

Printed in China

Contents

Preface and Acknowledgements

One of the greatest and most influential philosophers of the Twentieth Century, Ludwig Wittgenstein, would sometimes advise his students to abandon their studies in favour of something more useful – usually medicine, a profession to which Wittgenstein was himself drawn. His motivation was without malice. Wittgenstein sought to save intellects he admired from drowning in a subject (philosophy) and an environment (academia) within which he felt suffocated and from which he frequently tried to escape. Between 1941 and 1943, for instance, he worked as a dispensary porter at Guy's Hospital, London. But others have preferred a less generous interpretation. Karl Popper accused Wittgenstein of misreading the nature of philosophy, seeing it as linguistic game of intellectual puzzles rather than as something capable of offering insight into real moral and metaphysical problems. Popper was himself being somewhat misleading. Wittgenstein was attempting to dislodge philosophy from the kind of hubristic pedestals constructed by those like his former mentor Bertrand Russell, without necessarily reducing it to the status of a crossword puzzle. If we acknowledge language as a rule- and convention-governed tool (immersed within a particular 'way of life') then we can perhaps distinguish real problems from artificial ones.

Still, I wonder how often Wittgenstein considered other areas of philosophical endeavour. Medicine may be vital, but a considerable amount of research has shown that the effectiveness of doctors, nurses, drugs and machines that go *ping!* depends enormously upon the socioeconomic environment they inhabit. Wittgenstein's stint at Guy's occurred at a time when the profession, and all the other UK public services, were about to experience what might be called a piecemeal revolution. The establishment of the NHS was certainly inspired by a host of non-philosophical matters and yet, amid the bombs, the wreckage and the daily horror, this was a time during which social and political ideas were influencing social policies and public reform to an extent that the UK has rarely witnessed since.

This book is not concerned with that historical anomaly. Instead, it is another volume in my attempt to understand something of those ideas. In developed countries social policy accounts for about half of government

vii

spending and a quarter of national wealth – sometimes more, sometimes less. So when (if?) you vote 50% of what you are voting about is social policy. Yet unless those services have a theoretical and, I will argue, ideological orientation then those votes become the equivalent of shouting into the wind. We need porters, nurses, teachers, social workers, public administrators, etc. etc., but unless we possess some idea of what makes it all worthwhile then we are stumbling around in the dark. This is why the subject continues to fascinate me.

Many thanks to the referees and, as always, to Jo Campling.

List of Figures

Introduction

When he moved into his new home, Gad's Hill Place near London, Charles Dickens had the door to his study disguised as bookshelves. Yet if you looked closely you would see not books but fake spines that Dickens had ordered embossed with humorous titles. The nine volumes of *Cats' Lives* was one, the three volumes of *Five Minutes in China* was another. There was also the multi-volume *The Wisdom of Our Ancestors* which dealt with various subjects; its companion, though, *The Virtues of Our Ancestors*, was confined to just one book so thin that the title barely fitted the spine. As well as being a satirical comment on the Victorian inclination to revere predecessors who were nevertheless regarded as immoral to nineteenth century eyes, the joke, to me, suggests something in addition. Namely, our tendency to view ancestors as being at the summit of a height from which we have fallen *and* as being left behind at the base of a slope up which we are ascending. Ancestors as both our superiors and inferiors.

It was this puzzle that partly compelled me to write a follow up to *Welfare Theory*, one that would flesh out some of the tasters given in its final chapter and elsewhere. Since this text dealt largely if not exclusively with 'classic' theories of social policy I wondered whether there was an audience (and, more importantly, a lucrative market) for more contemporary ideas. The prospect was daunting because while it is just possible to devise a net wide enough to capture the great and the good of yesteryear, how do you snare that which is racing passed you? The answer is, you can do so only imperfectly. Any such summary is necessarily a form of intervention that moulds the reality of what it catches: it is a selection of snapshots. My own voice is more prominent in this book as a result and what you are to read is as much a snapshot of myself: my interests, my reading, my ignorance and my usual bias towards the UK. So as well as receiving an overview of some recent developments you are also invited to disagree profoundly with the positions that I take. In fact if you do not disagree with at least some of what I say then one of us is not doing their job properly – no don't look at me, it's bound to be your fault.

That said, other criteria have helped determine the content. Firstly, and to minimise repetition, I have excluded those areas which slot most neatly into *Welfare Theory* and so would be best left until a second edition of the same. Yet even with this self-discipline I have found it impossible to avoid revisiting such issues as reciprocity, altruism and class. Secondly, I have restricted myself to theoretical developments post-1990, referencing the most up-to-date literature whenever possible, though pre-1990 contributions are obviously brought in when necessary. Finally, I have omitted a treatment of environmentalism since I have little to add to what I have said in other publications for Palgrave (e.g. Fitzpatrick & Cahill, 2002) and there seemed little point in transplantation.

So the overlap between this book and *Welfare Theory* has been kept to a minimum. This means that if you have read the earlier work you will hopefully benefit from reading this one also; if you have not then while what follows tries to be accessible it does assume a degree of familiarity with social and political theory, and welfare policies, that would have to have been acquired from somewhere.

One matter it is worth repeating here concerns my general approach to political and social questions and problems or, to put it more grandly, my worldview. This consists of significant though by no means exclusive reference to ideological ideas, perspectives and influences. Compared to the 1990s, especially after the events of 1989–91, those declaring that 'ideology is dead', or some such, are now less prominent than they were. This may be because the proposition was just dumb to begin with or it may be because they believe the argument to have been won, in which case why bother reiterating it? There are perhaps three principal reasons why ideology is now dismissed by many.

Firstly, by the early 1990s 'discourse' had become a highly fashionable concept and is now an indispensable element of the academic vocabulary (see Chapter 2 also). There are many different ways of defining discourse. Sometimes it is used with reference to Foucault's conception of a system of power/knowledge through which subjectivities emerge; sometimes, it is used as an umbrella term for speech, language and communication. Broadly speaking the term's popularity reflects the twentieth century's linguistic turn away from the naïve belief in the transparency of language, back to a more pre-modern notion that the knowable world is infused with dense meanings that have to be constantly unpacked and interpreted. More specifically, it denotes a way of considering ourselves and our environments as texts, of no longer treating objects as being simply beyond language, as the unqualified origins of a word's meaning. The thing you are sitting on does not determine whether it is a chair, a *chaiere* or a *cathedra*; instead, objects are themselves the appropriations *of* language and so the artefacts of their cultural contexts. The relationship between sign (the unit of meaning) and the referent (the object) is always contingent. At the post-structuralist extreme, even the sign has broken down so that there is no necessary link between the signifier (the sound or image) and the signified (the concept). Signifiers point not to signified nor to referents, but to each other. The resulting stream of signification, the differential interplay of meaning, is what some call 'discourse'.

Ideology can therefore appear to be a hopelessly blunt tool by comparison. On the one hand it makes reference to a form of agency (e.g. the actual proponents of an ideology) that a discourse-inspired analysis breaks down. Actors are simply not the unified, in-control, coherent subjectivities that appear in ideological critiques. On the other, the concept easily collapses into an agentless structuralism where ideologies reside within autonomous systems of which we are the bearers, the functions.

Yet so long as we avoid these twin dangers is there any reason why ideology and discourse cannot be made to work together? For while discourse draws attention to the importance of cultural specificities, constructions and contingencies, ideology is a necessary reminder of how and why the cultural is itself shaped in and through the material. If we are not to treat everything as cultural – since how is this any better than treating everything as material? – then culture and matter must exhibit a mutual irreducibility, i.e. neither can fully explain the other.

As such, ideology becomes relevant again when we realise that the solution to the assumed crimes of essentialism is not a straightforward anti-essentialism but an analysis that is not afraid to re-draw boundaries. Without transgression boundaries become ossified and our intellectual endeavours become inflexible: an ideological analysis then declines into a justification of manifestos, revealed truths and a fanatical search for heretics. Yet without boundaries transgression becomes a self-referential and narcissistic pastime; a kind of intellectual consumerism performed by those more concerned (if they are bothered at all) with the cultural representations of poverty, needs, suffering and domination than with the sheer materiality of such social relations.

Now, please be aware that in this book I have not attempted an analysis that presupposes how the ideological and discursive might conjoin. There is a simple reason for this. The premise of the following is that contemporary theories revolve around the necessity of conjoining the material and cultural while reflecting the difficulty and contestability of doing so. To weld the ideological and discursive together would in a sense be premature, it would imply that I have the solution to what is perhaps the central dilemma of contemporary theory. So while my voice is occasionally noisy in the chapters to come this was a step I was unwilling to take. I return to these points throughout the book and attempt a summing up of this central dilemma in the Conclusion.

The other two reasons for dismissing an ideological approach can be reviewed more briefly. Some insist that ours is a post-ideological age in which pragmatism must rule. We cannot know in advance what kind of building we inhabit, or will inhabit in the future, and so have to construct a kind of intellectual architecture from the bottom-up without a readymade blueprint. Politics is therefore no longer about boxing social reality into the categories translated from an abstract metaphysical realm, but about clearing spaces and allowing new associations to form. Yet this anti-ideology criticism fails on several levels. Firstly, ideology is not necessarily about imposing blue-prints but can also be about orientation and guidance as new models and architectures are composed. Without such orientation a pragmatic approach risks becoming no more than a weathervane to prevailing trends, an altern-ative form of dogmatism that insists the 'real is rational' or 'there is no al-ternative'. Therefore, secondly, a pure pragmatism is already saturated with ideological assumptions and perceptions, whether its adherents care to acknowledge this or not.

A final reason for dismissing ideology involves the insistence that the world itself has moved on. With some form of democratic capitalism being the only game in town there is no room left for ideological contrasts to move. The ideological war is over, even if some minor skirmishes remain, and there are new battles to be fought. Ulrich Beck, for instance, was inspired as much by hostility to a class analysis as fascination with the new hazards illustrated by Chernobyl or Bhopal. Those new battles may involve reference to nationalist and/or religious fundamentalisms that do not accord with ideological tradi-tions. But this argument, too, depends upon a static reading of ideological analysis. To propose that the demise of communism reduces the room for ideological struggle is true only if the political and social space of democratic capitalism is being enclosed in advance, usually by those most vocal in defence of its possibilities and opportunities. In truth ideology need be no more trapped by its traditions than a post-ideological approach – and see the critique of Beck in Chapter 4 and Fitzpatrick (2001a: 187–8); and it is used here to trace the contours of the social field and identity where that field tends towards openness and where towards closure.

So, I am not claiming that an ideological approach is perfect and I do risk appearing a young man (youngish, anyway) imagining he looks cool in his grandfather's clothing. Certainly, an ideological framework cannot do every-thing, but then show me what can. In any event, it is the slant I feel most comfortable with.

What kind of framework is appropriate out of the many to choose from? Freeden (1996), to take one example, distinguishes between cores and periph-eries where each ideological constellation is characterised by a nucleus of ideas and principles that is relatively stable, and a periphery that witnesses the coming and going of more contingent, transitory elements. I decided to explore another method inspired by Freeden's but distinct from it. Recurring at several places throughout this book is a contrast between circumstance, choice and con-sequence. 'Circumstance' refers to the environmental conditions which precede our arrival and out of which we are shaped, the atmosphere we breathe and incorporate as we grow, the social, cultural and economic positions into which we are inserted. 'Choice' refers quite simply to the decisions and actions that originate from us as conscious beings who possess some degree of autonomy. By 'consequence' I mean the immediate effects we have upon one another, the copies of ourselves we leave on our surroundings.

It is trite to observe that none of these reference points is complete without the others. To over-emphasise circumstance is to risk treating individuals as little more than receptacles of their environments, as robots programmed elsewhere; giving too much stress to choice risks ignoring the limits of our autonomy and exaggerating our freedom of movement; an over-emphasis on consequence might risk treating the present as only ever an after-effect of what has gone before. No, the real interest comes from *how* we try to combine these terms, from the weight each is accorded and so the point at which we start. Consider the following diagram.

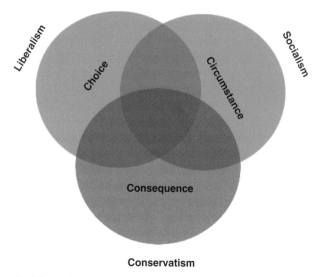

Figure 1   An Ideological Venn Diagram

Socialists are those who start with circumstance, i.e. with the environmental determinants through which we are socialised. This is why socialists have given greatest prominence to a socioeconomic analysis that centres upon, but is not necessarily limited to, class.[1] Liberals are those who start with choice, such that freedom of choice is the default position where the burden of proof is upon those who would limit choice in any way. Conservatives are those who emphasise consequence. Since the effects we have upon one another are so considerable there is a constant need for restraint and self-discipline that comes through an ethic of duty and responsibility.

This diagram is obviously crude. There are many variants of the above ideal-types that are dispersed around the circles and shaded areas, some journeying towards the main shaded area in the middle and some not. A multi-dimensional model would also make room for other spheres, e.g. the feminist emphasis upon gender. Nevertheless, this is the basic framework applied here. The book is therefore informed by three perspectives. Modern conservatism is the heir to the conservative tradition, though one which tends towards the liberal sphere; social democracy is here defined as the descendant of the social or welfare liberalism that flourished at the end of the nineteenth and beginning of the twentieth centuries, one that has veered towards the socialist sphere, though as we will see recent developments have swung it more in the direction of 'consequence' and so a renewed emphasis upon social duties; the 'new radicalisms' are approximate heirs to the socialist tradition, though incorporating a much wider set of theoretical sources and concerns. Modern conservatism, social democracy and the new radicalisms are not to be regarded simply as the contemporary equivalents of their ancestors – as agued above, ideology is more plastic and changeable than this – and nor do they inform each and every one of the following pages, but they are an effective basis for understanding some important new theories of welfare.

This is largely because those new theories have themselves evolved from their older antecedents. To some extent the 'classic' welfare state was what was left in the wake of the great ideological clashes over economic development, political democratisation and social change. It represented a kind of *negative consensus*, the residue our combatants left behind them as they moved on to the new battles inspired by those older wars. State welfare offered something for everyone. For if few people were completely happy with the forms assumed by welfare systems at any one time and place, few people were completely unhappy with them either. As the attraction of that negative consensus has faded – without vanishing entirely – so ideological critique has become more rather than less significant, as competing value-systems attempt to win the kind of all-out victories that the welfare state once stifled. In a post-classic era the terrain may have altered but the progeny of their more elderly adversaries are still very much in evidence.

This basic point is made in Chapters 1 and 2 where we update ourselves on some recent developments and additions to political ideologies. Modern conservatism is defined in terms of its adherence to free market liberalism and libertarianism, and to neoconservatism. The latter has become very fashionable in recent years and we review its key trajectory from Leo Strauss onwards. Social democracy has evolved in several directions. Third Way social democracy has by now been endlessly discussed, though there is also another group of theorists that I gather together as the 'new productivists'. Those further to the Left have also been busy reappraising such issues as equality, redistribution and cultural recognition, and some important contributions are collected together in Chapter 2 under the title of the 'new radicalisms'.

The next two chapters then begin to illustrate what this new terrain looks like. Firstly, there are debates over the meaning and scope of individuality. In Chapter 3 we start by examining the recent interest in agency and its attendant concepts (motivation, reciprocity). Aspects of community were discussed in *Welfare Theory* but we here return to ideas that the earlier book did not have time to analyse: trust, stakeholding and social capital. Theorists of class have sought to revive a reference point that many others have abandoned and attention is given to the recent work of Hardt and Negri. In Chapter 4 we then apply disagreements over individuality in order to explore competing explanations of contemporary insecurities, risks and anxieties. Chapters 3 and 4 are therefore concerned with the freedom of movement which different ideologies attribute to contemporary individuals.

Chapters 5 and 6 then examine two adjacent and ambitious attempts to redefine individuality that challenges many of the (ideological) assumptions of earlier chapters. In Chapter 5 we ponder whether it is possible any longer to locate the critical distance needed to understand the terrain in which we find ourselves. Firstly, do we now live in an information society? We assess the recent responses of Scott Lash and Manual Castells to this question and reflect on the implications for social critique. Secondly, what influences are Information and Communication Technologies (ICTs) having, or are likely to have, for welfare systems? What are the advantages to be exploited and the pitfalls to be avoided? Chapter 6 considers the interface of genes and environments and the claim that because humans are now more capable of 'self-evolution' than ever before the very meaning of identity and the self alters considerably. The potential of biotechnological interventions are reviewed, as are their implications for several policy-related areas.

In both chapters, however, I contend that the more extreme aspects of those radical challenges fail and that the framework sketched out in the earlier chapters – and in this Introduction – is more robust than its critics allow. The remaining chapters then set out to identify where the new social terrain may be said to be relatively open and where relatively closed. After our technological turn Chapter 7 then returns more explicitly to the human scale that debates about ICTs and new genetics sometimes risk drowning. Social psychology has long hovered in the background of social policy and this chapter tries to make its role more prominent. Debates about emotions and emotional labour have become fashionable in recent years and here we appreciate why. The same can be said of the body and we again set out to understand why this is and what it says about the contemporary direction of social policy.

Chapter 8 then turns to the debate about governance that has risen to prominence as old assumptions about state and society have faded. The discussion of governance is specifically directed towards two forms of ambiguity in contemporary society. The first of these is then examined by reviewing a host of ideas relating to crime and criminology; the second by outlining the debates concerning surveillance and surveillance society. If these concerns indicate one possible kind of future for social welfare Chapter 9 begins by outlining some recent contributions that direct attention to the importance of cultural differences and possibilities, giving lengthy consideration to the links between welfare regimes and to multiculturalism. Chapter 9 also reflects on the cultural role of the media and the extent to which the media impacts upon perceptions of welfare and so upon the future direction of social policy.

As I acknowledged earlier, these themes are inevitably rooted in my own obsessions and limitations. There is admittedly a certain arbitrariness to the organisation of this book; its themes could be reshuffled in a number of alternative ways. While the following narrative is a kind of mould I am not claiming that the clay is yet solid and inflexible. I have attempted to be systematic and fair while not seeking to disguise the passions which motivated me to write this book in the first place. Some will also complain, as some complained of *Welfare Theory*, that the following pages attempt to do too much, that the agenda is too crowded. *Mea culpa*. I could spend anywhere between 10–20 years expanding each of the following chapters into a full-length book and still not be able to do them justice. The problem is I was planning to spend that time on other pursuits – you know, mountain climbing, deep-sea diving, television watching, that kind of thing. Besides, I thought that some of you would be inspired to follow through on these subjects, especially if you were able to see them together, in juxtaposition. In any event I have learned my lesson and vow not to let go of your hand as we set off on our tour. Promise.

Best hang on to your hat with your other hand though.

1

Modern Conservatism Versus Social Democracy

Introduction

From the 1940s to the 1960s, in most developed nations, social democracy appeared to be designing the future. *Laissez faire* ideas had died with the depression and then the war as social conservatives turned their boats to a political tide whose destinations were other than those for which they had previously aimed. Even where Right-wing parties continued to be strong (USA, UK, Germany) the initiative seemed to lie with the Left; and although 'consensus' is too facile a description of post-WWII society, the skirmishes between Right and Left rarely erupted into all-out war. By the 1970s social democracy suffered from an excess of failure and of success: the failure to maintain a delicate balance between opposing economic forces; the success of creating new sociocultural relations whose members were rapidly outgrowing the post-1945 settlement. And while destabilising itself social democracy also succumbed to a series of economic shocks and political challenges. By the 1980s the initiative lay with a Right-wing determined to mould the world into an image whose shape would subsequently be made to appear inevitable and unavoidable. This final transformation has arguably been accomplished by social democrats who, faced with the same choice that conservatives had faced a generation earlier, eventually came to play the characters that had been authored by others. The years of and since the 1990s have therefore been curious. Right-wing ideas have dominated and yet the Right itself has sometimes appeared to lack confidence in its domination, convinced that the manoeuvres of the cultural Left (postmodernists, relativists, the politically correct) are subtly undermining the moral values of capitalism.[1] The Left, meanwhile, regained its voice(s) but not without discord between those who

1

would and those who would not echo the economics of deregulation and privatisation.

The story of the 1990s is too vast to be told in a single chapter and we will return, throughout this book, to many of the fronts along which Right and Left continue to clash. The intention below is to sketch some of the recent manifestations in the long-running ideas of Right and Left under the respective headings of 'modern conservatism' and 'social democracy'. I will say more about the Right, partly because it has made most of the running and partly because the next chapter will be dedicated to some recent developments in Leftist thought. Essentially, we will see that conservatives have sought to consolidate the inequalities of free market capitalism, whereas social democrats have sought new forms of equality that tend to eschew the language and many of the traditional implications of egalitarianism.

Modern Conservatism[2]

By conservatism I here refer to the broad spectrum of Right-wing thought (cf. Fitzpatrick, 2001a: 120–8).[3] There are many accounts of conservative ideas on offer (Eatwell & O'Sullivan, 1989; Freeden, 1996: Chs 7–10; Honderich, 2003) but what appears to be central to it is the demand for 'ordered freedom'; the limbs of conservative thought then branch out according to different views of what order and freedom might mean and how they might conjoin.

A brave attempt to identify a core to conservatism has been made by Kekes (1998). According to Kekes conservatism is that which rejects the formation of abstract ideals against which existing society can be compared. Instead, conservatism works from the inside out, exploring that which enables people to lead good lives and seeking to minimise the factors which prevent this from happening. Conservatism certainly offers support to a number of principles (civility, equality, freedom, a healthy environment, justice, order, peace, prosperity, rights, security, toleration and welfare) but refuses to prioritise amongst them. Therefore, conservatism is more of a disposition than a manifesto, one characterised by four general commitments: (1) scepticism towards notions of an ideal society or single good way of life; (2) a certain amount of value pluralism, though falling short of relativism; (3) traditionalism, or the idea that values derive from participation in traditions that both precede and survive us; (4) a constructive pessimism which recognises the failings of human nature and the limits of social action. Conservatism, then, is concerned with the political conditions of the good and so recommends as little interference as possible with individual conduct.

There are several grounds upon which this account can be challenged, though. Firstly, because it characterises conservatism as being opposed to rationalism – the idea that there are secure foundations for knowledge, morality and belief that can be discerned through the use of reason. For while conservatism certainly implies some degree of non-rationalism (Oakeshott, 1962) abstract ideals and rationalistic criteria are by no means alien to it (Pilbeam, 2001). Therefore, many conservatives *do* favour some of the above principles over others depending upon how each might be conceptualised. Secondly, the definition of conservatism as a philosophy of non-interference also captures some but not necessarily all facets of conservative thought. As we will see below, there are conservatives who would interfere continuously to preserve what they consider to be the best life for humanity.

So if it is difficult to compress conservative ideas into a core, we can at least make recent theoretical developments more manageable by distinguishing between the following two schools of conservative thought.[4]

Free market liberals & libertarians

Relatively few innovations have been made here since the halcyon days of Nozick (1974) and Hayek (1982) (see Fitzpatrick, 2001a: Ch. 3). For instance, in recommending that state welfare be replaced by voluntarism and competitive private charities Shapiro (2002) draws upon a familiar litany of claims: inheritance and brute luck ('circumstance') matter little, charitable donations are better than social rights, capitalism permits considerable social mobility, markets are always more efficient than states. It is, though, worth focusing on the contributions of Gauthier (1986) and Narveson (2001).

Whereas Nozick (1989) came to admit that he could not provide foundations for his libertarian principles, failing to develop a convincing account of human nature, Gauthier (1986: 55) believes that we should look to 'mutual agreement' rather than to natural rights for such foundations. Although subjective preferences are paramount he maintains that moral constraints on attempts to maximise those preferences are warranted because they will thereby make us better off. Put simply: individuals are more likely to prosper if they act with a view to the good of others rather than just their own. This doctrine of 'constrained maximisation' therefore implies that a moral sensibility should supplement an instrumentalist (means-end) rationality. The just society would consist of those who contract to that cooperative model. This is a Hobbesian account in that mutual constraint is held to be advantageous rather than inherently right or wrong; what makes it a market liberal one is Gauthier's conviction that communities organised according to the principle of self-interest will yield the greatest advantages because this is in tune with the preferences most people express. So where Nozick started with the principle of self-ownership Gauthier derives that principle, and all which follows from it, from this idea of a mutually beneficial contract.

In addition to those who query whether this notion of constrained maximisation is persuasive (see Morris & Ripstein, 2001) it might be questioned whether a philosophy of mutual advantage can accommodate the inequalities – in bargaining power and in capacities to participate in cooperative schemes – that exist all around us (Kymlicka, 2002: 134–5). Mutual constraint is beneficial only to those who are equal enough to consent to it in the first place, whereas the mutual constraint of the Prince and the Pauper is much more likely to favour the former. So in the absence of overall equality, where unrestrained consent is not forthcoming (due to inequalities in talents and endowments), then one of two things must happen. Either we end up with distinct and separate communities for each level of inequality in natural and social resources, as people disperse to contract only with those to whom they are equal in resources; or diverse levels are incorporated within an overarching Hobbesian schema, leaving us with the likelihood of some (the Paupers) being constrained more than others (the Princes). We could, of course, attempt to compensate for inequalities of talents and endowments but this smacks of the very redistribution that Gauthier is arguing against.

What of Narveson, meanwhile? He proposes that interference in liberty derives from actions and actions alone: 'non-actions' do not count. This is because while actions are identifiable the number of non-actions is infinite, rendering the very idea meaningless. So when I do not promote your liberty this does not mean I have thereby interfered with it; and while it may be regrettable if I let you starve I have not interfered with your liberty here either. Agreeing with Nozick's defence of private property (Fitzpatrick, 2001a: 45–6) Narveson claims that although past injustices would have occurred this is not germane to the present pattern of ownership. If my grandfather successfully defrauded yours then this is/was a matter for them, not you and me. Rectifying destitution – due to past injustices or not – is a matter of charity rather than justice, for,

> The incredibly rich may violate the liberty of the desperately poor, to be sure – but also vice versa … . Fundamental rights are universal and not loaded in anyone's favor, though the situations or the heritages, genetic or social, of some doubtless make it probable that they will acquire greater properties or degrees of influence or any number of other kinds of goods than another, possibly less fortunate (in those respects) persons. (Narveson, 2001: 99)

There can be no justification for any form of egalitarianism since people do not, by and large, desire social equality:

> The only premises that can validly generate rules that everyone will reasonably be subject to must be held, or be deducible from what is held, by every person. (Narveson, 1998: 84)

What might we say in response to Narveson? Firstly, do non-actions count after all (Honderich, 2002: 72–88)? It presumably depends upon the context. My failure to help you tie your shoelace does not interfere with your liberty, but what if you have fallen in a lake and are in evident danger? Although it was not I who pushed you into the water it would be an injustice (and not simply a lack of charity) if I did nothing to assist you since your right to life is now within my partial control. So while Narveson is correct to bemoan the infiniteness of non-actions what matters are the contexts within which performance (and non-performance) occurs. Secondly, Narveson is simply unconcerned with what I have already called 'circumstance'. Nozick's acknowledgement that past injustices constitute a problem for libertarians is simply nowhere present in Narveson's worldview. Thirdly, Narveson assumes that charity is better for society than paternalist bureaucracies but ignores charity's psychological and social effects upon the receiver, being concerned only with its beneficent effects upon the giver. Fourthly, he shares with Gauthier an assumption that bargaining power between actors is actually or potentially equal. In the first of the above quotes Narveson manages to assume (a) that agents will possess equivalent degrees of power (the poor may exploit the rich) and (b) that inequalities of power will nevertheless accumulate in favour of the advantaged. After all, if people are entirely responsible for their social positions (if the initial circumstances into which we are born don't matter) then why find this problematic?

Fifthly, whereas Gauthier is willing to define society as the cooperative endeavour Narveson (2001: 196; cf. Gray, 1993) insists that there is no such thing as cooperation over and above the market. If markets consist of institutionally defined incentives and disincentives then this is equivalent to Narveson justifying market relations in terms of market relations. Perhaps aware of this he defines the market not simply as a system for the exchange of private property but as the realm of freedom and choice *per se*. Who then could fail to prefer market freedom to state coercion? Given a choice between (1) the state restricting some liberties in order to boost the number of liberties overall and (2) fewer liberties, Narveson prefers (2). Sixthly, Narveson (2001: 70–1, 85, 201–03) is pretty much concerned to treat the real as rational, to ossify existing distributions of wealth and expenditure. Bizarrely enough, by treating preference as sacrosanct he is compelled to acknowledge that where people are happy with public ownership then good luck to them! His defence of libertarianism amounts to saying that the burden of proof should always be on the side of the non-libertarian, yet what is to stop non-libertarians from reversing this burden in the other direction? Finally, he overlooks the possibility that there are degrees of self-ownership. He believes that socialists' commitment to redistribution of external endowments must also commit them to the redistribution of internal ones (talents and body parts). But if this slippery slope is not inevitable then Narveson, ironically, ends up conforming to his own caricature of socialism: imaging that if the redistribution of internal endowments is illegitimate then *no redistribution whatsoever can occur*!

A few theorists like Gauthier and Narveson apart *laissez faire* liberals and libertarians have been content to apply their basic ideas to a range of new issues and debates, some of which we will be visiting in the chapters to come. Therefore, what the 1990s mainly represented was the 'naturalisation' of *laissez faire*, the saturation of economic and political discourse with its assumptions and axioms to the point where the burden of proof is upon those who would 'turn back the clock'.

Frank (2001), to take one example, offers a comprehensive review of America's business culture and the literature that repeats the populist mantras of corporate capitalism: 'there is no alternative', 'government doesn't work', 'trade unions are unnecessary', 'regulations are destructive', 'the welfare state is pernicious', 'inequality is good'. Yergin and Stanislaw (1998) typify this literature in treating 'the market' – by which they really mean 'unregulated markets' – as the end of history, as the victor of the twentieth century battle between those who successfully defended *laissez faire* capitalism and those who sought to attack it (communists, welfare liberals, unions). Such assertions reached a crescendo in late 1990s America at a time when the US economy appeared healthier than its European counterparts. The underlying message of such books is that corporate domination is natural and just, an important message at a time when half of the world's richest economies are corporations.

But what is particularly impressive is the way in which many Left-leaning parties have accepted the arguments of the business class, leading some to identify a crisis of governance where corporations increasingly assume the role once occupied by political parties (Monbiot, 2000; Hertz, 2000; Klein, 2000). One consequence is a new form of legitimacy crisis where, because voting becomes an inadequate means of influencing political elites, electoral turnout falls, far Right parties revive and many disengage from politics, democracy and serious social problems in order to engage in alternative experiences where their voices and contributions are more obviously welcomed. Furthermore, the inequalities that free markets create also come to appear inevitable, to the point where it is widely believed that although inequalities can be mitigated what was once called the 'strategy of equality' (Titmuss, 1970) is no longer imaginable.

So the 'ordered freedom' supported by free market liberals and libertarians involves an hostility to anything more than the minimal state and particularly to any system of redistributive welfare. They are also non-perfectionist. Perfectionism here implies that some versions of the good and the good life are objectively and demonstrably better than others, so that social experts are entitled to guide, persuade and perhaps even coerce people accordingly. To be non-perfectionist is to believe that there are many different versions of the good and that people should be left alone to decide for themselves what is best. Free market liberals and libertarians believe that this is what justifies *laissez faire* capitalism since, rather than impose beliefs upon people, it simply permits the effective coordination of economic transfers and interactions between individuals who may hold any number of different beliefs and values. Freedom therefore involves voluntary exchange and diverse versions of the good, ordered through the coordinating mechanisms of unregulated markets.

We have to appreciate, however, that there are degrees of perfectionism and non-perfectionism. A strict non-perfectionist will argue against the banning or regulation of anything, including hard drugs and child pornography. Yet few commentators go as far as this, observing that because our preferences derive from particular traditions and historical conditions then not even free markets should embody an 'anything goes' form of morality. This is why most free market liberals and even libertarians can be classed as conservatives, for although they are broadly non-perfectionist most are also content to orient themselves to the contours of actually-existing capitalism – as noted above.

So, while they are non-perfectionist free market liberals and libertarians are also conservative since they are content to interpret market exchange in terms of existing property regimes and patterns of distribution, and ignore the possibility of alternatives to both (Haworth, 1994). This is why some of the real innovations in recent years have been in the development of a *Left*-libertarianism where the ideal of individual freedom is combined with an egalitarian division of productive resources (see next chapter).

Neoconservatism[5]

There is another strand of Right-wing thought that is obviously and openly perfectionist. Here, market capitalism is celebrated also but free markets are not regarded as the sufficient condition of a good society. Instead, social institutions, values and practices must be shaped so that the destructive tendencies of liberal modernity are vanquished and capitalism embodies and propagates the correct set of moral, cultural and religious virtues. Neoconservatives and the Christian Right are those who believe in limited governance when it comes to economics but not when it comes to morals, behaviour, faith, belief and knowledge.

Although he died in 1973 the guru of neoconservatism continues to be Leo Strauss (1968), perhaps the main influence behind the Republican Party's 1994 *Contract with America* and so upon Bill Clinton's subsequent shift rightwards. Strauss believed that liberalism provides an inadequate defence against totalitarianism because it is based upon secularism and relativism.[6] By treating belief in God as simply one among a plurality of different possible beliefs, liberalism has undermined spiritual values and so eroded the fibres of social order. Consequently, contemporary society has lost itself to alienation and rootlessness, leading to breakdowns in civility, duty and family life. We therefore need a revival in public and religious values, in moral and cultural authorities, as a means of once more distinguishing right from wrong. As a kind of modern day Platonism, it does not matter whether these authorities actually speak the truth, merely that what they speak is believed to *be* the truth by the great mass of people: a single 'noble lie' is better than a lot of competing, unnoble truths. Democracy therefore has to be detached from liberalism and the public will turned away from rationalistic individualism towards a populist conservatism where people are educated to accept their place within an unequal social order.

That Strauss based his ideas upon a simplified distortion of liberalism (Drury, 1997: 7–19), or that it is not clear why his noble lie would be preferable to the totalitarianisms from which he fled, since any philosophy that treats people as useful idiots already seems to carry a demagogic potential, has not stopped Strauss from becoming one of the main influences on con temporary conservative thought and politics, as disseminated through the work of those such as Kristol and Himmelfarb.

Kristol (1995) argues that market inequalities are a reflection of natural inequalities so that any attempt to interfere with them, e.g. through a welfare state, is an unnatural attempt to portray the wealth-creators (especially corporations) as villains and the unproductive as victims. A new religious sensibility (the re-establishment of church and state) is therefore needed to rectify this unnatural state of affairs, to revive orthodox moral codes that reject the countercultures of the 1960s and so to bolster family values and populist nationalism. Neoconservatism is therefore founded upon the three pillars of corporate capitalism, moral and religious orthodoxy and nationalism. Himmelfarb (1995) calls for a return to Victorian values, though not necessarily to the Victorian society which commonly failed to embody them. It is state welfare that has created poverty, not only by its direct effects upon crime, illegitimacy and dependency, but by categorising people as needy, poor and helpless it has constructed the very social phenomena to which it claims to be responding. By rewarding vice and penalising virtue it only encourages more of the former (a 'moral hazard'). Therefore, she agrees with Kristol that moral legislation is needed to bolster a free market economy, e.g. schools that teach sexual abstinence in order to reverse the tide of promiscuity, pornography and sexual violence, and promote stable family life. Market and family dependency is the solution to state dependency.

Both Kristol and Himmelfarb demand that an economic revolution in favour of free markets be conjoined with a moral revolution in favour of bourgeois ethics (the work ethic, thrift, marriage, father-led families, self-reliance). This requires not simply the correct financial incentives but also, because people are not primarily rational actors, a system where 'people are told, from childhood on, what the right things and the wrong things are' (Kristol, 1995: 365). Himmelfarb (1995: 244–5), in particular, is careful to stress that their critique is directed against modern culture rather than against the poorest *per se*: the immorality of the underclass is often reflected in the immorality of an 'overclass'. Nevertheless, it is clear from where they believe most social problems derive. Since the poor have (at least in a welfare state) nothing to lose then their vices are more likely to accumulate, generation after generation, than the vices of the affluent because the latter, by virtue of their being well-off and not dependent upon the state, must already possess greater elements of the requisite moral character. The game is given away by neoconservatives such as James Q. Wilson (1993) who focuses upon the immoralities of those who 'drain' public resources and by Murray (see below and Chapter 6) who believes that differences in behaviour lead not only to differences in moral character but to the poor having a genetic configuration different to that of the non-poor (Murray, 2000: 30).[7]

What neoconservatives tend not to do is consider evidence from other countries. For instance, because the Scandinavian social democracies have levels of state expenditure about 3–4 times higher than the USA it must follow, on neoconservative logic, that they also possess levels of crime, illegitimacy and family breakdown which are 3–4 times higher than those in the US. The fact that they do not is not a fact with which neoconservatives appear comfortable. Might it be, then, that they are misreading what they call 'demoralisation'? That social problems are due not to the American welfare state being over-generous but perhaps to its not being generous enough? Might the combination of extensive means-testing in the context of a low wage economy be to blame? Should we not focus instead upon class inequalities, racism and other socio-structural factors (W. J. Wilson, 1997)? As we shall see in the next chapter, it is perfectly possible to agree with aspects of the demoralisation thesis but to attribute this not to the moral depravities of the poor but to a conservative-dominated economic culture. To conclude, critics might regard neoconservative moralism as nothing more than the kind of cant sniffed out long ago by Oscar Wilde: 'Really, if the lower orders don't set us a good example,' reflects Algernon in *The Importance of Being Earnest*, 'what on earth is the use of them?'

Nevertheless, such criticisms have not prevented sustained attacks on state welfare by the likes of Murray and Mead. Murray (1984) argues that the 1960s *War on Poverty* had created more poor people rather than less since generous benefits encourage family breakdown (by rewarding single households more than married couples) and underemployment (by making waged work less rewarding). Good intentions had therefore led to regrettable outcomes by changing the pattern of incentives to which people are exposed. Murray's initial inclination was therefore to treat individuals as rational actors, making decisions based mainly upon financial calculations. Fairly quickly, though, he came to accept the neoconservative idea that what matters most is moral character and he believes that single motherhood is at the core of contemporary social problems (Murray *et al*, 2001). Therefore, although his basic recommendations have not changed (the abolition of welfare for almost everyone) his emphasis is very much upon the importance of stigma as a means of inducing correct behaviour among the poorest.

Murray (1990) is one of the few neoconservatives to have engaged in international comparisons and he has suggested that the UK also possesses an underclass of the undeserving, albeit it at an earlier stage of development. However, more extensive surveys, sensitive to effects of social inequalities on behaviour (rather than vice versa), have not borne out Murray's thesis (Dean & Taylor-Gooby, 1992; Walker with Howard, 2000). Murray is therefore vulnerable to the accusation that the data upon which he bases his ideas is highly selective, designed to prove what he wants to prove (Lister, 1996; Deacon, 2002: 40–41). Even more controversially, Herrnstein and Murray (1994) insisted that IQ is distributed unequally by nature, such that those at the bottom of the income distribution are less naturally intelligent. Since, especially in the USA, blacks are more likely to be poor than whites the implications of this view are obvious and contentious and led to a storm of protest against the authors (see Chapter 6).

Mead (1986), for his part, accuses the welfare state of stressing social rights at the cost of ignoring social and moral obligations. Public order depends much more upon active participation in the life of a community: what we can give rather than what we take. The underclass consists of those who take rather than give which, despite the negative influence of state welfare, Mead attributes ultimately to their behaviour. What is needed, therefore, is a system of moral rewards and sanctions backed up by compulsion wherever necessary. If the excluded will not include themselves then they must be forced to do so. Mead (1997) calls this the 'new paternalism': coercion into the very social mainstream that most of the underclass want to join, even if they do not yet possess the resolve to make it happen. But if Murray's data is slender, Mead's is almost non-existent (Deacon, 2002: 54–61) and his views are ultimately based upon the belief that any job is better than no job. This, of course, makes *a priori* assumptions about job and non-job activities and it is not difficult to think of scenarios where people are entirely justified in refusing paid work where it would damage their sense of self, their long-term prospects and their emotional attachments. As with Murray, Mead overestimates the extent to which the poor are different from the non-poor or can be regarded as the cause of their circumstances.

But if neoconservatism is based upon a contentious support for moral authoritarianism it is at least more considered than that of the Christian Right. Or rather, given the Straussian emphasis upon spiritual regeneration, it is not unreasonable to regard neoconservatism as the moderate wing of the Christian Right. According to Durham (2000) the Christian Right is defined almost entirely by what it is against: federal government, regulation (of gun ownership, for instance), internationalism, welfare dependency, abortion and contraceptives on demand, multiculturalism, affirmative action, political correctness, gays and lesbians, promiscuity and cohabitation, theories of evolution, social equality. Therefore, the Christian Right are foot-soldiers for a God who is as appalled as they at how out of control society has become. The extreme wing of the Christian Right therefore demonstrates an evangelical zeal that the intellectual arguments of the above authors rarely betray. Here, since the world has been turned upside down – so that it is the poor who oppress the rich, women who oppress men, blacks who oppress whites, and the rest of the world that oppresses America – how much more urgent it must be to turn things the correct way up again, to reassert God's will upon the Earth.

We can therefore speculate as to why neoconservatism and the Christian Right have not taken hold anywhere else. American conservatism is a social movement (Kristol, 1995: 373–86), one that reflects America's continued image of itself as classless land of limitless possibility. Because it is supposedly classless America's affluent have little sense that they owe their position to inheritance and luck; the notion of *noblesse oblige* ('we'd better give something back to society since we have been more fortunate than others') is therefore missing, replaced by a self-satisfied and impatient individualism ('the poor are poor because they are not as virtuous as us'). And because America is so vast and still relatively young its conservatism is less likely to view society as organic and fragile. Indeed, although many neoconservatives are ex-Marxists they have retained their former view that society can be radically reengineered. The attempt to spread a less hubristic vision leads to occasional fashions for a 'compassionate conservatism' (Olasky, 2000), although some regard this as little more than a re-badging of the 'new paternalism' (Kutchins, 2001). So although there are authors in Britain and across Europe who agree with some neoconservative ideas (O'Hear, 1999; Sacks, 2000) theirs tends to be a philosophy of restraint rather than rage.

To summarise, neoconservatives also believe in 'ordered freedom', though they interpret this as a set of correct beliefs that people will follow freely once the required spiritual and moral framework is in place. It is not the freedom to choose anything within a coordinating marketplace but the freedom which comes with the recognition of duties and necessity, the acknowledgement of religious ethics. Therefore, neoconservative capitalism involves free markets but also forms of governance that redirect the preferences and aspirations of agents towards morally virtuous behaviour. Economic inequalities are to be celebrated not simply as an unintended but inevitable consequence of market exchange but as necessary for the common good. There are biological inequalities which, while not justifying an aristocratic society, determine a bell-curved distribution of income which is fairly constant across all countries, across all times (Kristol, 1995: 176–7). What is intolerable are not economic inequalities but the moral inequalities of character that derive from the attempt of welfare liberals to interfere with this natural order.

A final thought

Although a number of objections to both schools of conservatism have been noted above there is one that has not been mentioned and which I will sketch here before developing it further in the chapters to come. Conservatives accuse the Left of treating wealth as if it is freely available for redistribution and for ignoring the fact that wealth has to be earned. Productive resources do not drop like manna from heaven, as Nozick (1974: 160) put it, and so the attachment of wealth to the wealthy is not an in-justice but a reflection of desert. The Left has made two counter-arguments in reply. Firstly, that labourers are the real wealth producers so that present distributions reflect past and ongoing expropriations of wealth through ex-ploitation. Secondly, that productive people *do* drop from heaven in the sense that where each of us is within the social hierarchy is largely a matter of familial inheritance and brute luck in the distribution of talents. Therefore, if no-one deserves their inheritance or talents then just distribution cannot be based upon desert. The first of these arguments has been largely discredited: labour may be *a* source of value but cannot be the *only* source. The second is stronger and has led some conservatives to abandon desert as a key principle. Libertarians usually follow Nozick in speaking of 'entitlement' instead, but this has to follow from some notion of just original acquisition and, as critics have argued, there is no firm basis for this (Fitzpatrick, 2001a: 45–6). Most conservatives therefore retain reference to desert but struggle to reconcile this principle with the distribution of resources in actually existing capitalism.

One possible solution is to argue that, despite some injustice, all is for the best in the best of possible worlds. Kekes (1998: 9) acknowledges that poverty, discrimination and injustice affect 10–20% of people in modern society but points out that,

> ... the other 80–90% are enabled by the prevailing arrangements to live good lives.

And, in any event, the 10–20% of unfortunates are still better off than they would have been in the past. This approach therefore resembles the Utilitarian propensity to sacrifice minorities if this is to the benefit of the majority.

Another approach – taking us back to the categories defined in the Introduction – is to acknowledge the role of luck and circumstance but to suggest that these factors are still relatively minor determinants compared to effort. However, this runs up against the huge differences in material resources that prevail in most nations. Therefore, if luck and circumstance do play a much greater part in human affairs then this does not necessarily dis-credit Right-wing thought but it does suggest that only a *social* conservatism can give a rounded picture of how people interact individually and col-lectively with their social environments. Therefore, the role of state social policies in realising freedom, solidarity and well-being can be reaffirmed – and Christian Democracy can be said to re-enter the picture at this point.

This attempt to give a rounded account – to allow for luck and circum-stance, choice, desert and consequence – is one that has also exercised the Left, as we will see in the next two chapters once we have reviewed some recent developments in social democratic thought.

Social Democracy

Social democrats are those who desire to bring capitalist economies under some form of collective control using statist and gradualist reforms that are more ambitious and interventionist than those favoured by the above thinkers or even by supporters of a social market capitalism. Most conser-vatives are content to justify market-based inequalities so long as these are not morally or socially destructive. Social democrats, though, borrow from the traditions of modernist thought the urge to step outside the parameters we have been given, to reengineer where we are by imagining alternative social realities according to universal principles and ideals. Traditionally, this has made the Right a defensive set of prescriptions in contrast to the Left's more offensive assault upon what it perceives as social injustice. Social democracy has therefore derived from two Leftist traditions: a reformist kind of social liberalism and a more radical form of democratic socialism (Fitzpatrick, 2001a: 128–32). Since the 1970s, though, this alignment has unravelled and the Left has become more defensive (Giddens, 1994). With the exhaustion of Keynesian welfare and the ascendancy of Right-wing ideas, the Left spent many years struggling to regain its philosophical confidence, political edge and electoral voice. The main victim (especially after 1989) has been democratic socialism, leaving the social liberal wing to dominate. Less bookended than previously by socialists to their Left, social liberals have adopted a radical pragmatism of the Centre as a means of countering the Right's hegemony. By the mid-1990s this strategy was beginning to bear fruit with the emergence of what we shall call the New Social Democracy (NSD) around which much subsequent debate about the future of the Left, and of state welfare, has been organised.

Neorepublicanism and pluralism

To explore the NSD we first have to understand the important philosophical context it inhabits. Many on the Left have come to believe that equality cannot be achieved without a strong sense of community and solidarity (Roche, 1992; Miller, 1999) since why should people pull in a certain direc-tion unless they see that others are also expending their fair share of effort and time? Whether fairly or unfairly quasi-egalitarian systems (like state welfare) are often regarded as not doing enough to foster the requisite sense of mutual participation. But rather than obsess about the 'undeserving poor' (see above) these thinkers believe that as much attention should be paid to the 'undeserving rich'. So in addition to their traditional liberal and egalitarian concerns many social democrats now believe that a greater sensitivity to communal belongingness and responsibility (what I am calling 'consequence') is also needed.

It is against this background that neorepublicanism has emerged. The republican tradition recommends a politics of the common good and of civic virtues; *neo*republicanism is the attempt to recreate these in a society when the simple fact of consumerism, mobility and individualism cannot be wished away. In policy terms this does not mean dismantling social rights but it does mean fixing those rights quite firmly to a set of social duties (Gutmann & Thompson, 1996). There are two distinctions and qualifications of which we need to be aware. Firstly, neorepublicanism stands in contrast to a pluralism which stresses not merely the fact but the intrinsic value that comes from society making room for a plurality of wants, activities, identities and interests. However, neorepublicanism and pluralism are ideals to which few attach themselves exclusively, and many theorists can be located somewhere between these extremes. Secondly, this first distinction intersects that between liberalism and socialism, but note that many neorepublicans and pluralists on the Left borrow elements from both the liberal and the socialist camps, with few pitching their tents exclusively in either. We therefore have two distinctions which, in cutting across one another, creates the following four sectors – but remember that the positions of their 'representatives' are more nuanced than my brief descriptions allow.

Carens (2003) and Pettit (1997) are exemplars of a socialist neorepublicanism in their belief that participation in society is undermined by the inequalities of power that capitalist market relations create. Reforming and eventually replacing the latter will therefore enable the desired level of participation to emerge. A more moderate version of this position is also visible in White (2003) whose ideas I will review in Chapter 3. Dagger (1997: Ch. 12) can be found among possible liberal neorepublicans since he grounds autonomy in a strong sense of community, but a community whose common good involves enabling people to live self-governed lives as members of a political society. Liberal pluralists include Galston (2002) for whom individual rights must limit the scope of government activity and majority rule. That said Galston prefers an expansive conception of individual and collective responsibilities that, via the principle of reciprocity (see Chapter 3), imposes more duties upon citizens than many liberals would permit. Finally, an example of a socialist pluralist is yours truly. Fitzpatrick (2003) acknowledges the importance of both equality and responsibility but argues that these principles have to be made compatible with a diversity of social goods and activities since squeezing everyone into the same box seems less than desirable.

There is something to be said for and against each of the above but let me confine myself to some broad criticisms. The potential problem with neorepublicanism comes when we consider how and when to enforce duties when they have not been performed according to social norms. If enforcement is strong then we have to rely either upon state coercion – which has hardly been fashionable recently – or more informal moral sanctions by the community – which to be effective can be equally as repressive. Carens (2003: 163–76) tries to find a way around this by imagining not a legal/physical enforcement but the internalisation of norms such that the desire to make a social contribution (by which he means full-time work) would be automatic. Yet while all societies involve internalised norms the liberal tradition he invokes makes greater room for what is and is not considered to be normal. Similarly, even when people are performing their stipulated duties how do we judge whether they are performing them well enough? Should we closely monitor each and every action or adopt a much looser, hand-off approach – one that sends us back in a pluralist direction? Of course this is a dilemma for any society but particular for one that supposes the centrality of duty. So neorepublicanism emphasises duties but at the cost of the voluntarism by which the performance of duties is made meaningful instead of automatous.

But if pluralism gets us out of that dilemma does it create others? The more limited the enforcement, the more we invite a libertarian society where nothing more than voluntary exchange is permitted. We may try to swerve away from this destination towards a more egalitarian and solidaristic society but how can this be made to work unless people recognise the attraction of mutual compliance and feel compelled to participate in the cooperative schemes out of which social goods are made? And if the mechanisms of enforcement are loose then are we not inviting free riders to sit down and enjoy themselves in an environment that they have not shaped and so whose benefits they have not earned?

My intention here is not to resolve this debate but to establish where contemporary trends lie. Since, as I noted in the Introductory chapter, most political theorists push towards the centre of the Venn diagram, while continuing to prioritise one principle above the others, it is misleading to portray past social democrats as having ignored the importance of duty. However, given the recent fashion for neorepublicanism (often going under the moniker 'communitarianism') – even in self-proclaimed pluralists like Galston (former advisor to Bill Clinton) – the commitment to social duties is being made more explicit while the commitment to social equality has been diluted. As a result while social democrats have traditionally been content to embrace liberal and socialist elements there is a sense in which many (certainly in the English-speaking nations) have now reverted to social democracy's origins in nineteenth century social liberalism, leaving them happier to be bookended by conservatism. This leads us into a discussion of the NSD.

New Social Democracy

Going under a number of different guises – the radical centre, the new centre, the Third Way, progressivism – the NSD dates from the mid-1990s and is effectively the intellectual and practical response that Centre-Left parties eventually made to the many years of the Right's dominance. The basic solution was not to capitulate to every aspect of conservatism (although many ideas and reforms were accepted as *fait accompli*) but nor to salvaging what came to be termed 'old' social democracy (Keynesianism, state central-isation, nationalisation, class conflict, producer-oriented reforms, vertical redistribution, public sector expansionism). Instead, the emphasis was upon applying social democratic principles, values and goals to a socioeconomic environment that was taken to have been irrevocably shaped by modern con-servatism (Commission on Social Justice, 1994; Gray, 1996; Levitas, 1998; Giddens, 1998, 2001; Hombach, 2000; Driver & Martell, 2002). Therefore, the NSD was committed to social justice but to that version of social justice which was most consistent with free market capitalism. It was a practice in search of a philosophy in search of a practice, hoping to transcend what it held to be the sterile oppositions of Left vs. Right while continuing to appeal to the very ideas which gave that opposition its force. And by 1998 the NSD did indeed appear to be the 'next big thing' in western politics, with social democratic parties in government in the USA and throughout Europe. And if not all of them were converts to the new, hardly any of them were con-servers of the old.

The theorist with who the NSD is most closely associated is Tony Giddens. Giddens (1994) insists that in order to explain social exclusion we have to focus upon recent changes in the meaning and implications of social agency. The excluded are those who are least able to negotiate the risks and uncertainties of late modernity (see Chapter 3). Giddens therefore advocates a system of 'positive welfare' which is based upon his notion of 'life politics'. This means that whereas the classic welfare state helped people to cope with *changed* circumstances that could be anticipated (unemployment, sickness, old age) a new welfare system must enable people to actively *shape* their lives with greater awareness and control in the face of future circumstances that cannot be anticipated or predicted with any accuracy. The social structures and economic forces with which we are faced are less determinate than their predecessors – and so harder to insure against in traditional terms. Third Way social democracy therefore necessitates a social investment state where equality implies inclusion in society's way of life rather than a flatter distribu-tion of income and wealth (Giddens, 1998, 2000). Indeed, while Giddens is not hostile to redistribution if its beneficial effects can be demonstrated, his notion of inclusion might well be consistent with the maintenance of consid-erable inequalities. Insurance against risks is no longer merely 'social' but is also a cultural and psychological state of reflexivity, calculation and readi-ness; and cradle-to-grave provision is now redundant in a society where our biographical portfolios must be constantly updated along with changes in our work, familial and geographical circumstances. Because contemporary society is radically mobile and uncertain our social institutions and life trajectories have to be similarly flexible and adaptable. The NSD offers a political space within which this can be thought through since, willing to mix ideas from a variety of sources, it is not attached to the ideological *rigor mortis* of traditional Left and Right.

A number of criticisms of Giddens's recent work have been advanced. One criticism is that he overstates the extent to which the 'old' social democracy (and so the classic welfare state) is redundant (Pierson, 2001). Giddens is perhaps more willing to look at evidence which backs up his Third Way hypothesis than he is at evidence which does not. Therefore, he consequently overestimates the extent to which the NSD really is capable of reconciling ideas from a variety of ideological sources so that the flexibility of the NSD's rhetoric does not necessarily translate into practical reality (Fairclough, 1999). Giddens can be accused of accepting too much of the conservative agenda, then. His oft-repeated assertion that 'rights imply responsibilities' is one more often directed against the exclusion of the poorest than that of the wealthiest (Fitzpatrick, 2003: 21–4).

However, we are running ahead of ourselves and we need to look more closely at the NSD itself. The literature on the NSD is vast and so explanations of it have been sliced and diced in a myriad different ways. The following five principles, however, seem to be broadly representative (see Fitzpatrick, 2003: Ch. 1).

Community

The NSD attaches itself to 'civic community' in the same way that the old left was supposed to be attached to 'state collectivism' and the new right to 'market individualism'. Hence, it employed the rhetoric of communitarianism (called neorepublicanism in the previous section) and social capital (see Chapter 3). The essential point here was to mark out a political space that its potential enemies on the left could not equate to the market and its potential enemies on the right could not confuse with the state. If community refers to the associative networks of solidarity that pertain within civil society, linked to but not reducible to the state and market, then it permits an economic and political flexibility that utilises the strengths of both public and private, national and local, social cohesion and market mobility.

Meritocracy

One implication of this strategy is that social equality, while held to be desirable, could not be imposed 'from above' but would have to emerge from within, and be consistent with, the interstices of individual aspiration and market relations. Therefore, new social democrats emphasised opportunity against what they perceived as the inhibiting limitations of 'outcome equality'. Meritocracy is the result of equal opportunities plus freedom of choice, demanding not the reduction of inequalities *per se* but of those that do not derive from effort and hard work. The state therefore has the duty of providing the educational, welfare and labour market reforms that embody equal opportunities, but citizens bear the responsibility of utilising those opportunities. Thus the need for 'active welfare', or provision that emphasises insertion into the labour market, rather than a 'passive welfare' that pays people to be idle. Equality does not, then, require the 'levelling' of the affluent but a more complex emphasis upon the capacities and life chances of all social groups.

Reciprocity

This formula of opportunities in return for effort translates into the notion of reciprocal citizenship, where rights imply responsibilities, in contrast to the passive citizenship of unconditional entitlements that the old social democracy is alleged to have embodied. Reciprocity is therefore consequential upon the principles of community and meritocracy: we owe to the community in proportion to what we obtain from it and have no claims upon the resources which others have deservedly earned for themselves. We return to this in Chapter 3.

Inclusion

So social justice is less about a simple equality than about multiple forms of inclusion within society's way of life. Exclusion is therefore not identical to a 'lack of material resources' but is a dynamic process of social marginalisation that has a number of diverse sources. It follows that inclusion requires not the redistribution of income but the more effective distribution of decent wages bolstered, where necessary, by income-related transfers. Policies should therefore be targeted upon the supply-side, i.e. what does or does not make people employable: the presence, or otherwise, of skills and qualifications that constitute not a one-off apprenticeship but a portfolio that requires frequent updating throughout one's working life.

Pragmatism

The compass that orients the above principles to changing circumstances is that of pragmatism, defined not in terms of expediency but of adaptation towards a post-ideological environment. Where public goals can be best delivered through the private sector (or a combination of public and private investment and management) then so be it. People are interested in results and so care little about *how* those results are delivered. Ideals are important but not if they distract us from real world circumstances.

What these principles add up to is arguably an 'equality without egalitarianism'. In line with a school of thought going back at least to Marshall (Marshall & Bottomore, 1992) the NSD is not concerned with inequalities *per se* but with *unjust* inequalities, i.e. those that are not matters of effort and desert. Tackling child poverty is therefore one of its clear links to the 'old social democracy'; though inequalities that are the consequences of genuine merit (risk taking, hard work) are perfectly justified. Yet whereas egalitarians in the tradition of Tawney (1931; Bobbio, 1996) believe that this requires upper and lower limits upon the 'social space' within which individuals are allowed to move, e.g. limits upon how much wealth they can accumulate, the NSD is committed to meritocracy without limits. They are attached to equality of opportunity (basic compensations for luck and circumstance) but not to the idea that such compensation also requires equality of outcome since this is believed to place too great a restriction upon choice and aspiration (Fitzpatrick, 2001a: 26). So, while concerned about discrimination in terms of gender, ethnicity, ability and sexuality, the NSD is much less ambitious when it comes to distributive justice. Its equality is one of raising the social floor rather than lowering the social ceiling.

Critics of the NSD therefore feel the following five points to be crucial (see Fitzpatrick, 2003).

Firstly, having given up on the goal of radically reforming capitalism, new social democrats have left themselves with the tools of ethical exhortation and administrative compulsion. This means that its appeal to community, aspiration and obligation has frequently been moralistic and authoritarian, shading back into the punitivism of conservative discourse: if millions are still socially excluded, despite the opportunities on offer, it follows that they are somehow, to some degree, excluding themselves. The NSD has therefore adapted the distinction between deserving and undeserving and so overseen a blurring of social and criminal policies (see Chapter 8).

Secondly, it has accelerated the shift towards a consumerist culture within the public sector. With European levels of expenditure unlikely to be matched for the foreseeable future modernisers in the UK Labour Party adopted a managerialist ethos of efficiency towards the public sector. Hence the enthusiasm for targets, league tables, performance-related pay, outsourcing, competition, private sector funding and management-speak and perpetual quality audits (see Chapter 8). That the public sector produces goods that cannot often be assessed according to the same criteria as market goods is a lesson that new social democrats have struggled to relearn. The revaluation of public sector values that it has articulated has therefore been a double-edged blessing since top-down measures may actually make things *less* efficient by crowding out professional autonomy, knowledge, morale and dedication. In addition, some argue (Schwartz, 2004) that this consumerist culture is actually bad for consumers too since a surfeit of choice can actually disempower by creating anxiety, confusion, opportunity costs and psychological inertia. Most people are as concerned with quality as they are with quantity, so that even in a supermarket environment (let alone a public sector one) they seek to balance a sense of security against the experience of freedom. The mantra of 'more choice' may actually be counterproductive as the values people seek in a public sector context, e.g. communal identification with others, becomes crowded out by the marketplace.

Thirdly, the NSD has neglected the importance of social processes and structural conflict. It has concentrated upon the individualistic surface of society and largely ignored the deeper factors that constrain or enable individuals' potential. Meritocracy is therefore a weak replacement for egalitarianism since 'opportunity' either does or does not possess meaning depending upon the distributive context. For instance, the opportunity to attend university is less meaningful where the middle class can effectively buy access to the best schools, tutors and other forms of educational resource.

Fourthly, the link between rights and responsibilities is either philosophically unremarkable or politically contentious – indeed, the former is reiterated as a means of diverting attention away from the latter. Therefore, the NSD's discourse constructs duties in a particular way that it then skilfully represents as the *only* way. By associating exclusion with the problems of crime (always individual, rarely corporate), drugs, benefit fraud, truancy, etc. it implicitly suggests that 'exclusion' means the exclusion of the poor from the mainstream and not of the mainstream from the poor (still less of the superrich from the mainstream) (Jordan with Jordan, 2000). The move is also performed by distinguishing between passive and active welfare – as if no-one had thought of labour market activation prior to 1997! The real difference, then, is not between passive and active welfare but between a welfare state that previously reflected the values of solidarity, e.g. through social insurance systems, and one that now boosts low pay mainly through means-tested tax credits and transfers.

Finally, the NSD places too much emphasis upon the restorative powers of paid work. So long as employment (*any* employment) is available and offers a decent income then there are few social problems for which it has not been touted as a panacea. But what this ignores is the quality of the jobs on offer and the quality of the long-term prospects that they provide. In the absence of such quality workfare policies always tend towards the punitive. Additionally, the NSD tends to downgrade the importance of non-paid work. With obligation defined as 'the duty to participate in the labour market' new social democrats have struggled to reconcile this injunction with a recognition that carework, in particular, possesses social value (see next chapter). The heavy accent upon paid work has opened up fissures and contradictions across a range of family and welfare-related policies.

The new productivism

While not necessarily employing the discourse of the Third Way there are several authors who also want to revitalise the Centre-Left by jettisoning some of its traditional ideas. The main idea to be abandoned, or at least severely diluted, is that of vertical redistribution, i.e. the redistribution of material resources to the least well-off. This does not mean that egalitarianism is discarded but that it is conceived in 'horizontal' rather than 'vertical' terms.

The starting point for this school of thought involves the assertion not only that social democracy's demise has been greatly exaggerated but that it is better equipped than its rivals to meet the challenges of the future (Brown & Lauder, 2001; Hutton, 2002). According to Goodin *et al* (1999), social democracy trumps both market liberalism and Christian Democracy because in addition to achieving its favoured principles (social justice and equal opportunities) social democracy is also the best means for achieving *theirs* (efficiency and growth; solidarity and stability). Therefore, social democracy is stronger than even many of its supporters imagine.

Nevertheless, this does mean that the more revolutionary aspirations of the social democratic tradition have to be rethought. Huber and Stephens (2001) make the point that because high labour market participation rates, of women as much as men, are the *sine qua non* of social democracy then social policies have to facilitate the creation and maintenance of a high employment economy. Huber and Stephens therefore offer support to the Dutch model: a high employment economy does not have to be based upon full-time employment alone, but can also imply a proliferation of part-time jobs and flexibility in terms of both job sharing and work schedules. Social policies should therefore be geared towards this kind of part-time labour market and one which goes further than even social democracies have yet managed in establishing equity of choice and experience between men and women.

Esping-Andersen (1999, 2002) agrees with this kind of strategy. By drawing upon theories of post-industrialism (Fitzpatrick, 2001a: 157–63) he insists that we have to find a third alternative to the unenviable choice between a service economy based upon low unemployment and high levels of income inequality (the American model) or one based upon high unemployment and high replacement ratios (the European model). In short, the

Golden Age of welfare capitalism has been superseded by two forms of post-industrial economics: the social exclusion of the working poor and that of the non-working poor. Esping-Andersen therefore seems to agree with the argument which says that the welfare state has reached the political and economic limits of its expansion, such that we cannot simultaneously achieve each of the following goals: employment growth, wage equality and modest levels of social expenditure. We face a 'trilemma' where we can achieve two of these goals but not all three (Fitzpatrick, 2003: Ch. 4). We cannot achieve equality for all in the here and now. His favoured alternative involves an acceptance that some forms of inequality are unavoidable while ensuring that no-one is *permanently* excluded. State welfare should therefore be based upon a 'mobility guarantee' where many of us experience periods of under-privilege (especially when we are young) but where these periods are of temporary duration only.

What Esping-Andersen is drawing upon is a new 'life-course' literature which focuses upon stratifications of and across time. Leisering and Leibfried (1999; also Gershuny, 2000) accuse most poverty research of being locked into a static, inflexible analysis that treats poverty and exclusion as fixed characteristics and overlooks the extent to which they transcend class boundaries. Structures, institutions and biographies are far more complex than this, they maintain. While some are undoubtedly trapped in long-term poverty, for most of us poverty is something that we risk and occasionally fall into throughout our life histories. Welfare policies should therefore provide not so much a safety net into which we can plunge as a bridge that will enable us to cope with these transitional periods. At the heart of these authors' concerns is the desire to see greater progress towards what is often called the 'work-life balance'.

So, what such commentators are pointing towards is what I have here called a 'new productivism'. The welfare state has always been productivist in that it has prospered the most when based upon low unemployment. However, in a post-industrial economy that conservative governments were able to spend many years shaping, and with more and more people squeezing into the middle class, the traditional emphasis upon vertical redistribution from rich to poor is now held to be less realistic and relevant than before. Therefore, high levels of labour market participation require supply-side activation policies (rather than 'passive' benefits and Keynesian macroeconomics), 'bridging' strategies (such as a mobility guarantee) and more effective horizontal redistribution across the life course. Yet although the new productivism certainly shares certain features with the NSD its egalitarian commitment remains stronger and it is less concerned with demonising the 'old' social democracy (Esping-Andersen, 2000: 763).

Even so, the new productivists can still be charged with adopting too individualistic an approach, one that neglects the positional dynamics of power struggles in favour of a biographical subjectivism (Fitzpatrick, 2004a,

2004b). For while it might be the case, to take one example, that much class analysis has relied upon a conception of stratification that is too simplistic, hierarchical and invariable, there are many examples where this is not the case (see next two chapters). So although they call for a more complex theory of structural, institutional and biographical interaction, the new productivists risk ignoring the continuing need for collective and collectivist solutions.

This is one of the reasons why their emphasis upon paid work is potentially dangerous. Esping-Andersen (1990) once characterised social democracy as a strategy of decommodification, i.e. of freedom from the market (see Chapter 9). In practice, decommodification has meant nothing more than a *partial* freedom based upon strong and enduring periods of participation *within* the market. Yet even if the distinction between commodification and decommodification may be overdrawn (Room, 2000) the idea of 'freedom from' is still valuable. Without this notion of 'freedom from' as an operational ideal the new productivist emphasis upon active labour market participation may be insufficiently distinct from the new paternalist argument we reviewed above, a society in which the duty to earn is held to override all other forms of social value and contributory activity (Standing, 2002). Consequently, ecological and emotional sources of value risk being occluded by the productivist stress upon employment (see Fitzpatrick, 2003: Chs 4–6).

Conclusion

These schools of thought represent some of the key ideological developments of recent years. Free marketeers and libertarians continue to reiterate the basic ideas established in the 1960s and 1970s, about the ability of unregulated markets to coordinate the free choices of individuals more efficiently than government. However, theirs is still a conservative doctrine given the features of existing capitalism which are sneaked into their philosophical premises. Neoconservatives and the Christian Right argue for a capitalism of economic deregulation but also of moral and cultural intervention. However, the attempt to reconcile the principle of desert with prevailing distributions of wealth leads either to incoherence, or to blatant unfairness, or back to the kind of social (and European) traditions of conservatism that they reject. New social democrats attempt to renew the Centre-Left tradition by borrowing ideas from diverse ideological sources but arguably underestimate the continuing role that structural inequalities play in determining our life chances. The new productivists also wish to renew social democracy by stressing the temporal dimensions of poverty and inequality; yet they, too, might be accused of downplaying the importance of class structures and positional conflict.

So we can see that conservatives seek to consolidate the inequalities of free market capitalism, whether through economic or moral justifications or both, whereas social democrats are committed to addressing inequalities while detouring around the traditional concerns of egalitarians. But while Right and Left have been squaring off against each other in these terms what else has been happening? Has anything moved in to fill the space once occupied by democratic socialism? What kind of radicalisms are attempting to open up a new front at odds with the conservative and social democratic mainstreams?

2

The New Radicalisms

Introduction

What follows is not intended to be a comprehensive overview of what I am calling the new radicalisms as this would be too big a task for a single chapter but it hopefully does identify a stream of debate that offers alternatives to the ideas explored in the previous one. Today the Left is less a coherent manifesto than a signifier around which a diversity of movements can be said to cluster with varying degrees of consistency and deliberation. The more it has been vilified by its opponents the more this signifier has regained a credibility that it arguably could never have obtained by itself. So although not everything which is radical is Left, nor everything which is on the Left is radical, there still exists an intellectual space beyond the mainstreams of conservatism and social democracy which we cannot ignore.

It was the 1960s, when the post-war settlement was not yet under threat and opposition to restrictive moral, cultural and sexual codes was flourishing, that represented the high-water mark of the post-war Left, but its momentum proved to be unsustainable. The Left therefore dispersed into seemingly endless refractions of itself: on the one hand into the politics of identity, of language and into single-issue causes; on the other, into a pragmatic politics of accommodation with changed social realities. But the faultline I wish to explore below, and will be returning to throughout the book (especially Chapter 9 and the Conclusion), is specifically that between materialist and culturalists.

For the former, the social is somehow shaped by material interactions, whether these be understood as consisting of human nature, productive forces or some other candidate, that possess a reality independent of what we can say about it. Social injustice therefore consists of society's inability or unwillingness to reorder the material into distributive forms beneficial to everyone and the crisis of the Left has derived from the growing fear that this was perhaps an unrealistic goal after all. For the latter, a simple materialism was always naïve in that it overlooks the extent to which matter is rooted in cultural and discursive contexts such that it cannot be understood independently of the social frames that provide it with meaning. Matter is everywhere constructed by the social subjects who embody it. Social injustice is therefore due to a lack of attention given to 'the cultural', broadly defined, and the crisis of the Left represents a period of transition away from the Utopian aspirations that can lead to Stalinism and towards a political philosophy more sensitive to the particularisms and contingencies of social interaction.

So we have an array of materialists, who continue to define themselves as socialists, Marxists or as liberal egalitarians, and a series of culturalists who have been influenced variously by postmodernism, post-structuralism and communitarianism. Furthermore, there have been many on the Left who have straddled the divide with whatever degree of coherence or deliberateness.

Many will dispute this account and accuse it of over-dramatising the Left's divisions. The schism is only apparent, some will argue, and vanishes once we take the trouble to provide a more sophisticated explanation of the material and the cultural. Yet many attempted resolutions tend to reconfirm the above account by either reducing the cultural to the material or *vice versa*. Indeed, the incommensurability of the two perspectives may suggest that we resolve the dispute by refusing to seek a final, once-and-for-all reconciliation, but I will have more to say about this in the conclusion to this chapter and in Chapter 9.

This chapter does not provide a full account of this schism but it does hope to articulate the main ideas that have emerged along the faultline just described. To this end we review some recent theoretical developments in egalitarianism (as an example of materialism) and in discourse studies (as an example of culturalism). Finally, we will review some recent innovations in feminism in order to appreciate why and how some are seeking to move beyond the schism and the political paralysis to which it has arguably given rise.

Egalitarianism[1]

While the goal of strong social equality may no longer attract many political parties it remains central to Left thinking (also Callinicos, 2000):

> Reason should certainly alert us to the gross inconsistency in founding a social order on principles of merit and then rewarding people for qualities that come to them through no merit of their own. (Phillips, 1999: 72)

There is therefore a wide range of analysis and commentary upon which to draw and recent theorising has to be understood not as an attempt to reconstruct basic justifications for equality but as attempts to strengthen the theoretical justifications that predate the onslaught of recent conservative philosophers. Much of this 'strengthening' has concerned the links between equality and other concepts, for one of the implications of Temkin's (1993) expert analysis is that equality runs into paradox and incoherence if treated as a stand-alone principle.[2] So what are the 'links' with which recent theorists have been concerned? We might identify the following concepts as crucially important: class, markets, resources, freedom, desert and luck, respect and sufficiency, priority. Below, we review each of these in turn (and see Fitzpatrick, 2001a: Ch. 2).

Class

There remains a body of ideas motivated by class and particularly by Marxist explanations of class relations – see the next chapter also. Marxism has typically offered more insights into inequality than equality, being based upon the idea that those who create wealth have it stolen from them due to unequal distributions of productive assets. It then follows that social systems and institutions have to be understood primarily as manifestations of class inequality and the means of its reproduction across time and space. Jones and Novak (1999), for example, read post-WWII social democracy as a brief respite from capitalist repression before the state – in the 1980s – reverted to type. Welfare systems are therefore revealed as forms of discipline directed against the poor and vulnerable:

> For the poor and the working class more generally, the state continues to become more authoritarian and restrictive, more concerned with their control and containment and unconcerned with their worsening plight. This policing state, when compared with its immediate social-democratic predecessor, reflects an acceptance of widening social inequalities and poverty. Increasingly stripped of its positive welfare functions and abandoning any pretence of social obligation and rights, the state reverts to more draconian measures of maintaining order. (Jones & Novak, 1999: 174)

The values of social democracy are not necessarily rejected but social democracy is here regarded as somewhat naïve in its post-WWII confidence that capitalism could be tamed and irrevocably altered with relative ease. Similarly, Lavalette and Mooney (2000, 2002) revisit the collective struggles of the distant and recent past as a means of demonstrating, in the tradition of E. P. Thompson, how a radical analysis can reveal the complex interactions of society's micro and macro levels.

Yet Marxists have generally found it much harder to indicate what communist equality would amount to. A post-class and post-scarcity society is presumably one where social relationships are no longer mediated by states and markets. Yet assuming that some form of mediation is still needed, e.g.

because human errors cannot be completely eradicated, then what form should these take? Direct democracy has been one favoured response (Macpherson, 1977) but this either requires a highly sophisticated and co-ordinated set of actors and institutions or, if this is unrealistic, a system that makes democracy rather less direct and utopian. And, as always, Marxists must face the problem of transition (Wright, 1994). Has class struggle been displaced onto a global stage? Is class struggle now just one of many sites of radical resistance? Has 'immiseratation' sublimated into other forms? These are all worthwhile questions out of which a compelling political strategy may one day still form, but the fact that such fundamental issues still need to be probed after two centuries of (it is alleged) capitalist exploitation and repression could indicate that Marxist conceptions of inequality and equality, i.e. as distinct from social democratic ones, are still underdeveloped (see Cohen, 2000).

Markets

Consequently, many recent theorists (including some Marxists) have attached themselves to the traditions of social democracy and liberal equality, producing a number of interesting debates. For example, the late 1980s and early 1990s saw a great deal of attention given to market socialism, the idea that socialism can and should be based upon market exchange rather than central planning.[3] At its most modest, this may result in no more radical an ambition than that displayed by the NSD. But for many, market socialism implied the widespread collective ownership of social resources and usually, though not always, some form of extensive workplace democracy (Miller, 1989; Nove, 1991). Markets would therefore allocate goods with efficiency but without the waste of both human and non-human resources that *capitalist* markets produce. For whereas capitalist markets are based upon private ownership and profit, socialist markets would operate within the context of just institutions and so be shaped by other criteria. John Roemer (1994, 1996), for instance, imagines a system of social dividends by which shares in the economy are collectively owned but are 'rented' out to individuals during their lives. So with property rights equalised the distribution of income, even when affected by markets, would be more equal than at present. Market socialism has therefore appealed to liberals, since it retains the spaces of individual freedom and of decentralised decision making, but also to Marxists, since it arguably transcends the economics of capitalism. A market socialist system would therefore have little need of state welfare since the problems of unemployment and low pay, and all the other social dilemmas attendant upon them, would allegedly disappear.

Critics, though, allege that market socialism is not realistic since it could fully satisfy neither of its main objectives (see Pierson, 1995). Some on the

Left maintain that the anarchy and wastefulness of markets can only be over-come through planning – preferably democratic and decentralised if the errors of state communism are not to be repeated (Ollman *et al*, 1998). Market forces have to be severely constrained, rather than merely redirected, if the selfishness and the inequalities that they engender are not to be repro-duced. The Right agree that market socialism would simply collapse back into market capitalism but accept this as desirable (Gray, 1992). For what would happen if publicly owned enterprises and banks decided to become private bodies? Either the market socialist government would have to allow this and permit the re-emergence of capitalist acts between consenting adults, or it would have to prevent it and so recreate the kind of dictatorial centralisation that market socialism was supposed to overcome.

Resources

One possible response to such criticisms involves tying the egalitarianism of productive resources into the more mainstream tradition of social democracy. If the case for collective ownership can be made from within this tradition then popular support for it might make the above criticisms less acute.

One attempt to offer a radicalised social democracy has been proposed by Bowles and Gintis (1998). Their ideas are based upon the thesis that inequal-ity *impedes* economic performance and productivity rather than enhancing them. We therefore have to distinguish between redistributive policies that do damage productivity and those that do not. The redistribution of income falls under the first heading since it has an adverse impact upon incentives and so ultimately upon competitiveness. However, a redistribution of assets will have no such effect (unless you assume that these will be misused by those who are naturally undeserving) since, by giving everyone a stake in the economy and so boosting the productivity of those who are currently kept unproductive, overall economic performance will improve and competitive-ness remain undamaged. Therefore, it is possible to envisage *less* income redistribution leading to *greater* equality if assets are distributed equally. What do Bowles and Gintis mean by assets? Firstly, home ownership should be promoted and, where necessary, subsidised by the state. Secondly, children should have rights to their parents' income when parents act ir-responsibly. Thirdly, educational vouchers would empower both parents and children. Finally, productive assets should be transferred to workers so long as additional measures are in place to ensure that risk-aversion does not lower competitiveness.

This kind of 'asset egalitarianism' therefore carries potential appeal both to social democrats – and some have made connections between it and the NSD (White, 2001) – but also to socialists given its alleged implications for equal-ity and the socialisation of the economy.[4] If by assets we mean capital and wealth then such socialisation may be permissible; though if we mean something else, e.g. education, then its radical appeal is more modest. Bowles and Gintis appear to straddle the divide – and theirs is very much a 'new productivist' emphasis – and so occupy a space that is worth keeping an eye upon in the future. Yet by associating egalitarianism so closely with productivist concerns (the need for competitiveness, efficiency and growth) Bowles and Gintis arguably undermine the other aspects of equality that are not served by a productivist approach. For example, unless increased productivity serves to reproduce the natural and emotional bases upon which it depends then productivism (whether egalitarian or non-egalitarian) may not be sustainable in the longer term, leading to social and ecological crises that egalitarianism cannot address alone (Fitzpatrick, 2003: Ch. 5).

Freedom

Egalitarians have also been long concerned to argue that equality and freedom are not the opponents that conservatives insist, not only because equality can enhance the freedom of those who need it the most but because equality can enhance some types of freedom against other, less preferable types. A recent twist to this story of reconciliation has been provided by Left-libertarianism (Fitzpatrick, 2001a: 51–2).

Although Left-libertarianism has a long history (Vallentyne and Steiner, 2000) its resonance is fairly recent since it defends the kind of individualistic conceptions of freedom that have prevailed in recent decades but seeks to reconcile this with an egalitarian system of ownership (Steiner, 1994; Vallentyne, 2000) or at least a minimal standard of guaranteed income (van Parijs, 1995). Its first premise is that because individuals are the full owners of themselves then any violation of self-ownership is unjust. Therefore, there are quite severe constraints upon the extent to which individuals may be forced to do things against their will. However, whereas for libertarians on the Right this is what justifies free market capitalism, Left-libertarians combine this premise with a second which says that natural resources should be thought of as jointly owned so that only common interests can determine the use of resources. This is partly because there is no prima facie case for private property rights in those resources – Nozick's (1974: 175–82) defence of 'just original acquisition', i.e. the Lockean proviso, is held to be irreparably weak, clearing the way for a collectivist and egalitarian alternative (Fitzpatrick, 2001a: 51); and because of the role played by 'brute luck' in human affairs (see below). But rather than engendering the complete abolition of private ownership Left-libertarians believe that private owners should be required to pay a rent to the community equivalent to the full competitive value of the resources they have 'appropriated'. So Left-libertarians agree that individuals own themselves but insist that self-ownership only prevails within an egalitarian system of property ownership. This system may resemble a welfare state of sorts, though one presumably shorn of its paternalist and bureaucratic apparatus, or it may imply something far more radical, perhaps the kind of asset-based egalitarianism that we discussed earlier.

Libertarianism does enable a degree of rapprochement between Left and Right. Nozick (1974: Ch. 10) famously observed that in a free society those who wish to form communistic communities are perfectly free to do so; they simply cannot impose their preferences upon the rest of us. For critics, though, this is naïve, another example of Nozick defining freedom as 'non-interference by others' and ignoring the extent to which freedom can be curtailed by forms of structural domination that do not necessarily require person-to-person interference. Barry (2003) has been more ambitious, proposing that if egalitarians can abandon their attachment to a strong state and the idea that undeserved abilities should be redistributed, and if market libertarians can give up the pretence that only choice matters, then both sides can find agreement in the need for redistributive land taxation and in an economy within which mutualist firms and organisations flourish.

So, although they will agree broadly with the kind of social reforms advocated by others on the non-libertarian Left, Left-libertarians arrive at these reforms via a different route. Cohen (1995: Ch. 4) argues that this route is nevertheless an important difference and that there arises an inevitable conflict between *full* self-ownership and an equality of conditions. Where people are born with unequal talents then an inequality of conditions will result since even where they possess identical sets of external goods some (the talented) will use their goods more effectively than others (the untalented) over time. We may attempt to compensate for those inequalities of talent – perhaps because they are undeserved – and enforce an equality of conditions, but this would require the untalented to have a say over when, how and where the talented utilise their talents and so contradicts the idea of full self-ownership.[5] Cohen therefore maintains that full self-ownership is incompatible with egalitarianism and suggests that we must either abandon the latter (as Nozick maintains) or the former. Cohen concludes that egalitarianism has to be based at best upon *partial* self-ownership where the individual's use and control of their person is not total, such that others have a stake in your rights to yourself. If we accept this argument it presumably means that Left-Libertarianism fails as a viable approach.

Desert and luck

As noted in Chapter 1, although admired by the Right the concept of desert has long been associated with the Left also. For Marxists it is first necessary to observe the socialist principle 'to each according to his labour' if we are to eventually pass beyond socialism into communism. Nevertheless, many on the Left have been uneasy with the concept since it suggests that if rewards should be proportionate to contribution then the unproductive poor are as exploitative as the unproductive rich (Kymlicka, 2002: 178–87). Liberals like Rawls (2001: 61–79) also make reference to desert in his assertion that justice is a doctrine of reciprocity such that people can exclude themselves from the group of the 'least well-off' and so from the benefits conferred by the difference principle. Even so, those such as Dworkin (2000) feel that Rawlsian justice is incomplete because he failed to build the concept fully into the heart of his philosophy.

Much recent liberal and egalitarian political philosophy has therefore been concerned to reconcile desert (and related ideas of choice and responsibility) with some notion of social justice, to give a more well-rounded egalitarian philosophy. What this involves is a theoretical rapprochement between that for which we cannot be held responsible (natural and social inheritances, brute luck, the actions of others) and that for which we perhaps can (ambitions, uncoerced choices and efforts of will). Determining the precise 'cut' between these is, however, difficult and inevitably contentious.[6] If I write a best-selling book (fat chance) to what extent do I deserve the rewards as a free agent and to what extent should those rewards revert to the community since the book has also been produced by factors for which I am not responsible (a good education, loving parents, comfortable social background, etc.)? Our answer to that question must affect our view as to what levels of taxation and social expenditure are justifiable. Basically, the greater the role played by circumstances, inheritances and luck then the higher the levels of tax and expenditure which might be justifiable; but if individuals are regarded as the main authors of their lives then lower levels of tax and spending could be appropriate.

Dworkin (2000: 287–99) is one who has laboured with such questions and insists that, although circumstances shape choice, so long as an individual identifies with the choice in question then they *can* be held responsible for the resulting outcome, whether good or bad. However, others insist that Dworkin is overestimating the importance of free will in human affairs, since our choices are rarely either free or coerced but consist mostly of adaptation to given circumstances. And if our social environment is unjust then such 'adapted preferences', whether we identify with them or not, are themselves nothing more than reflections of unjust circumstances. Therefore, we should not give that much weight to principles of choice, responsibility and desert after all.

Roemer (1998) is one of those who takes such an approach, constructing his theory of equal opportunities upon the concept of 'social types', i.e. the categories into which individuals can be said to fall depending upon a host of variables – age, income/wealth, occupation, social background, and so forth. Roemer's basic idea can be best explained through an illustration. One of the social policy dilemmas we face is in deciding when the financial consequences of ill health should fall upon the individual concerned and when upon society collectively. If someone contracts lung cancer after years of smoking then where does the responsibility lie and onto whose mat should the health bill fall?[7] Most of us might be tempted to follow Grandpa Simpson in proclaiming 'a little from column A and a little from column B', but Roemer offers an approach more sophisticated than this kind of fence-sitting, 50/50 response. Let us say that we have four wards of cancer patients according to the rubric of Figure 2.1

	Affluent	Poor
Young	*Ward 1*	*Ward 2*
Old	*Ward 3*	*Ward 4*

Figure 2.1   Examples of Basic Social Types

Roemer asserts that those upon whom the greatest individual liability should fall can be found in Ward 3, i.e. those who have lived affluent lives, and so experienced relatively low levels of stress, and who have had time to curb their smoking habits. Those upon whom the lowest individual liability should fall can be found in Ward 2, i.e. those who are poor and have had less time to develop healthier lifestyles. Wards 1 and 4 lie in between, with the relevant variables balancing each other out. In short, where we draw the line between choice and circumstance will alter depending upon the social type in question – whereas the standard 50/50 response collapses all social types into one.

Now this example is simplistic since it only involves two variables and Roemer acknowledges that actual social types are multiple and complex so that distinguishing between circumstances and choice is extremely difficult (as well as being a matter of value interpretation) – see next chapter also. Nevertheless, Roemer's theory confirms the suspicion of egalitarians that, when properly designed, progressive systems of economic and social policies could redistribute resources from those whom circumstance has blessed to those whose choices are severely constrained by impoverishing environments. And if determining the ways and the extent to which choice and circumstance meld together is difficult, a brief glance at those who would simply attribute social inequalities to choice (e.g. Choi, 2002) suggests that the effort is worthwhile nonetheless.

Respect and sufficiency

Other egalitarians are more than a little dismayed by such approaches. For Anderson (1999) the idea that people should be compensated for bad luck is objectionable since it defines them in terms of characteristics popularly held to be inferior and so denies them the respect which is owed to us all. What she calls 'democratic equality' still insists upon the abolition of oppressive hierarchies but is firmly based upon a doctrine of moral equality. This stress upon respect is also central to Schmidtz's (2002) defence of 'prior possession'. We cannot treat resources as if they are, ever were or ever could be owned jointly: the property rights of those who 'got there first' (firstcomers) must be defended as a matter of respect and of liberty. This does not mean that 'late-comers' lose out necessarily since they will gain from the wealth created by firstcomers and, in any event, justice has to start from where we are.

What Anderson in particular does is to offer support for a principle of sufficiency, the idea that a just distribution of resources is one that leaves everyone with enough but does not object to inequalities in non-essential goods, e.g. consumer goods. This accords with a politics of minimum standards which was at the heart of Beveridge's conception of the good society – rather than equality *per se* – and which some regard as the *sine qua non* of income maintenance (Veit Wilson, 1998). The problem is in defining what we mean by 'enough'. If sufficiency is quantified in modest terms then redistributive reforms can be correspondingly moderate, though for more thoroughgoing egalitarians like Anderson it has to imply much more than this. But whatever the implications Arneson (2002) insists that sufficiency is an inadequate principle upon which to build social reform; a single line of sufficiency leads to the potential neglect of those above the line whose position can be improved and of those below the line who can be helped even if they cannot be raised above it.[8] This may mean that we should specify multiple lines of sufficiency, though Arneson prefers an alternative approach, as explained below.

It might also be pointed out that Schmidtz's version of respect risks ossifying existing patterns of distribution to an extent incompatible with social justice. While latecomers may have much to gain, significant numbers will presumably not gain as much as the lucky descendents of firstcomers. The importance of 'circumstance' therefore reappears since while some will have 'got there first' due to their own efforts others will have simply been lucky. So while private property is justifiable (circumstance cannot account for everything) property *rights* are not *given* since the nature and justice of property is derivative upon an antecedent weighting of circumstance and choice, *and* how that weighting alters over time as society becomes either more or less just. While an egalitarian system may violate individualistic rights of private property a non-egalitarian one ensures that we do not possess equal shares in those resources, e.g. our common inheritance, upon which choice and desert cannot reasonably be said to encroach.[9]

Priority

Parfit (2001) has pointed out that 'equality' is often mistaken for 'priority' such that whereas the former is concerned with the relative distance between the top and the bottom the latter is concerned only with the absolute position of the bottom. For 'prioritarians' justice consists of improving the position of the least well-off and although there are occasions when this demands an egalitarian distribution it is also possible to envisage scenarios where this is not the case. Where Poorman can only be assisted by redistributing resources from Richman then such redistribution is both prioritarian (since Poorman's position has been improved) and egalitarian (since the gap between the two has narrowed). However, egalitarians are vulnerable to the 'levelling down' argument in a way that prioritarians are not. Imagine two countries where everyone in Country A owns two houses while in Country B 50 percent of the population own two houses and the other 50 percent own three. On strict egalitarian grounds Country A is preferable and yet this appears to be counterintuitive. After all, those in Country B who own two houses are no worse off then anyone in Country A: their possessions are still the same even though there are others who possess three houses. The egalitarian support for Country A therefore represents a levelling down in comparison to Country B whereas a prioritarian is neutral between the two countries. Indeed, if the choice were between Country B and Country C (where everyone owns one house) then egalitarians will prefer Country C even though the absolute position of the least well-off has now been worsened. Parfit is not suggesting that egalitarianism be abandoned but he is demanding a clearer distinction between support for an equality of relative positions and for improvements in the absolute position of the least well-off.

Take the four distributive scenarios in Figure 2.2 – the horizontal axis represents time, the vertical a combination of income and wealth and the dotted lines the trajectories of the top and bottom quintiles.[10]

Scenario (1) is both egalitarian and prioritarian since the absolute position of the bottom improves and the distance between the bottom and top narrows. Scenario (2) is prioritarian but not egalitarian since although the absolute position of the bottom improves the relative distance widens. Scenario (3) is neither egalitarian nor prioritarian while scenario (4) is egalitarian but not prioritarian. Now, whether we are egalitarians or prioritarians scenario (3) is eliminated as a desirable option and, if we are both, then scenario (1) appears to be the most desirable. The difficulty comes in adjudicating between (2) and (4).

Prioritarians will support (2) but not (4), egalitarians will support (4) but not (2); and there are convincing arguments on both sides. Since under scenario (2) the absolute position of the least well-off improves as much as under (1) then why does what is happening at the top matter? Under scenario (4) the absolute position of the least well-off declines as much as under (3) but perhaps their status improves since the position of the better off declines even more (which is to say that Country C might be preferable to B since, even though they lose a house, the poorest in country B might benefit from transition to C because it embodies a greater equality of status, e.g. in terms of how socially valued they feel).

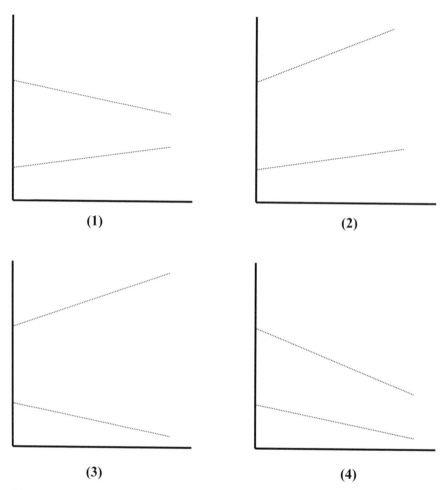

Figure 2.2   Equality and Priority

In reality, the conflict between egalitarians and prioritarians is likely to be less extreme, as illustrated in Figure 2.3.

In scenario (5) the poorest do less well than in scenario (6) but since the position of the richest also improves less favourably then the resulting inequality in (5) is less than that in (6). An egalitarian will therefore prefer (5), despite the poorest being less well off than in (6); whereas a prioritarian will prefer (6) for this latter reason, regardless of the greater inequality. The disagreement between them centres around whether the absolute position of the poorest can be separated from their relative position. For instance,

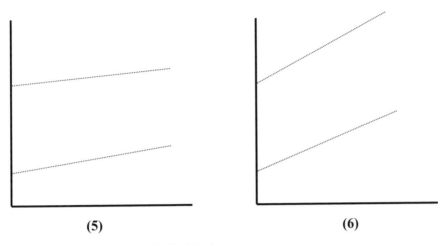

(5) **(6)**

Figure 2.3 Equality and Priority Revisited

Arneson (2002: 196) has come round to the view that priority is superior to equality *per se*:

> ... what matters morally when getting a benefit to a person is in the offing is not how badly off that person is in comparison to others. What matters is the degree to which the person is well off or badly off as measured on an absolute or noncomparative scale.

Arneson is more determined than Parfit to associate prioritarianism with a 'moderate egalitarianism' since securing gains for the worse off depends upon the amount of benefit that can be secured for both worse and better off. Yet what ultimately matters is this absolute scale and not inequality as such.[11] Even so, the egalitarian can still claim that the absolute and the relative cannot be separated out so neatly. The possibility of devising Arneson's scale depends, as he readily acknowledges, upon an absolutist definition of well-being, but if – as I noted in Fitzpatrick (2001a: 10) – neither a purely absolutist nor a purely subjectivist definition is entirely adequate then can such a scale really be meaningful? If social status matters and if status implies a strong qualitative dimension then the superiority of (6) over (5) is not so clear after all.

Two key questions appear unresolved, then. Firstly, can we separate out priority from equality as much as Parfit wishes? Secondly, although he re-acquaints priority with equality, can 'absolute position' be separated from 'relative position' as much as Arneson imagines? To put it another way, must the avoidance of levelling down (whether in scenario (4) or (5)) *always* be regarded as a side constraint upon what we should and should not do? It is not counterintuitive to suggest that subjective well-being *may sometimes* rise even when objective or absolutist well-being declines. In Britain the experience of WWII might be cited as such an example and since this period helped to inspire post-war reforms we might hesitate to ground social policy and social justice upon nothing more than prioritarian principles.

Discourse

As noted in the book's Introduction discourse has become a popular term in recent years although there is little consensus regarding its sense or frame of reference (Howarth, 2000: Ch. 1). For some, it denotes the way in which we understand and act upon the social world in and through the productions and circulations of language and meaning. It therefore replaces 'ideology' since this concept still implies totalising forms of knowledge, power and action that have become anathema to many. For others, discourse does not signal a new ontology or epistemology but, instead, has to be theorised as a product or reflection of pre-discursive objects and relations. It is therefore a second-level concept. On this reading, discourses do not penetrate 'all the way down' but articulate a world that is, to some degree, independent of and prior to language.

One way or another, though, the concept seems to refer to the importance of language, power and categorisation. The idea that language is a transparent medium of exchange had finally died by the middle of the twentieth century and had been replaced by the idea that we are everywhere preceded by language so that subjectivity is spoken by the grammar of our social origins. The question then is whether language is to be understood as a structured system of signs or as an open stream of difference; whether as still external to a subject who arrives from outside language's external borders or as a subjectless play that erases modern conceits of agency and autonomy. The disagreement here feeds into and out of disagreements over power.

Does power follow a singular logic or is it, as Foucault (1975, 1977) insists, a technology of disciplinary norms that produces bodies, a body being that which 'freely' reproduces the power that gave birth to it (see Chapter 7). For Foucault, truth is not that which speaks *to* power but that which always speaks *of* it and social institutions do not need to repress, in the conventional sense, the subjectivities through which they practice. It is this interpenetration of power, subject, knowledge and institution that Foucault describes as discursive. Critics, though, allege that this is to collapse the polarities of regulation and resistance so that by being made to appear everywhere each ends up appearing nowhere (McNay, 1993). So while Foucault may awaken us to ever-present conflicts of 'bio-power', by ignoring the ethical field linking philosophy to politics he provides comfort to the hierarchical agencies of oppression and inequality.

Finally, then, is classification to be understood primarily as classification *by* agents or as the distribution *of* agents into classificatory boundaries along the flows of power? Is the subject still at or at least somewhere near the centre or must we think in different terms, of centreless grids, networks, webs and labyrinths within which subjects appear only fleetingly, the residual afterimages of liberal humanism that still reflect occasionally in the mirrors which modernity erected to flatter itself?

To delve into these debates it is useful to distinguish between realists and post-structuralists. Realists insist that language is a second-order reflection of a material substratum that discourse can never fully penetrate or constitute; post-structuralists believe that when we talk of 'the world' we are referring to no more than the production of meaning through discursive interaction and cultural context. Here, then, realists and post-structuralists can substitute for what I earlier termed materialists and culturalists. This is no doubt to repeat the very errors of which the latter constantly complain. Yet it does capture one of the many faultlines on the contemporary Left which, for all its implications for social theory and reform, cannot be ignored. Two recent schools of thought illustrate what is at stake here. They are both inspired by post-structuralism but the following account will show why realist critiques of them remain persuasive to many.

Governmentality

The governmentality literature (Dean, 1999, 2003; Rose, 1999a, 1999b) draws upon Foucault in particular and insists that 'governmentality', or the conduct of conduct, is a rationality that saturates the social and inhabits the self, rather than being external to it. Practices of calculation, categorisation and partitioning are not simply the means of governing objects but the means by which new objects arise for governing. So these authors are not simply repeating the mundane point that governmentality implies more than government and state, but that government and state are themselves inscribed within the domains of particular discourses. States police in so far as they are policed and populations are rendered up for the regulatory gaze as bodies that have already been constituted as surveillable, as subjects that are governed through their freedom and are free only in so far as they are governed. We are therefore presented with an alternative to liberal and Marxist perspectives, both of which (but for different reasons) regard freedom and governance as opposites. Governmentality is capable of revealing why 'liberal authoritarianism' is not such a oxymoron after all (Dean, 2002; cf. King, 1999).

This approach therefore offers a new account of the origins and trajectories of welfare states, one that does not offer *ex nihilo* theorisations of actors and classes but which traces into the minutiae of social experience the administrative practices out of which the surfaces of subjectification can be said to condense. For example, new means of keeping order were demanded by the modern growth and concentration of populations, leading to the 'massification' of bodies through quantitative techniques (censuses, statistics), distinctions between poor/unproductive and affluent/productive, and the pathologisation of 'the poor' as either deserving or undeserving. The development of modern welfare systems might therefore be seen as the continued discursive incarceration of 'problematic groups' and as the consolidation of a welfare subject whose freedom is enhanced through the collectivisms of social insurance, stable employment, social work and all forms of compulsory cradle-to-grave provision (Garland, 2001a) (see Chapter 8).

Yet while the governmentality literature opens up exciting new vistas for analysis it is not always clear whether it offers the basis of a counter-critique to conservatism. If it locates potential sites of resistance within the everyday – the possibility of micro-resistances by which we can momentarily distort what the disciplinary gaze can and cannot see – it remains reluctant to knit those sites together; for if we are always within a domain of governmentality then there is no 'outside' and so it follows that any overarching counter-critique must carry within it the signatures of our future governance. O'Malley *et al* (1997) outline a 'weaker' version of post-structuralism, one where the governmentality literature might engage more creatively with critical theory, yet they do not explain how this association may be performed as this is precisely what any kind of post-structuralist approach (whether weak or strong) seems to preclude. It is only by slipping back into the confines of humanist and naturalist social science that Rose *et al* can fail to notice that their normative criticisms of free market liberalism are disallowed by their conceptual premises.

So, the moral outrage of the Foucauldians is directed at the micro-effects of a capitalist system that they refuse to visualise at the macro-level in the belief that visualisation closes down the possibility of new narratives and new descriptions. Rose (1999b: 95) insists that,

> One must discard the presupposition that one can criticise regimes of power to the extent that they falsify and distort human subjectivity and utilise the extent of this falsification as a yardstick by which power can be evaluated...

Here, the evaluation of power is ruled out of court and we are left without a centre of power and responsibility that would permit a macro-critique, the aim of which would be the redistribution *of* power and responsibility. So although they direct our attention to the governance of subjectivity and the micro-social, the theorists of governmentality resemble foreign correspondents who are unwilling to intervene at a higher level in the events upon which they are reporting. The governmentality debate offers useful insights into the ways in which modern systems empower and disempower yet it is not clear from it why we should regard disempowerment as morally and socially problematic.

Post-Marxism

Post-Marxism represents a synthesis of two traditions, Marxism and post-structuralism, though here the influence of Foucault is more muted. Heavily influenced by the ongoing work of Laclau and Mouffe (1985; Laclau, 1990, 1994, 1996; Mouffe, 1992, 1993, 2000) post-Marxism advocates a radically plural democracy that rejects the universalisms of critical theory (cf. Derrida, 1994).

The basic approach is laid out in *Hegemony and Socialist Strategy*. Whereas Gramsci (1971) conceived of hegemonic struggle as a tug-of-war between workers and bourgeoisie, Laclau and Mouffe argue that there are a multiplicity of 'subject positions' such that struggle does not occur between pre-given interests and identities but is always the means by which interests and identities make themselves through the recognition of others in an incessant process of alliance and conflict. Meaning is never fixed so that the social is never fully identical to itself, implying that critique can never hope to encompass the totality of the social field. Instead, the social is an articulatory practice whose identity is only ever partially stabilised by discursive formations, formations which are always subject to instability due to the contingency of systems, their openness to difference. Therefore, the social is always and everywhere political, circulating between the attempt to fix meaning and constant reminders of the impossibility of doing so. Society can never form a closure since it consists of antagonisms that can always rupture the relatively stable points of a social order.

The significance of these ideas lies in their simultaneous rejection and affirmation of the Marxist tradition. On the one hand, Marxists were excoriated for attempting to discern essences and universals within the supposed depths of society and history, and for representing themselves as the intellectual and practical embodiments of those depths – the Leninist/Maoist conceit that leads ultimately to the gulag. Yet Laclau and Mouffe nevertheless insist that once these conceits are stripped away then, due to its concern with struggle (albeit one traditionally focused upon the teleological clash between capital and labour), Marxism is well placed to theorise the plurality of conflicts that flow across a mutable series of axes. Post-Marxism therefore calls for the radicalisation of democracy where the social is always reopened to itself, but without any utopian dreams of finality and totality.

There is a sense in which the greatest triumph of post-Marxism lies in the events that have occurred since its emergence, events indicating that society may indeed never be as closed as many imagine: the fall of Apartheid, the implosion of Soviet Communism, counterreactions to corporate capitalism, global terrorism. It therefore represents an alternative to the dreams of a final unity with which humanity has long haunted itself: the attempt to bring God and God-substitutes down to earth, the dreams of absoluteness and totality through which fundamentalisms (whether religious or secular) are constructed. For those who dream of unity are usually disappointed by its lack in a present that seems suddenly imperfect, often succumbing to pessimism and the paranoid feeling of betrayal by 'heretics' who have consequently to be eliminated.

Yet post-Marxism has also been subject to a number of persuasive criticisms (Geras, 1998; see Smith, 1998; cf. Howarth, 2000: 111–25). Firstly, that it is a form of discursive idealism which ignores the materiality of objects and fills the world with nothing more than language. Post-Marxists reject this accusation by acknowledging that materiality exists independently of discourse but nevertheless insist that there can be no such thing as pre-discursive *meaning* since meaning is only ever discursive and an object only carries meaning in so far as it inhabits a system of signification. An object becomes recognisable by being named. This ontology, though, does seem to rest upon a passive conception of materialism, where discourses act upon objects but objects cannot reciprocate, except through more discourses. To be convincing, the rejection of a realist/idealist distinction either has to permit a greater role to material determination or else fall back into the idealism with which some critics charge it.

Secondly, post-Marxism has been accused of relativism. If discourses can only ever be judged from within their own contextual framework, if there is no extra-contextual space, then we are left with no rational reason to prefer, say, Marxism to anti-Marxism or liberalism to anti-liberalism (see Chapter 9 also). To resist this accusation post-Marxists seem to follow Rorty (1998: xvi–xxxiii) in rejecting the epistemological distinction (relativism/universalism) upon which it is founded. For Rorty, relativism is a product not of post-modernism, which is committed to the 'positionality' or context-dependence or truth, but of those who go searching for absolutes. But, against this position, even if we abandon the search for a God's eye view does this mean that we cannot search for *any* form of absoluteness or objectivity? It may be true that,

> Destroying the hierarchies upon which sexual or racial discrimination is based will ... always require the construction of other exclusions ... (Laclau, 1990: 33)

but unless we can cogently demonstrate to those beyond our contexts that these other exclusions would be morally *superior* to sexism and racism then a politics of anti-discrimination can do nothing more than appeal to those who have already been raised within its tradition.

Finally, then, post-Marxism risks a political naivety that is parasitic upon the very philosophies that it claims to dispel. Neither Apartheid nor the Berlin Wall fell because people rejected objectivity and universality in the name of post-structuralist difference; they fell because they were widely held to violate the human rights that most hold to *be* objective, absolute and universal. There is undoubtedly a need to combat dogmatism and fundamentalism – and the dilemma of contemporary liberalism lies in attempting to reconcile this need with assertions of objective universality (e.g. Gray,

2000) – but this does not necessarily mean that we should see ourselves as nothing more than the bearers of our contexts.[12] Is pluralism better served by abandoning foundationalism or by people agreeing to disagree about what those foundations might be? The force of post-structuralism depends upon its not being widely accepted by the very pluralists that it celebrates. This also indicates why post-Marxism cannot deliver a knock-out blow to critical theory since the continued existence of the latter, for all its supposed errors, is indispensable for the identity of the former (Fitzpatrick, 2002a).

These criticisms aside, post-Marxism has wielded some influence upon social policy research. Torfing (1999: Ch. 12) applies a discourse analysis derived from the work of Laclau, Mouffe and Slavoj Žižek to the historical development of state welfare as a means of understanding current dilemmas, changes and strategies. For all intents and purposes this replicates the kind of analysis we reviewed in the previous section where the focus is upon governmentality rather than rational agency (liberalism) or class struggle (Marxism). Torfing concludes by agreeing with Jessop that we have entered a new mode of regulation based upon global competition and post-Keynesianism (Fitzpatrick, 2001a: 161–3) but he calls for an account that is less economistic and functionalist than that of the regulationists:

> People act upon discursive constructions of the 'real world' rather than upon the hard facts themselves. Or, rather, they act upon which is constructed as facts in and through discourse. (Torfing, 1999: 241)

Yet it is not clear that such 'radical constructionism' would be any more sophisticated than the economism it is intended to replace, particularly given the criticisms which we have just reviewed.

Feminism

Is there a way around this standoff between realists and post-structuralists, materialists and culturalists? What I intend to review below are some recent theoretical innovations which, deriving from feminist debates, may allow us to do so. We leave to one side those which tie into debates reviewed elsewhere in the book (and see Fitzpatrick, 2001a: 139–45) or those where the theory has a specific methodological or policy-orientation. What follows is therefore not an attempt to cover every aspect of the feminist 'third wave' (Lister, 2003a).

Masculinity

Much has been made in conservative circles of how feminism has plunged men and masculinity into a crisis, precipitating a rise in social problems as young men find that the positions in society they would formerly have occupied have been taken by women, leaving their aggressive and domineering instincts with nowhere else to go but into lawlessness, promiscuity and self-harm (Pizzey *et al*, 2000). Social demoralisation therefore follows from the attempt to impose artificial equalities upon the natural order. Feminism has been generally slow to counter this accusation, although the literature is now growing in volume (Whitehead, 2002) and 'men's studies' no longer raise as many eyebrows as it once did.

Of key importance in this respect is the work of Susan Faludi (1999). Having previously launched impressive salvos against the anti-feminist backlash (Faludi, 1992) she sets out to empty masculinity of the conservative content that it often assumes. Her basic conclusion is that the crisis of masculinity is real and should not be dismissed by women as male whinging. However, rather than this crisis being due to feminism and improvements in women's social position it is really due to an economy which has less use than previously for skills traditionally associated with men, to consumer markets that now subject men to the same commodified insecurities as women, and to a culture where many men regard gender equality as a threat rather than an opportunity. Feminism has contributed to this culture to some extent (by focusing upon the dominated rather than the dominant) but it is ultimately due to mainstream ideologies failing to adapt to feminist challenges that go far beyond the demand for equal pay or more childcare. The conservative accusation is therefore particularly galling since it advocates with one hand the kind of competitive, free-for-all economics the effects of which it wants to halt with the other.

Faludi therefore suggests that the next stage for feminism lies within a new association between women and men, a recognition that neither can make much progress without acknowledgement that they share the same problem: not 'male oppression' or 'female oppression' but the oppressive relations which are inscribed within our cultures and economies of power. In short, what both need is more rather than less equality and new means of describing themselves in terms of the other. Of key importance here is the concept of care since it can be claimed that the demoralisations of self and society are due to care being eclipsed by ideologies of productivity where work continues to be largely identified with employment.

Care

The literature on care is now vast due to its considerable implications for our understanding of citizenship, work, dependency and equality (e.g. Tronto, 1993; Sevenhuijsen, 1998; F. Williams, 2001; Noddings, 2002; Lister, 2003a) – see Chapter 7 also. Feminists make several claims about care:

- Care is a valuable form of work even when it is unpaid
- Most paid carework is *under*paid and unpaid carework tends to be undervalued

- This is because carework is performed mostly by women and so its low status reflects patriarchal assumptions about usefulness and productivity
- The entry of more women into the job market has not altered this substantially, although men do now perform more carework than before
- We need policies that provide more effective support for caregivers
- We need reforms that encourage a more equitable split between men and women of caregiving activities

Therefore, we have to understand citizenship as reflecting a much broader conception of social participation, one where caring, earning and 'earning by caring' are more equally valued. This implies that the public/private distinction should no longer be gendered, i.e. equivalent to that of male/female, and a recognition that rights and responsibilities are performed in the domestic sphere as much as in the workplace. Work can therefore be redefined as 'working for others', for those to whom we bear expressive attachments, rather than simply 'working for another' through the wage contract. The fetishisation of independence (Sennett, 2003) – whether through the labour market or otherwise – is therefore challenged on the basis that since we are all the givers and receivers of care then a straightforward division between independence and dependency is both simplistic and, because independence is identified with job market success and fulfilment, hegemonic. Care therefore implies equality in the distribution of caregiving and receiving between men and women, but perhaps also in terms of the wider political economy since care seems to require a more effective work/life balance and so not only the redistribution of time but a redistribution of the resources needed to make time meaningful (Williams, 1999; Fitzpatrick, 2004a, 2004b).

The debate about care therefore ties into those we have reviewed above. It has egalitarian implications, ones that are not necessarily limited to that of gender, and it also relates to the wider appreciation of the social role of discourse. Some take this in a post-structuralist direction. Here, gender differences are understood as discursive constructions where the feminine has been 'the other' of a humanness constituted in masculinist terms (Butler, 1990; Haraway, 1991). Breaking away from such 'phallogocentrism' requires a new symbolic or imaginary order that renarrates the self in non-essentialist – and therefore non-masculinist – terms. Equality derives not from the equalisation of given identities but from the deconstruction of identities and the emergence of new regimes of power and subjectivisation. Care might then be thought of as a process through which our partial identities meet, understand and combine more effectively.

Others, though, prefer to locate both equality and discourse within a more materialist frame where it is not believed that the traditional concerns of poverty, exploitation and oppression can be adequately replaced by a politics of difference or identity (Phillips, 1999; Segal, 1999). There is still a need for collective actions that derive from ideological strategies, even ones that risk invoking totalising critiques, in a world where transgressions have become more rather than less difficult due to the inhibitions of capitalism rather than of modernity *per se*. Here, care is a means for re-engaging with the political economy of patriarchal capitalism.

The disagreements at work here reflect those within the contemporary Left as a whole and we will review below an influential attempt to deal with them. Beforehand, though, it is sensible to indicate why care cannot, by itself, provide a new philosophy. Most obviously this is because care can sometimes be oppressive. Think of the saint who is more concerned to assist the poor as a sign of divinely-inspired charity rather than address the social causes of poverty; or think of the disabled person for whom care might be less preferable than a greater degree of independence. Secondly, by attending to the particular, some theorists of care tend to demonstrate hostility to universal principles that they accuse of being too abstract and rationalistic (Fitzpatrick, 2003: 114–8). Yet although universalism can be a way of ignoring the particularity of harm and vulnerability this hostility risks detouring around recent attempts to conceive of universalism in more complex, flexible and sensitive ways – see below. An abstract rationalism is merely reproduced by those who would abandon it in favour of an ethic of emotionalism (Gilligan, 1982). Care may certainly contribute to but can never replace a theory of justice.

Redistribution and recognition

This is what makes the recent work of Nancy Fraser so potentially significant. Long concerned to develop a feminist postmodernism for the Left, Fraser (1989) has begun to tie together a number of threads in ways that bear relevance not only for political radicalism but for radical social policies also. While still drawing upon postmodernist ideas Fraser has wanted to move the debate on and establish that postmodernism is not simply a celebration of difference (a resistance to logics of totality) but of respect for differences that are in some way socially valuable. To this end she has made connections with those seeking to establish new cognitive, ontological and social frameworks. So what is important for Fraser is not difference *per se* but recognition, and not recognition *per se* but one that joins with doctrines of social justice to facilitate a reconciliation of Leftist materialism and culturalism.[13]

One of those with whom Fraser takes issue is Axel Honneth. Honneth (1995, 2001) argues that that the theoretical case for justice must rest upon an acknowledgement of recognition as that which is essential to social norms and identities. If recognition is taken to encompass love, esteem and legal equality then we have foundations sufficient for the understanding of socio-economic injustice. Whether the problem is racism or unemployment we should perceive injustice as disrespect for the moral autonomy and psychological integrity of the person. Fraser contends that this is to overestimate the extent to which recognition can support the philosophical and political weight that Honneth would rest upon it (Fraser & Honneth, 2003: Chs 2 and 3). Instead, it is best to conceive of reality as consisting of several points of entry, none of which is epistemologically superior to the others. For instance, rather than collapse the cultural (status) and the economic (class) together it is better to view them as integrated yet analytically distinct nevertheless. Cultural and economic injustices feed off one another but neither can be entirely mapped on to the other.

Fraser notes how social justice and recognition are usually treated as incompatible because the former is interpreted in terms of universal rules (the Kantian 'right') and the latter as a question of ethical judgement (the Hegelian 'good'). But according to Fraser (2001) recognition also involves justice-claims where 'misrecognition' entails forms of institutional exclusion and subordination that can be demonstrated according to universally-valid criteria. Challenging misrecognition therefore means ensuring a 'parity of participation' by distributing material resources in such a way that economic structures are just and accord an equal respect to all social participants. Equality of recognition should therefore *not* be accorded to those who either do or would deny participative parity to others and social justice therefore implies the just distribution of both material and cultural resources.

Fraser's work is therefore significant for two reasons. Firstly, it rescues universalism from those who would distinguish it from all domains of particularity by either subordinating the particular to it or it to the particular. Fraser's work therefore converges with those who have also sought a 'situated' or 'grounded' universalism from with the traditions of critical theory (e.g. Benhabib, 1992) and so offers feminism a useful means of reconciling a politics of materialism with one of culturalism. Secondly, it embraces the two wings of recent Left politics. Fraser (1997: 59–62) proposes adoption of a universal caregiver model whereby caregiving and wage-earning are regarded as the purview of both men and women, requiring reforms that facilitate and encourage men and women to move equally and freely between public and private spheres. This seems to imply a strong redistribution of resources (egalitarianism), as well as an acknowledgement that we require alternative social relations that embody new discourses and meanings (of citizenship, useful work, dependency, etc.). Fraser's ideas have subsequently influenced those who work more directly in the field of social policy: Williams (1999) outlines seven policy-related points at which the need for cultural recognition and for socioeconomic equality intersect; Lister (2001) argues for a welfare agenda of both redistribution and recognition whereby the poorest are empowered to become actors in the political process of service design and delivery.

This approach has not gone unchallenged, though. Young (2000: 92), for instance, accuses Fraser of relegating the cultural to a subordinate level, of dichotomising the politics of identity and difference as 'merely cultural' and so of reproducing the very oppressions that she claims to be addressing. In short, Fraser thinks that she has reconciled the material and cultural but has actually kept them apart conceptually and so underestimated the extent to which they interpenetrate. Honneth, too, complains that Fraser separates social reality out onto different analytical levels until it becomes almost impossible to reconnect them (Fraser & Honneth, 2003: Ch. 4). In reply Fraser (1997) maintains that unless we do separate out the material and the cultural as ideal-types then we misinterpret the links between cultural struggles and capitalist ones.

Yet aspects of such disagreement have become more subdued over time. Fraser acknowledges that any distinction between the material and the cultural had to be heuristic, requiring a new understanding of each sphere as somehow both autonomous and yet 'interfused' with the other. The welfare state, she claims, is as cultural as a film (Alldred, 1999: 132). Young (2000) has made greater room in her recent work for issues of distributive justice that cannot simply be treated as cultural recognitions and misrecognitions. None of this amounts to a simple rapprochement, but does perhaps indicate a mutual acknowledgement that no perspective can fully contain both itself and the best insights of its opponents.

Concluding Thoughts

This chapter has given some flavour of the intellectual ferment that continues to characterise the Left. At one extreme we have materialists for whom the concept of equality continues to be of central importance; at the other we have culturalists who focus, instead, upon discourse and difference. Neither on its own appears entirely convincing. There does not appear to be an over-arching theory of material equality capable of capturing all aspects of injustice. Yet theorists of discourse cannot entirely dissuade us away from a more traditional, 'realist' perspective. I have suggested that recent developments within feminist theory offer a possible rapprochement – not to be confused with a synthesis. Through a discussion of gender (in the form of masculinity) and care we arrive at Fraser's attempt to conjoin redistribution (social justice and class) with recognition (status and culture).

Where does this leave us? It may imply, as hinted at the beginning of the chapter, that any resolution of the Left's schism cannot wait upon a final reconciliation since there is no such thing as a reconciliation which will not engender new disagreements and so a need for new reconciliations. Yet rather than allow this realisation to transform us into post-structuralists *per se*, if finality is undesirable (and anyway impossible) then we have nothing to fear from the heuristic ideals that culturalists otherwise oppose so long as we keep this clearly in mind. Therefore, the dichotomy which Fraser has articulated, and which I have made central to this chapter, may ironically be both more and less post-structuralist than post-structuralism. Perhaps the task is not to transcend the schism on the Left but to refuse to take it too seriously.

This is why I have referred to the new *radicalisms*. For this is what the movements of the Left already do, they practice what they do not preach: the march and the campaign never wait upon theoretical completion – at least not any more. If so, then this implies that justice is never whole, self-contained or without fractures and interruptions: the material and the cultural never quite match up, and nor should they. This is a point I will return to in Chapter 9. Before we can arrive at that ultimate destination, though, we have to appreciate a series of debates around which conservative, social democrats and new radicals clash. We begin by exploring questions of agency, community and class.

3

Agency, Community and Class

Introduction

Having spent the opening chapters reviewing three of the key political per-spectives at work in contemporary welfare theory the rest of the book is spent discussing some of the main debates of recent years into which they may be said to intervene. The main intention is to explore the debates themselves rather than fitting them rigidly into the above political boxes. However, I seek to explain as we go along why and how those perspectives make their respective interventions. We begin in this chapter by looking at questions of agency, community and class. The first two have certainly impacted upon political and academic debates in recent years, with class having declined in influence. Still, the premise of this chapter is that we cannot fully understand any one of these concepts without some reference to the others.

Agency

A thought-provoking claim is made by Deacon (2002; cf. Deacon & Mann, 1999) when he argues that the subject of social policy has not paid enough

attention to questions of agency because of its collectivist bias and its commitment to social equality:

> The defining characteristic of the quasi-Titmuss paradigm, then, is that it is uninterested
> in questions of agency and is hostile to the idea that one of the purposes of welfare is to
> shape the behaviour and aspirations of those who receive it. (Deacon, 2002: 14)

Consequently, the Right has been able to mould and dominate debates concerning behaviour, rationality and motivation, promoting a discourse which
emphasises punitive and individualistic principles that the Left has not been
able to counter adequately. As such, the NSD at least represents an attempt
to wrestle the initiative away from the Right and so should not be blamed
for attempting – however poorly at times – to reconfigure the Left's agenda
(Deacon, 2002: 116–7). Along similar lines Sennett (2003: 59) argues that,

> Radical egalitarians have sometimes argued that if material conditions can be equalized,
> then mutually respectful behaviour will spring forward, 'naturally' and spontaneously.

Are these allegations accurate? Has the Left really neglected agency? Or,
alternatively, has it simply spoken in a different idiom, one that might not
easily translate into the mainstream political vocabulary? There is good
reason to believe that the Left *has* addressed questions of agency in the past.
Sennett's allegation surely misrepresents a two hundred year old tradition in
which it was expected that the mutualism and solidarity of the labour movement would enable a society of strong equality and social ownership to be
eventually built. Socialists did not ignore respect, they placed it in a particular
theoretical and historical framework. This is discernable in Titmuss's view
that,

> ... people are conditioned by their environment which in many ways, large and small,
> insidious and blatant, forces them to dwell on the physical things, the observable phe-
> nomena, the bricks and mortar of existence. (Alcock *et al*, 2001: 20)

Now this may or may not offer a credible account of the interaction between
social structures and individual actions, and it may not make explicit reference
to *agency*, but agents are present here nonetheless as those who dwell on
'bricks and mortar' as ways of coping with the bigger problems in their lives.
Why, then, is arguing that individual freedom is conditioned and constrained
by economic forces any less a concern with agency than the Right's argument
that freedom may be conditioned and constrained by political ones? The
former offers a socialist (or at least a social) interpretation and the latter an
individualist one but to argue that only the latter suits an agent-centred
account is a conservative proposition that the Left is entitled to reject.

But, if this allegation is misleading, what of the present? With the socialist
movement having faded, at least in developed countries, is there a need to

evolve a new vocabulary better suited to our 'post-socialist' condition? Might Deacon and Sennett be correct to allege that since we cannot import ideas from the past the Left *should* be exoriated for its intellectual inertia? To explore these questions let me analyse one of the most important contributions of recent years to this school of thought (cf. Jordan, 1996; Lister, 2003b).

LeGrand (2003) proposes that we think of both public sector professionals and the recipients of public services according to the following ideal types. The assumption that people are fundamentally self-interested is to assume that they are *knaves*; if they are assumed to be basically altruistic and public spirited then they are *knights*; if people are thought of as passive, with little capacity for independent action, then they are *pawns*; whereas if they are active agents then they can be defined as *queens*. A taxonomy which measures professionals as either knaves or knights and recipients as either pawns or queens yields an interesting map of welfare ideologies. Social democrats have traditionally thought of providers as knights and recipients as pawns, i.e. the former engineer policies for the common good that the latter should be grateful to receive; free market conservatives (and new social democrats) have seen providers as knaves and recipients as queens, i.e. policy makers are self-serving, unless checked, and recipients capable of acting like sovereign consumers. LeGrand argues that social policies should be organised so that recipients are indeed defined as queens but that they are robust enough to sustain either knightish or knavish behaviour on the part of professionals. He argues that quasi-markets can fulfil this criterion of robustness.

LeGrand therefore offers a post-socialist theory of agency that could appeal to many on the Left. There are, though, several flaws with it. Firstly, it does not deal with the issue of reciprocity (see below) and so with the quality of those relationships which fall outside the matrix of market exchange. Secondly, it applies an individualist reading to a range of associated but nevertheless distinct dichotomies (self-interest/altruism, structure/agency). For instance, LeGrand (2003: 14) accuses the Left of viewing the poor as pawns, as victims of the structural constraints imposed by our socioeconomic environment. This then leads to a culture of excuses in which nothing is expected of them. Yet (as with Sennett) this is a crude characterisation. The Left has usually regarded poor people as victims only when viewed in isolation; in their capacity to act in collective movements the poor have been interpreted as anything but passive! Similarly, the Right may wish to regard welfare users as queens but there are other forms of social association related to welfare, e.g. family and nation, in which they largely expect people to accept the hierarchies and rules of given institutions. Third, LeGrand (2003: 82–4) is biased in favour of market solutions to welfare problems and does not explore the possibility of developing new forms of democratic voice (Fitzpatrick, 2002a). Finally, his call for robustness is somewhat confused. As a sop to the Left LeGrand (2003: 167–8) insists that quasi-markets work as effectively, if not more so, when accompanied by knightish and altruistic behaviour. Yet if they are to be robust quasi-markets must presumably be neutral between knights and knaves, suggesting that they are not capable of creating knights in and of themselves. So where are the knights to come from? LeGrand does not say, perhaps assuming that they will always be there for us to rely upon. But if quasi-markets are neutral between knights and knaves then perhaps there is nothing that can or should prevent the latter from dominating. In short, robustness offers a de-politicised form of politics that brackets the attempt to create policies designed to improve human character – and the political controversy over what this implies. Although a theory of agency it assumes that agency is a given, e.g. it identifies queens as consumers who prefer exit strategies to those of voice.

What these criticisms suggest is that if agency is separated from the background conditions of society then what results is a limited and unbalanced conception, as if by forcing open the eye Titmuss tended to keep shut we have closed the other eye he kept firmly open. We can further appreciate why this is by examining two of the main categories around which the debate on agency has recently been organised: reciprocity and reflexivity.

Reciprocity

Reciprocity seems to have replaced altruism in the lexicon of social policy. Having received its classic statement by Titmuss (1970; Page, 1996) altruism denotes an act of selflessness in which self-gratification and the expectation of return are not the prime or immediate motivation. Altruism is undoubtedly a key human characteristic but is it, or could it ever be, *the* key characteristic since even its defenders seem to accept that altruism is present only infrequently or under exceptional circumstances (Geras, 1998)? This, added to the explosion of self-interest in recent decades (see Chapter 6 also), has made altruism deeply unfashionable. By contrast reciprocity can potentially connect to the conservative emphasis upon duty, the social democratic emphasis upon solidarity and the radical emphasis upon direct, unmediated mutuality.

So is reciprocity superior to altruism and to what extent should the former be enforced? Let me begin by addressing the second part of this question. Some have argued that inherent self-interest requires a welfare state of sticks and carrots where the job of social policies is to make self-interested motivations and actions work towards the common good by applying a series of income-related incentives and disincentives (Murray, 1990; Bane & Ellwood, 1996; Field, 2003). Reciprocity therefore requires policies and institutions to discipline those who are or may become ill-disciplined. Key aspects of this assumption are visible within the NSD, usually allied to rhetorical appeals to moral fairness and national identification:

> Respect is at the heart of a belief in society … . It makes real a new contract between citizen and state, a contract that says that with rights and opportunities come responsibilities and obligations … . From the 1940s to the 1970s government sought to address social and economic problems through intervention and state planning. Social democrats in Britain and the US who held a liberal view of the 'permissive society' divorced fairness from personal responsibility. They believed that the state had an unconditional obligation to provide welfare and security. The logic was that the individual owed nothing in return. By the early 1970s this language of rights was corroding civic duty and undermining the fight-back against crime and social decay. (Blair, 2002)

One problem with enforcing obligations is that it may be unfair and directed against the least advantaged (cf. Fitzpatrick, 2001a: 67–70). This is the case where the cure for unemployment is thought to be workfare sanctions.[1] To argue that those subject to enforcement will benefit from it is unpersuasive since there may be other ways of benefiting them which are more respectful of their dignity, autonomy and sense of responsibility. And there may well be basic entitlements (to shelter, to health care, to a minimum income) to which all have an unconditional right, perhaps because a large part of our social wealth has been inherited from previous generations, generating a right to a basic equal share for all (Fitzpatrick, 1999a: 58–60). Yet enforcing obligations may also be counter-productive even in its own terms, since it may undermine people's sense of self-respect and so have deleterious knock-on effects elsewhere. Or it may limit the meaning of reciprocal contributions to a narrow channel of activity, e.g. workfare can squeeze out respect for and commitment to childcare. In short, systems of enforcement should perhaps be more flexible and diverse than Murray *et al* imagine, where sanctions are a last resort once the emphasis upon rewards and incentives have been exhausted.

But the ultimate problem in determining *how* to facilitate reciprocity is in deciding *what kind* of reciprocity we want. It is simplistic to treat reciprocity as if it is just one thing. Rather than being an 'element' reciprocity is instead a 'compound' formed out of other concepts and imbided with political contestation or, to put it simply, we might contrast an 'altruistic reciprocity' with a 'selfish reciprocity'. The former embodies an ethos of gift-giving and of 'paying it forwards' i.e. the acts of generosity we receive are passed on to others rather than simply returned, as in a commercial transaction, to the giver. The latter is one in which reciprocity implies 'paying it back': now I have benefited you I expect something in return. Assuming that both forms of reciprocity are important the Left will presumably want welfare systems to encourage the former as much as possible. In other words, a straightforward appeal to reciprocity does not eliminate the essential choice to which Titmuss drew attention, between an environment of social justice and one of market-based commercialisation.

It is for this reason that some refer to 'fair reciprocity'. For White (2003: 18) equality in the distribution of the social product requires that reciprocal obligations be performed in the cooperative endeavours out of which that product is generated:

> ...where the institutions governing economic life satisfy other demands of justice ... to a sufficient extent, citizens who actually claim the high minimum share of the social product necessarily available to them under these institutions have an obligation to make a decent productive contribution, proportional to ability, to the community in return.

But note the proviso that background conditions be just and egalitarian. Where this is not the case then enforcement adds to the injustice already dealt to the least advantaged. Fair reciprocity therefore requires that the state guarantee just background conditions and concern itself as much with exclusion at the top as exclusion at the bottom.

Through the concept of fair reciprocity White at least attempts to reintroduce conservatism and social democracy to a strong version of social justice and equality. As indicated in Chapter 2 the greater the role played by circumstance (luck, inheritance, social structures) in human affairs then the less people can be said to deserve their social positions and so the more social equality might be justified as a means of correcting for undeserved disadvantages; but if circumstance is less important then the less we can claim to be the products of undeserved circumstances and so the more social *inequality* might be justified. By downplaying the role of circumstance in human affairs, by apparently insisting that the unemployed claimant bears the same social responsibilities as the Duke of Westminster, conservatives and new social democrats prevent the creation of the very background conditions that would make their appeal to duties and reciprocity more legitimate.

Yet White's approach is still not entirely satisfactory (for a longer critique see Fitzpatrick, 2005). Firstly, there is a deficit of democratic consent in his ideas: people have little choice but to claim the benefits of social cooperation they receive and to claim them in ways that have already been determined – the emphasis again being upon waged work. Secondly, he gives too much prominence to free-riding and overlooks the extent to which (a) we are *all* free riders to some extent and (b) an element of free riding might sometimes constitute a necessary form of social exchange – see the discussion of tit-for-tat in Chapter 6. Finally, the 'fuzzy boundaries' between what is and is not a socially productive contribution cannot be policed as systematically as White imagines. In short, while White is concerned with social justice he is less connected to the contrasting motivations (altruism and selfishness) that Titmuss identified as crucial to the operation of social justice.

So it is not clear that rights and duties correlate as closely or as simply as some imagine. Goodin (2002) offers a matrix capable of generating 45 different ways of defining reciprocity. His matrix stretches across three dimensions. Firstly, there is a dimension of 'conditionality' where obligations may or may not exist independently of one another and the performance of your obligations may or may not require others to perform theirs. Secondly, there is one of 'temporality' where obligations may or may not be performed simultaneously. Finally, there is the dimension of 'currency' where discharging an obligation may consist of reciprocating with a wider range of goods than one has received. In short, not only does the political mainstream have a very narrow conception (1 out of a possible 45) of how rights and responsibilities should correlate but this conception seems designed to consolidate existing relations of power; for when resources are distributed asymmetrically,

> ...to insist upon strict and immediate reciprocity has the effect of reinforcing relations of social subordination .... It works by catching people when they are weak; and, by requiring them to repay immediately when they are hardly able to do so, it keeps them that way. (Goodin, 2002: 592)

Therefore, the kind of robustness to which LeGrand appeals sidesteps some of the hard political choices that have to be made.

In retrospect, then, Titmuss may be more sophisticated than many of his latter-day critics, and can be reinterpreted as arguing not for a society of saintly knights but for a reciprocity that is looser, more mature and multidimensional than those who operate with a commercialised model of self-interest and state-enforced sanctions. So for all its talk of trust and social capital (see below) the enforcement of reciprocity, in the name of agency, might compare unfavourably to Titmuss's welfare state where people are encouraged to follow the example of others and make contributions to the social good without the state, armed with a checklist of social duties, constantly looking over their shoulders.

Although they too take issue with Titmuss, Burns *et al* (2003) construct a model of reciprocity which highlights the importance of social connections but also embodies the recognition that such connections cannot be forced into place by tickbox moralists. They call for a form of 'hands-off intervention' where government facilitates communal self-help but does not get involved too directly since such involvement is self-defeating, often undermining the very motivations and capacities of those communities themselves (cf. Hibbitt *et al*, 2001). Unfortunately, they maintain, the current obsession with paid employment risks taking us in the opposite direction by leaving people with less time, energy and resources for the kind of communal interactions upon which our formal economies and labour markets depend.

So the debate concerning agency and reciprocity is arguably far more subtle and varied than many of the above authors seem to imagine. Although the Right's emphasis upon duties is certainly very powerful it is designed to obscure the many other versions of agency and reciprocity that could be supported and to distract attention away from social conditions. Perhaps the real question is not why the Left has traditionally ignored these issues but why it is now accused, by many friends and enemies, as having done so.

Reflexivity

Reflexivity can mean both 'reflectiveness' and 'reflex' and these meanings should not be confused although they may certainly conjoin. The former is most often associated with Giddens (1991, 1994; Beck *et al*, 1994) and his thesis that our contemporary self-image is that which subjects itself to constant examination, refracting itself into multiple versions and endlessly reconnecting these fragments through a variety of narrative strategies: it is the self-image of self-images. Agency therefore becomes a never-complete biography of micro-texts that reconstruct themselves constantly, a DIY assembly kit for which there are no instructions other than those we make up as we go along. Here, in advanced modernity, there is a general absence of certainty and the proliferation of risks that evade actuarial calculations since they are themselves the manufactured products of past calculations and attempts to control the social environment by insuring against external nature.[2] Therefore, our ideas about politics and society must become more flexible and reflective, capable of transcending the bounded territories that have previously been kept separate, and 'post-traditional' in the sense that to avoid tumbling into fundamentalism traditions must keep no part of themselves hidden from the investigative gaze.

Beck & Beck-Gernsheim (2002; Beck, 1992), meanwhile, focus more upon *reflex* and the modern destabilisation of modernity. Reflection becomes less of a possibility because we have less time in which to reflect and no critical horizon to which we can journey in order to picture the whole of the social field. Social life speeds up and becomes individualised as individuals slip free of social bonds and become the centres of themselves. Reflexes become indeterminate reactions to other reflexes and so we become lost within a complex of reflexivity – a social pinball machine. Our risk society therefore consists of responses to risks that will themselves generate new risks and so a need for new responses. None of this means that new bonds cannot be forged, it just means that social reintegration cannot be compelled from above. Indeed, Beck seems to advocate his own version of 'hands-off intervention' where communities define themselves as 'risk communities', required to cope with indeterminacy and vicissitude, and so encouraged to experiment with new forms of civic alliances (Beck, 2000: 163–5).

Part of the problem with both of these accounts is that they ignore the significance of political struggle. The trouble with those like Giddens is, according to Mouffe,

> ...their claim that a left/right divide, a heritage of 'simple modernisation', is not relevant anymore in times of 'reflexive modernisation'. By asserting that a radical politics today should transcend this divide ... they imply we now live in a society which is no longer structured by social division .... it is based on the illusion that, by not defining an adversary, one can side-step fundamental conflicts of interests .... It is all very nice to announce that there should be 'no rights without responsibilities' or no 'authority

without democracy', but how is one going to put such programmes into practice
without profoundly challenging the existing structures of power and authority? (Mouffe,
2000: 110–11)

Their version of the reflexive agent is therefore of a self unconstituted by
political conflict, of an environment from which hegemonic struggle has
been all but eliminated and where grand questions concerning the justice
or injustice of social background conditions are much less relevant than
before. Giddens (2002: 38–43) feels that he can recommend the radical
democratisation of social relations while recommending that equality be
redefined in terms of a competitive meritocracy. Beck (2000: 1) can assert
that 'The unintended consequence of the neoliberal free-market utopia is
the Brazilianisation of the west', as if the latter was never a conscious strategy
of *laissez faire* conservatism (Culpitt, 1999). Nor does he seem to consider
the possibility that individualisation is itself the *mediation* of class identity,
relations and conflict.

Social policy might therefore be advised to take a different approach to
reflexivity. Hoggett (2001) proposes a scale of reflexivity (in the sense of
reflectiveness) that cuts across a second dimension articulating the extent to
which the self can and cannot shape its environment. According to Hoggett
this typology enables us to distinguish between 'first-order agency' where
actors operate according to given institutional rules and 'second-order
agency' which confronts, resists and challenges systems and relations (both
social and familial). As such, second-order action represents a form of
rupture that reopens the division between agency and structure as a political
space and not simply as a sociological category. Greener (2002a) takes this
model over and, drawing on Bourdieu's work, locates it within a social
context of power relations that structure the meaning, distribution and
means of translation between various forms of economic and cultural capital.

We can see then that neither social policy nor the traditional agenda are as
alienated from ongoing debates concerning agency as Deacon and others
imagine. Their vocabularies are capable of encompassing a diversity of social
layers, from the holistic to the individualistic, holding all within its field of
vision and exploring the stable yet mutable social columns that connect them.
Essentially, the Left says that the more power we have to shape our societies
collectively then the more likely individuals are to act responsibly towards one
another – so, by obstructing the means for collective action, it is social inequalities which undermines free and responsible agency. Some have certainly succumbed to the temptation to oppose the crude behaviourism held by various
conservatives with an equally crude social determinism; but there is a major difference between recognising the need to reorganise its vocabulary and, as some
of the above authors recommend, abandoning it altogether.

The question I wish to pursue now is whether that reorganisation can be
supplied by some contemporary debates concerning community.

Community

The aim in this section is to review some ideas that Fitzpatrick (2001a: Ch. 4) was not able to cover in its discussion of citizenship. To this end I propose to engage with three of the most important contemporary debates concerning community and to do so with particular reference to agency.

Stakeholding

Although it has been in use since the 1960s it was really in the mid-1990s that this term attracted the interest of politicians, academics and other social commentators. Referring to the broad spectrum of those who are affected by an organisation (whether public or private), 'stakeholders' denotes a wider and more diverse population of interests than that of either shareholders or stockholders (Kelly *et al*, 1997). For whereas these terms refer merely to the holders of stocks and shares, stakeholders may also include employers, suppliers, customers and other relevant communities.

Attention has been generally paid less to the conceptual meaning of stakeholding and more to devising models through which stakeholding can be promoted across a wide array of economic, social and political arenas. This has sometimes left the term looking rhetorical and slippy, capable of being appropriated everywhere by everyone and leaving it without definitional precision (cf. Stoney & Winstanley, 2001). For Tony Blair (1994) it could imply a 'one nation' form of social identity through which people identify with, and recognise a duty to contribute to, the common good regardless of social background. For Will Hutton (1995) it suggests a new means of organising firms and markets that would push the UK more towards the European than the American version of capitalism. Hutton (2002) has long demanded that dominance by the short-term interests of the stockmarket be replaced by solidaristic objectives where people have a far greater say over the decisions that affect them, requiring lines of representation, participation and accountability that cannot be provided by tinkering at the corporate and administrative edges.

The welfare theoretical debates regarding stakeholding have been quite muted, partly because of its rhetorical vagueness and partly because it was quickly translated into a technical term (as in the case of 'stakeholder pensions') with little recognition beyond the circle of policy wonks. For new social democrats stakeholding has been closely related to their concerns with inclusion and exclusion or, more specifically, their attempt to voice those concerns without recourse to an ideology of redistributive egalitarianism, an attempt that many social policy commentators have regretted (Lister, 1997; McCormick, 1997). The debate has therefore been immersed within that regarding the NSD in general. However, continued reference to stakeholding, whether as a vague aspiration or a specific model, may tell us something important about contemporary conceptions of social communities.

Stakeholding seems to place the emphasis upon consensus rather than conflict, upon what connects rather than what separates. What is more significant is the social context within which use of the term has prospered, a context that defines itself as the after-effect of the failed social philosophies of earlier times. With state-centred collectivism and market-centred individualism having apparently been discredited, stakeholding appears suitable to a post-ideological era of pragmatism and managerialism. The battles of old (capital versus labour, private versus public) are held to be redundant, inaccurate descriptions of contemporary social realities. This explains the preference for voluntarism, albeit a preference tendered much more often to corporations than to, say, benefit recipients; for if conflict is not inherent to capitalism it follows that compulsion is unnecessary in order for the powerful to act with reason, responsibility and compassion.

But if those relations have not somehow melted away beneath the sociological gaze then neither have the battles of old, nor the ideological footprints that (for better or ill) have brought us to where we are. But by rejecting this view, many advocates of stakeholding are left to complain about the effects of inequality, exclusion and individualisation, while depriving themselves of the political and discursive means of addressing it effectively. Stakeholding risks being not simply an emphasis upon consensus (hardly a controversial aspiration in itself) but the erasing of inherent social conflicts and the idea that society consists of struggles over and through systems of power. For some of its advocates conflict becomes defined as a 'failed consensus', the temporary refraction of unity (promulgated no doubt by those who cling to old ways of thinking), which requires those who break the consensus to be levered into the mainstream (Field, 1998). But even the more ambitious models fail to go beyond a conception of the public interest (Hutton, 2002: 281) as if the meaning of 'the public' is already present and obvious. Stakeholding is therefore the cry of the pragmatist's social conscience, the desire for community in an individualised environment which the pragmatist cannot, or will not, see beyond. The stakeholder community is therefore a community of social atoms, an individualism attempting to describe itself in the language of solidarity; it is the image of an individualistic society trying to alter its reflection by raging at itself in the mirror.

This is not to argue that stakeholding is a concept that must necessarily be discarded. Stoney and Winstanley (2001: 618–22) review the more radical formulations that have in some sense been inspired by the idea of stakeholding and it is certainly possible to construct egalitarian models of social ownership that owe something to the debate (Ackerman & Alstott, 1999). Dowding *et al* (2003) outline a series of stakeholding models that would arguably distribute resources and assets more equitably than the present welfare system.

Trust

Similar thoughts might also apply to the recent fashion for trust (Misztal, 1996; Weber & Carter, 2003). Highlighting the importance of trust for societies and economies is by no means new and was a running theme of much nineteenth century commentary from Tocqueville to Durkheim, the basic idea being that trust is a force crucial to the communal integration, economic prosperity and moral health of society. This force manifests itself most obviously on a micro-level, in the trust (or lack of) that we demonstrate towards colleagues and acquaintances, friends and neighbours, lovers and strangers. To what extent are we prepared to offer part of ourselves to others and have confidence that our good faith will not thereby be betrayed or misused? Yet the acts and relations which characterise the micro-level also bear macro-level consequences for economy and society.

Economic welfare depends not simply upon the visible codes that govern property, contracts of exchange and employment, but ultimately upon the honeycombed channels and networks through which social interaction circulates. Where levels of trust are low then people are more likely to defect from economic relationships in order to gain advantage over others and so economies are likely to be characterised by suspicion, pre-emptive retaliations and competitive enmity. It is by no means clear that individual acts of self-interest automatically aggregate into the social good – as some followers of Adam Smith have imagined (e.g. Barro, 1997) – since competition depends upon forms of cooperative identification that the free market cannot, by itself, sustain. The skeletal frame of the economy therefore has to be understood as supported by, and interwoven with, the anatomy of culture (see Chapter 9).

Similarly, then, social welfare also depends upon communal instincts of trust. In low-trust societies individuals are less likely to make new connections or to sustain old ones, and so less likely to espy themselves in others through a common recognition of shared identities, national histories and cultural experiences. The emotional drawbridges are raised and with them the means through which social relations can be productive and healthy. Low-trust societies are those characterised by higher levels of stress, crime, isolation and incivility than high-trust ones (e.g. Halpern, 2001), for in high-trust societies there is a degree of intuitive and informal sociability that underpins that society's surface activities, an orientation towards a solidaristic order where, because the fulfilment of expectations can be reasonably anticipated, the expectations which are formed are more likely to be aimed towards the social good. So high-trust societies are characterised more by reciprocity and mutuality than by selfishness. In the case of both economy and society, then, the absence of trust has costs that are higher in the long-term than the gains which derive in the short-term from failing to nurture and maintain the relevant values and intuitions.

That trust itself depends upon a supportive institutional context, and has to be constantly nurtured rather than taken for granted, is something that both Right and Left can be accused of ignoring. The Right can be indicted with forgetting the role played by cultural bonds in the early development of capitalism and with depending upon a hollow conception of the social agent as little more than a utility-maximiser whose overwhelming priority should be the pursuit of self-interest in an impersonal marketplace (Fukuyama, 1995: 17–21). The consequence of applying this textbook actor to the real world is the erosion of trust and so to an economic culture where the more competitive self-interest attempts to perform the roles previously taken by solidaristic relations then the more the economy consumes its own body mass and wastes away. Consumers, workers, managers and investors begin to disengage and lose sight of their mutual embeddedness.

The Left can be charged with undermining the forms of socialisation through which trust is cultivated. The anti-family bias of the Left, according to one possible argument, ignores the extent to which the family is the main arena through which we learn to trust others, a lesson that can then be carried forward into the school, neighbourhood, workplace, voting booth and so on. And the class analysis of the Left perhaps opens a rift between capital and labour where both are encouraged to pursue narrow sectional interests rather than acknowledging their mutual dependency. The welfare state, then, can be accused of undermining trust by appropriating the roles that were formally performed by communities for themselves (cf. Purdue, 2001), by reducing the scope of voluntary activity and organisations, and by encouraging a 'rights culture' that perversely emasculates the political authority of those who provide welfare services:

> ...the growth of the welfare state accelerated the decline of those very communal institutions that it was designed to supplement. (Fukuyama, 1995: 313)

Some, though, have questioned the assumptions made by theorists of trust. In his extensive review of survey data Newton (2001) found that voluntary activities do not correlate strongly to social attitudes of trust, that trust among citizens is not closely related to trust between citizens and political authority, and that trust is a much more complex and diverse quality than is normally appreciated. Newton does not claim that trust is unimportant but he does supply compelling empirical evidence that, as with agency, reciprocity and stakeholding, the picture is much more complex than their more strident advocates would first have us believe. And with the highest levels of trust being found in Norway, Finland, Sweden, Denmark and Iceland (Newton, 2001: 211) – countries (with the exception of Iceland) with strong social democratic movements – the critique offered by those such as Fukuyama is weakened.

How might we explain these high levels? In general, theorists and researchers have distinguished between two types of cyclical movement. In a 'virtuous circle' trust in the political system, the public sector and one's fellow citizens means that people will transmit resources and loyalty to the state, enabling it to achieve its objectives effectively and thus attract further levels of trust in return; we are more likely to trust when we are, in turn, trusted. In a 'vicious circle' the lack of trust leads government to be less effective and so confirm that people were right to withhold their trust in the first place. But why do some countries maintain a virtuous cycle, e.g. Sweden, and others a vicious one, e.g. USA? Rothstein (1998) applies an institutionalist reading and argues that a universalist welfare system is more capable of generating trust than a selectivist one, since by being organised around a basic division between deserving/contributors and undeserving/non-contributors the latter perpetuates levels of suspicion and discrimination that universalism avoids. He argues that 'collective memory' is important, i.e. how the histories of social institutions are represented through contemporary political strategies and processes (Rothstein, 2000). Trust is generated when historical experience is constructed in ways that facilitate agents' faith in their institutional environments. Kumlin (2002) proposes that personal experience is also important, so that where users are treated more as customers empowered to hold producers to account then levels of support for public services will be high (Leadbetter, 2004). However, Svallfors (2002) demonstrates that the 'cyclical' thesis is simplistic and that, say, Americans may trust their social institutions as much as Swedes but trust them in different, culturally-specific ways.

As with stakeholding, then, the message is that we must be attentive to the ideological role that the concept of trust is being called on to perform, i.e. the cluster of ideas with which it is being most closely associated. Is trust a necessary adjunct to market individualism or do they point in opposing directions? Are contemporary policy reforms generating more trust or does the possible shift towards more insecurity and greater regulation of civil society (Chapters 4 and 8) undermine trust? Stakeholding and trust and potentially useful terms through which some older debates can be augmented but it is far from clear that we have been thrown onto a new social terrain for which they provide the only available compass.

Social capital

Recent debates concerning reciprocity, stakeholding and trust have revolved quite closely around the notion of social capital with the work of Robert Putnam being the key influence:

> Whereas physical capital refers to physical objects and human capital refers to properties of individuals, social capital refers to connections among individuals – social networks and the norms of reciprocity and trustworthiness that arise from them. (Putnam, 2000: 19)

Putnam traces the concept to earlier generations of sociologists, not least to Bourdieu's (1984: 12–14) idea that dominant economic groups maintain their dominance through the possession of cultural capital, i.e. versatility in and control of education, language and cultural references (see Chapter 9).

The strength of Putnam's contribution is twofold. Firstly, he weaves many different strands together, revealing the interconnections between agency and community with greater effectiveness than many of his peers, for instance:

> A society characterised by generalized reciprocity is more efficient than a distrustful society .... If we don't have to balance every exchange instantly, we get a lot more accomplished. Trustworthiness lubricates social life .... Civic engagement and social capital entail mutual obligation and responsibility for action. (Putnam, 2000: 21)

Nor is Putnam an unqualified supporter of all forms of social capital, recognising that it can be used as much for malevolent purposes as virtuous ones. The former are more likely to derive from 'bonding social capital', where groups with homogenous identities use their associations to exclude others. Putnam contrasts this with 'bridging social capital' where groups are open, outward looking and capable of encompassing people from across a diversity of social cleavages. The distinction is often hard to maintain but Putnam insists that the terms are not interchangeable and seems to suggest that the virtuous uses of social capital are most likely to appear when 'bridging' acts as a counterweight to excessive 'bonding'.

The second contribution made by Putnam is his thesis that (in the USA at least) social capital has been in decline for some time now, symbolised by the person who prefers to go bowling alone rather than in a team with others. He attributes this primarily to the replacement of the civic-minded generation who experienced the Second World War by later generations who are less entangled in communal life. What role does Putnam see for the welfare state in all of this? He challenges those who see social capital as inversely proportional to social expenditure and the size of government, as if growths in the latter must lead to a decline in the former (Putnam, 2000: 281–3). Rothstein (2003), similarly, believes that if government institutions are seen to be impartial then levels of trust in 'most people' will rise and so social capital enhanced: it is a selectivist, parsimonious and punitive welfare system that undermines social capital. The survey evidence is presently inconclusive. Scheepers *et al* (2002) find that social democracies have less social capital than liberal or conservative regimes – possibly implying a conflict between high social capital and the social rights of citizenship; but van Oorschot (2003) concludes that state welfare correlates *positively* with social capital (though not with relations of informal solidarity). In any event Putnam believes that state welfare must run with the grain of market capitalism since the latter is not inherently damaging to social capital either. Putnam (2000: 320–1, 358–60) therefore seems to adopt a Centre-Left position in favour of 'social capitalism' where equality and social capital, although by no means equivalent, go together and he has no patience for the accusation that it is poor households and benefit claimants who undermine social networks of trust and reciprocity.

There are three criticisms that we might throw at Putnam. Firstly, some have questioned his central thesis of decline. For instance, Wellman and Haythornthwaite (2001) object to his conclusion that social capital is less likely to be a consequence of computer-mediated interaction (Putnam, 2000: 177). They contend that cyberspace possesses certain advantages over the territories of social geography, not least of which is its capacity to facilitate new diasporic communities in addition to strengthening or renewing old social ties. Secondly, if it is true that social capital can be used as much for malevolent purposes as virtuous ones then surely an adequate account of social capital must depend upon an overarching theory of social justice. Putnam does not offer one, however, and despite his warm words of support for equality and state welfare his treatment of social capital is really left floating in something of a philosophical vacuum.

Finally, then, Putnam does not get to grips with one of the main controversies that has long surrounded this debate. What is the appropriate conceptual fit between economic, human and social capital? Many radical commentators (e.g. Smith & Kulynch, 2002) are suspicious of the term social capital because it is frequently allied to either a weak or even a nonexistent critique of capitalism, the suspicion being that the rhetorical cuddliness of the term is an ideological mask beneath which society is judged on the extent to which it functions in favour of capitalist imperatives. Putnam's examples of malevolent social capital encompass urban gangs and fascist separatists but he neglects a possible third category. This category would consist of those who *build* and deploy some forms of social capital in order to resist other forms, e.g. those which bolster hegemonic power (corporate systems, for instance). In other words, Putnam (cf. 2000: 152–66) smoothes over political conflicts where different forms of social capital confront one another, as in the anti-corporate conflicts of recent years – see next chapter.

In short, many are suspicious of social capital because it discards the political significance of class and renders 'capital' as a simple indicator of interpersonal connection rather than as a socioeconomic relation characterised by struggles over power. It is not clear, then, that we should abandon some of the earlier approaches where the fit between physical, human and social capital was assumed to be a lot closer. This is surely the case when Bourdieu talks of a 'conversion rate' between capitals where these are subject to constant conflict and fluctuation:

> The social positions which present themselves to the observer as places juxtaposed in a static order of discrete compartments ... are also strategic emplacements, fortresses to be defended and captured in a field of struggles. (Bourdieu, 1984: 244)

In the case of stakeholding, trust and social capital, therefore, I am left with the thought that although these concepts may be useful this is true if and only if they supplement some older questions, themes and issues. Therefore, if debates about agency are unconvincing without reference to a cogent theory of community and if contemporary theories of community are all missing something vital then might a more collectivist approach fill in the missing pieces?

Class

Is class the missing piece? While disagreeing on the details many social scientists continue to insist that we still live in what are class societies of one form or another (Westergaard, 1995; Marshall, 1997; Taylor-Gooby, 1997; Savage, 2000). In this section I will review two debates pertaining to class and social change.[3] The first returns us to questions of the extent to which we are in control of, and so can be held responsible for, our circumstances; the second concerns the opportunities for collective action within the current social conjuncture.

Circumstances

To what extent do individuals deserve their circumstances? Have they shaped them as a consequence of their preferences, actions and choices, or is it the case that circumstances are largely undeserved because individuals have little or no control over them? It is certainly true that, at least initially, individuals cannot be held responsible for their socioeconomic backgrounds and familial backgrounds (external resources) or their talents (internal resources), since to imagine otherwise is to pretend that young children have the capacity and opportunity to exercise social control. Yet does this mean that circumstances of inheritance and luck dominate human affairs *per se*, or must we insist that individuals mature to the point where they mould their given resources through free will and cannot cite circumstances as the determining factor in their lives?

As observed in the last chapter, Post-Rawlsian political philosophy has been struggling with these questions for some time and I have already explored the contributions, and possible limitations, of Dworkin and Roemer (cf. Arneson, 1989; Cohen, 1995). Yet what these developments have left us with is the extreme difficulty of determining the appropriate point at which choice can be said to take over from circumstance. One solution is to abandon the attempt altogether and return to those who would ignore circumstance. Nozick's argument in this respect is basically threefold. Firstly, he says, while it is true that we do not choose our class, family or talents they are endowments that belong to us nevertheless: I may not deserve my talents but because I own them they cannot, contra Rawls, be treated as 'morally arbitrary' (Nozick, 1974: 216–27). Secondly, because I freely develop the talents that I own it would be an injustice to deprive me of the products of my labour through redistributive measures (Nozick, 1974: 150–64). Finally, if it is just to redistribute external resources such as money, as egalitarians maintain, then why not internal resources also (Nozick, 1974: 226–7)? If we are permitted to redistribute whatever is undeserved then why not body parts and talents as well? But if it would be abhorrent to make ugly the naturally beautiful, or untalented the naturally talented, then why is it any more appropriate to deprive them of their earnings through taxation?

These are powerful arguments but, amongst other criticisms (Fitzpatrick, 2001a: 50) they do seem to bump up against the sheer weight of environmental constraints with which we are faced. Marshall *et al* (1997) go to great lengths to demonstrate that individuals have unequal opportunities to develop their resources along the lines that Nozick insists they can, and that these inequalities correlate strongly to the inequalities of class. With differences in educational attainment, for instance, correlating to differences in class then the 'fit' between class origin and class destination is still very close and shows little sign of having shifted over time. Of course, it may be that the less well-off are simply less intelligent, so that their social position can be attributed to nature rather than class, but recourse to this (highly contentious) argument would also undermine Nozick's claim that freedom to develop our talents is important. Rather than waiting for Wilt Chamberlain to become a world-class sportsman, in a society where nature is held to be the ultimate factor we may as well assess the external and internal resources of young children and determine the distribution of social goods on that basis. Marshall *et al* (1997: 165) conclude that,

> ...those who would reject people's claims to deserve superior reward on the basis of superior natural talent need not deny that the individual may be responsible for exercising that talent. What bothers them is the lack of responsibility for the fact that they, and not others, have it in the first place.

So if we should not attribute everything to choice we are still left with the problem of establishing the proper cut between it and circumstance. This perhaps throws us back to the ideas of Roemer (see previous chapter). But apart from the obvious difficulties in operationalising all of the class-relevant variables, Roemer's approach also leaves the problem of levering into the picture that which is non-class specific. Presumably, an affluent black household is ratcheted up the index of choice due to its wealth and then ratcheted back down again due to constraints imposed upon its members by racial discrimination. Is it therefore realistic to operationalise not only class and luck but also the many different forms of bigotry and institutional disadvantage that characterise our societies? No easy answer to this question seems currently available but egalitarians caution that if brute luck plays a considerable role in human affairs then social policies which reflect this, however imprecisely, are preferable to those which ignore it.

Nevertheless, it seems clear that simple assertions about agency that limit themselves to discussion of freedom, responsibility and community do not stand up to scrutiny once circumstances, including the socio-economic ones of class, are properly taken into account.

Collective action

Yet if unchosen and undeserved circumstances really do play such an important role in social affairs then can we ever really shape our social environments? If the weight of circumstance makes egalitarianism desirable then surely it also makes social equality virtually impossible to achieve! The solution to which political radicals have always reached is that of *collective* action, the idea that we can achieve collectively what we cannot do so separately. Collective action is a big subject that is dealt with in Fitzpatrick (2001a: 13–19) in terms of the problem of deciding what is a social good and how it can be realised. Below, I will here review two recent interventions into the debate about social change and the potential for radical mobilisation.[4]

Hardt and Negri (2000: 23) derive from Foucault and Deleuze the belief that we have entered a new society of control in which command is distributed democratically throughout the social field and pervaded through the brains and bodies of citizens (partly through welfare systems) to the point where alienation and discipline become the highest forms of desire, the very signs of autonomy:

> The great industrial and financial powers thus produce not only commodities but also subjectivities. They produce agentic subjectivities within the biopolitical context: they produce needs, social relations, bodies, and minds – which is to say, they produce producers. (Hardt & Negri, 2000: 32)

In opposition to this colonisation of the fields of agency lurks the proletariat, defined not as an industrial working class but a differentiated and stratified multitude of all those who sustain capital through their labour by being subject to its domination and exploitation. This labour has in an age of postmodern capitalism become immaterial, consisting of informatic labour (mediated by communication technologies), abstract labour (a further removal of the worker from their work) and affective labour (the production of feelings through services) (Hardt & Negri, 2000: 292–4). Labour is therefore a general social activity that encompasses reproductive as much as productive work.

We should not look for examples of systematic rebellion in this age of 'Empire' because struggles no longer translate from one context into another: instead of '...travelling horizontally in the form of a cycle, they are forced to leap vertically and touch immediately on the global level' (Hardt & Negri, 2000: 55) as a simultaneous economic, political and cultural attack upon the new 'virtual imperialism'. Through processes capable of overwhelming the codes of capitalism – migration, for instance – the multitude challenges the market's idea that humans are interchangeable by reappropriating space and constructing new social cartographies in demanding the right to control its own movement, to re-produce itself. It therefore offers the possibility of a global, postmodern communism.

These ideas have attracted an enormous amount of commentary, not all of it complementary. It is possible to complain that Hardt and Negri are being too postmodern: that, for example, they ignore the privileged claims that some workers might make by virtue of their position in the production process (Boron, 2005). It is possible to accuse Hardt and Negri of not being postmodern enough. Featherstone (2002) identifies as a weakness the belief of Hardt and Negri in the possibility of utopia: utopia as a reality encompassing the totality of the social field. This offends against the paradox, which Featherstone draws from Žižek, whereby freedom is only ever a resistance to the inevitably of control and so is negated whenever the impossibility of transgression is denied in the name of freedom itself. Therefore, utopia cannot be real but is always a receding horizon of otherness. Which of these criticisms is most cogent? The first objects to their support for *postmodern* communism but risks invoking the kind of essentialism (the industrial working class as *the* world-historical agent) which has led radical politics down too many blind-alleys. The second objects to their support for post-modern *communism* on the grounds that the latter invokes a utopian totality which is always dead on arrival; this objection lapses into a kind of post-political self-indulgence in which the impossibility of a final liberation is the price emancipatory movements of the future must pay for the errors of the past. Yet progress does not have to aim at finality to be real and desirable.

One possible solution to this bind may be represented by Holloway. Holloway's (2002: 176–85) take on Hardt and Negri is that they retain a productivist analysis orientated around changes in the mode of production, where the construction of humanity is taken to have shifted from industrial machines to the cybernetic intelligences of ICTs. While regarding labour as a form of biopower they still retain a deterministic and positivist reading whose ancestor must be the base/superstructure model:

> Today we increasingly think like computers .... Interactive and cybernetic machines become a new prosthesis integrated into our bodies and minds and a lens through which to redefine our bodies and minds themselves. (Hardt & Negri, 2000: 291)

Holloway (2002: 36) is influenced by Foucault also, distinguishing between 'power-to' (the power to do) and 'power-over' (the power to direct the doing of others). These powers are in a state of contradictory antagonism where struggle consists of the sometimes inarticulate demand,

> ...to liberate power-to from power-over, the struggle to liberate power from labour, to liberate subjectivity from objectification.

This liberation is possible because power-over depends upon power-to, just as capital is labour reified from itself and the powerful depend upon the powerless. The implications Holloway (2002: 41–2) takes from the fact of these dependencies is worth quoting at length:

> There are indeed a million forms of resistance, an immensely complex world of antagonisms. To reduce these to an empirical unity of conflict between capital and labour, or to argue for an hegemony of working-class struggle, understood empirically, or to argue that these apparently non-class resistances must be subsumed under class struggle, would be an absurd violence. The argument here is just the contrary: the fact that capitalist society is characterised by a binary antagonism between doing and done means that this antagonism exists as a multiplicity of antagonisms. It is the binary nature of power ... that means that power appears as a 'multiplicity of forces'. Rather than starting with multiplicity, we need to start with the prior multiplication that gives rise to this multiplicity. Rather than starting with the multiple identities (women, blacks, gays, Basques, Irish, and so on), we need to start from the process of identification that gives rise to those identities.

We therefore do not have to choose between defining power as a dichotomy (a binary unity) of dominator/dominated (Marx) or as a diversity of discursive subjectifications (Foucault) since power can track back to the suppression of doing by what is done, while being manifested along multiple lines of suppression. Rebellion therefore consists of the practical and intellectual search for new forms of social doing and cooperation – what Ellison (2000) calls a 'proactive form of engagement' – against those who fetishise the present and insist that there is no alternative.

Like Hardt and Negri, then, Holloway breaks away from the labour theory of value of classical Marxism and is content to define exploitation, alienation and domination not as the expropriation of a surplus in the process of production but, more simply, as the limitation of potential: the worker is generalised to include us all. But whereas Hardt and Negri arguably displace agency and subjectivity, so that capital and class are treated as external to one another, with the latter a biopolitical effect of the former, Holloway refuses to do this and contends that we could not be oppressed unless it was we ourselves who were doing the oppressing: what renders us powerless is our desire for power. Holloway, then, offers an approach capable of framing a number of revolutionary conjunctures that conjures the possibility of real utopias without totalities and finalities.

The possible virtue of Holloway is his constant admission that 'we don't know' what to do or where we are headed: a politics of modesty suited to the diverse resistances of global movements (see next chapter). Yet the converse problem with Holloway is that his is a dizzying orientation to an unmappable landscape. He recommends no specific means of intervention – other than the injunction to go forth and resist – because no specific mode of social (re)production is theorised, perhaps on the grounds that this would just be another form of power-over. Some may therefore suspect that this, too, is another postmodern Marxism and so feel nostalgia for the idea of capital and class as 'external relations', making possible the kind of determinate counter-strategies that link together islands of resistance in the seas of global capitalism – I return to this theme in the next chapter. Traditional notions of reform and revolution may have failed but, as I think Orwell observed, they were not all the same failure.

This represents one overview of the state of some very current debates. Although no easy resolution to the above problems is currently possible we might legitimately conclude that the birth of the death of class has been much exaggerated.

Conclusion

We began with the accusation that the 'quasi-Titmuss paradigm' has been hostile to issues of agency and I suggested that it would be simplistic to throw such an accusation at the Left. For the Left's concern is not to downplay the importance of agency but to contextualise it, to explain the social environments out of which agents are born and within which they move. Therefore it is true that we have to understand how state welfare shapes behaviour and aspirations but we cannot do so unless we appreciate how and why state welfare shapes and is shaped by a much wider socioeconomic context. I went on to suggest that, for similar reasons, contemporary debates about community are not up to the job of supplying the required context where these debates have revolved around stakeholding, trust and social capital. And I finished by arguing that class still provides an important conceptual framework, one to which many of the earlier discussions can be related, in terms of both circumstance and collective action. However, while class remains central to the reality of our societies it is far from clear whether it yields a rigorous political strategy and, if it does, what kind of strategy that might imply.

So if it is purblind to discuss agency and community without reference to class the opposite is also true. Each concept bears fractures that point in the direction of the others, yet it often seems those others are only able to fill the gaps by opening up gaps and ruptures of their own. We are left with the pieces of a jigsaw where the picture fragments the closer we come to attaining it.

As part of our journey towards that goal I want now to discuss a subject that was hinted at above in the section on reflexivity. It has become common and rather clichéd to describe ours as an age of risk, anxiety, insecurity and uncertainty. Yet before we agree with the many commentators who insist that this lends weight to a highly individualised interpretation of society it is worth trying to unpack the many possible sources of contemporary phobias and panics. By drawing upon the above insights we may discern that the actual picture is layered with many competing dimensions.

4

Insecurities[1]

Introduction

Some insecurities have their origin in nature (natural disasters), many straddle the boundaries of the natural and social (as is the case in risks associated with global warming, pollution, resource scarcity, etc.), while others may be categorised as largely or entirely social (as in the case of job insecurity). Some insecurities are real and others are imagined. However, many insecurities are real *because* imagined according to Thomas's Theorem where if we define something as real then it becomes real in its consequences. Think of fears about children's vulnerability that leads to excessive paternalism (don't go near strangers, don't stray away from home, don't walk to school) and so to a risk aversion that may serve to make children more rather than less vulnerable.

Why has a concern with insecurity, risk and anxiety become so important in recent years (Adams, 1995; Kemshall, 2002)? Do we actually live in a world that is genuinely more risky than before or is it that we have become more nervous as the demise of the cold war has failed to bring the wellbeing we had expected while making us more conscious of other threats? The difficulty in answering such questions derives from the fact that we look upon that world through a series of reflecting mirrors that can distort as much as they reveal. Insecurity seems to derive from uncertainty about the future combined with a lack of power to control that future. The problem is that many different accounts of uncertainty and power are available to us, and so many different ways of accounting for contemporary insecurities. In what follows I will draw upon the arguments of the previous three chapters to sketch the accounts offered by conservatism, social democracy and the new radicalisms, so that we can understand something of what is at stake in the social policies of the twenty-first century. We begin with an outline of each school's basic approach to insecurity, followed by a discussion of some contemporary debates that allows us to glimpse at the possible implications of the concept for social policy.

Accounting for Insecurity

Conservatism

Based upon the account in Chapter 1 we can infer that the conservative account incorporates both economic and cultural features (Fukuyama, 1995). Economic insecurities are thought to derive from distortions upon market relations that are mistakenly imposed by the forces of collectivism. This is based upon the belief that such relations are expressive of human nature (e.g. the desire for material satisfaction) as well as enabling everyone's preferences to be fulfilled via the market's 'invisible hand'.

The state is obviously one such force when driven by an interventionist and welfarist agenda whereby politicians and bureaucrats believe that they can engineer a prosperous and egalitarian society through managerial techniques. The inevitable effect of this agenda, according to conservatives, is that the decisions of market actors, i.e. the suppliers and consumers of goods, are constrained by having their freedom of choice limited and their incentives undermined due to excessive levels of taxation. Those on low incomes or without work are invited to become dependent upon the state by having their incomes artificially boosted through transfer payments financed by the taxes of others. Trade unions are another force of collectivism in their attempt to raise the price of labour to a point which employers cannot afford. The consequence is that markets do not 'clear', e.g. workers price themselves out of jobs, and so work below their optimum level of efficiency. Collectivism is therefore *the* source of economic insecurity by introducing unpredictable and arbitrary processes into the market (inflationary pressures being especially damaging) and so the welfare state is particularly culpable in its attempt to 'free' people from the market, to subject populations to the whims of centralised and centralising administrators and by undermining private property and individuals' self-sufficiency through redistributive measures.

Cultural insecurity, meanwhile, implies threats to the stability of social order and identity. Apart from a minority of anything-goes libertarians, who would simply let individual freedom rip, most on the Right are attached to the securities of place which they identify with tradition, family, neighbourhood and nation, since these provide the context for preferences and actions and so represent the cultural underpinnings of market society. 'Place' is seen as threatened, though, by liberal and socialist principles. As Burke

(1968) intimated, traditions and customs are undermined by the kind of abstract reasoning and social engineering to which both liberals and socialists are prone. The attachments to family and neighbourhood are also unravelled by the state interfering in the private sphere of family life and undermining the solidarities of local, civic association by dictating to it from the centre. Finally, national pride and identity are destabilised by the shame of patriotism and preference for a woolly internationalism that are demonstrated by most liberals and socialists, ignoring the fact that the group to which we belong, and from which we derive our sense of security and obligation to those whom we resemble, is primarily a *national* group rather than one based upon the cross-nationalities of class, gender, and so forth. The nation is seen by conservatives as being under threat both internally (by those who are encouraged by the ethics of state welfare to disrespect authority, property and law) and externally (by those coming from different national traditions who would undermine our identity either through inter-state integration and the formation of new political sovereignties or through the multi-ethnicities that result from too-rapid immigration and assimilation of alien cultures).

In sum, conservatives denounce the influence of a kind of 'liberal/socialist collectivism' for the economic and cultural insecurities that they identify. Conversely, then, security can be increased by sweeping away this kind of collectivism and replacing it with a market society based upon rules of law that reflect the cultural presuppositions of the nation in question. On an economic level this means reducing levels of taxation, narrowing the scope of the public sector, requiring and (if necessary) forcing people to be self-sufficient, re-emphasising the profit motive and the virtues of entrepreneurialism, decreasing the power of organised labour and removing almost all impediments to the free operation of market forces. On a cultural level it means reorienting society to the inheritance of our cultural traditions through effective education and socialisation. Rather than floating in a social vacuum market actors must be able to recognise the national heritage within which economic and political institutions are embedded. An emphasis upon decentralisation and the benefits of localism must be combined with a remoralisation of society (respect for law and order in particular) and an acknowledgement that nations are organic and cannot be remodelled swiftly without initiating social trauma. For conservatives, security therefore comes from synthesising a free economy with cultural and national stability.

Social democracy

Those further to the Left question whether this synthesis is coherent, realistic or desirable (Taylor-Gooby, 2000; Edwards & Glover, 2001; Standing, 2002). Its possible incoherence lies in the contradictory objectives that are being invoked: flexibility in the economy plus stability in national culture, deregulation of the former plus re-regulation of the latter. The problem is that once unleashed market forces are difficult to contain and so can cause cultural disruptions without the kind of state coordination and interventions that modern conservatives are reluctant to initiate – I return to this point below. Yet even if a coherence can be devised at a theoretical level conservative prescriptions seem to require a degree of social engineering that they otherwise abhor when proposed by liberals and socialists. Given social developments in the twentieth century, the conservative attempt to reverse the tide has over the last few decades produced social traumas for which conservatism may be the cause rather than the solution. The hostility to state welfare ignores the extent to which it has been perfectly consistent with the cultural evolution of particular societies – as conservatives in those countries are more willing to acknowledge.

Social democrats have therefore proffered an alternative account of security and insecurity. Here, it is the free market which represents an obvious source of insecurity since, although markets successfully manage to balance themselves in the academic textbook, in reality supply and demand fluctuate widely and unpredictably. Schumpeter's (1992: 81–6) phrase 'creative destruction' expresses the dynamism of markets except that the creativity is usually only identifiable at an intellectual and historical remove; for most of those experiencing the storms of economic destruction and innovation at the time the situation is far less conducive to feelings of safety and security. Therefore, markets must be given the kind of steadiness that they cannot supply for themselves and people must be provided with guarantees of income security that they can rely upon when markets fail. Hence the attraction of a Keynesian welfare state that stabilises markets on the one hand and provides social rights outside the market on the other.

And while the economy cannot sustain the degree of deregulation which conservatives recommend nor does the cultural sphere need to be shored up to the extent that they advocate. Ironically, the stronger conservatives attach themselves to cultural traditions the weaker those cultures can appear to be, necessitating an almost authoritarian emphasis upon family and nation which leaves conservatives unable to deal adequately with issues of gender and ethnic equality. The liberal strand of social democratic thought suggests that cultural change can be directed and represent a source of security *if managed properly*. Often this will involve going with the grain of public opinion though it can also involve leaping ahead of, and steering, public opinion – in the UK we might think of the increasing acceptance of same-sex relationships despite the hostility that originally greeted the decriminalisation of homosexuality in the 1960s.

For social democrats, then, insecurity derives primarily from a winner-takes-all capitalism that would sweep away all before it unless circumscribed by political boundaries whose ultimate guarantor is the democratic state. By contrast, in a society where the common good is balanced against individual freedom, where there is a strong role for the public sector, where social insurance prevails over the private insurance market, where wellbeing is regarded as a collective enterprise, where some measure of redistributive equality is pursued and where the distinction between 'economy' and 'culture' is far less severe than it appears to be for modern conservatives, then security is more likely to prevail than its antonym.

However, and as noted in Chapter 1, the details of traditional social democracy have come under attack from within that tradition itself. The NSD is based upon the belief that since the Keynesian welfare state has exhausted the limits of its possibilities economic intervention must shift from demand to supply and welfare intervention from passive rights to active obligations. Some aspects of conservatism are accepted, therefore, particularly the emphasis upon independence and self-sufficiency. But rather than this implying either the evacuation of state assistance or the simple re-founding of assistance upon a 'new paternalism', a conception of the enabling state is retained though this is now interpreted as enabling people to update their skills and qualifications to keep pace with the new economy, globally-oriented and technologically vibrant. The economy has developed to the point where economic insecurity is likely to emerge whenever we attempt to position the economy upon a single set of foundations, whether these be free market forces or the mixed economy. NSD draws attention to the fishing rod and enjoins us not to waste time altering the course of the river in which we are fishing. Security can never be fully guaranteed, therefore, but is more likely to dominate when we acknowledge the ineluctability of insecurity and apply a reflexive pragmatism to the uncertainties we face.

Similar considerations apply to the cultural realm. Giddens (1991) has reiterated the point that no cultural form can take its continuation for granted since self-legitimation through a simple appeal to the past is no longer possible in the forward-sweeping processes that characterise advanced modernity. Instead, individuals must constantly reinvent their cultural contexts through a reflexive appropriation of ever-changing circumstances and our identities – whether based upon customs, family, neighbourhood or nation – consist of the incorporation of new elements in a constant process of re-assemblage and hybridisation. The familiar is forever being made unfamiliar. Cultural security is therefore something of a chimera unless this is imbued with the impulse towards a radical democratisation by which we throw ourselves into an ever uncertain future and recognise that the security of our cultural identities is only ever relative since only ever a contingent and transitory compilation of fluctuating social meanings and boundaries.

The key term for the NSD is therefore 'reflexivity': the reflexivity of economic and cultural actors for whom a certain degree of anxiety, risk and uncertainty are welcomed as the inevitable conditions of security. Therefore, whereas conservatism and social democracy have traditionally regarded security and insecurity as zero sum, as mutually exclusive, the NSD is far less willing to separate the terms out.

The Need for Insecurity

With your indulgence I will spend more time fleshing out a new radicalist view on these debates since this is perhaps the least developed of the perspective we are contrasting (Davis, 1998; Bauman, 2000a, 2000b). What follows are some tentative notes rather than a full-blown lecture.

The premise of this section is simple. It would be very easy to regard ourselves as being in an entirely new social era yet, and as I indicated in the last chapter, it is facile to imagine that we suddenly find ourselves standing amid a landscape for which entirely new maps are required. The tectonic plates of society may shift constantly but to assert that the environment has recently been remodelled in its entirety is less a representation of the scenery and more a conceit of the mapmaker who has signposts to sell. So this section's premise is that we must talk of evolution instead of revolution, of reconfiguration rather than insurrection, of the development of continuities. Therefore, although the NSD may be admired for having discerned some important changes in our social environment, vis-à-vis the conjunction of security and insecurity, the old maps have not thereby been rendered entirely redundant.

So far as social policy is concerned this means that we may still conceive of needs as a key social concept while recognising that the means through which needs are fulfilled have altered. Traditionally, needs were defined as material and absolutist. But as the social system developed to meet those needs (however imperfectly) so the latter began to assume the cultural and socially relative properties more conventionally associated with wants and preferences. By their very nature desires can never be satiated and so the objects of desire are characterised as much by absence (the gap between expectation and delivery) as presence. Consumption becomes a form of addiction since the object can never fully supply what we expect to find. Possessions always point beyond themselves to their own contradiction – the promise that consumption will one day come to an end – and it is out of this endless pursuit of finality that the commodity form emerges. So as we succeed in realising basic needs we condemn needs in their advanced (non-basic) form to similar streams of commercialisation, although the shift involved here takes hold most rapidly in commodified societies, i.e. those with fewer non-market spaces and so with minimalist definitions of basic needs. Therefore, if we wish to understand the contemporary trajectory of need-satisfaction, the amalgamation of need and desire, we have to appreciate developments in those societies most consumed by commercialised logics.[2]

The implication is that needs, too, become characterised by lack, absence and deferral, characterised by a constant reminder of the impossibility of fulfilment. Yet these characteristics are not homogenous across time and space and will bear different implications in different contexts. In the commodified countries that I have in mind – supreme among which is the USA – what has come to dominate is fear and apprehension at a series of social phobias that lurk just beyond the confines of the panic room. But rather than being a major cause for concern this insecurity is itself a source of security: the more the home is (or is imagined to be) under threat then the greater the sense of shelter that it is thought to provide; the more alien the outside then the more protected we feel on the inside. As such, it is not that fears have replaced needs, or insecurity security, but that highly commodified societies need fear and insecurity as new sources of unfulfillable satisfaction. Needs and wants therefore conjoin around social objects that are simultaneously feared and needed, terrifying and yet perversely compelling: the poor, the indigent, the beggar, the criminal, the paedophile, the refugee, the Muslim, the terrorist.

In short, we seek security through insecurity, the equivalent of the child who throws away a toy in order to enjoy its return, of lovers who quarrel in order to experience reconciliation, of cinema goers enjoying a horror film, of voyeurs who stalk the edges of their lives in order to take control at the centre. And what explains this social condition? We increasingly yearn for collective experience as individuals for whom the experience must be a fortuitous coincidence, a transitory conjunction of separate lives, a reconfirmation of the death of collectivism. But if we feel ourselves less able to experience collective forms of security, because the need for collective experiences cannot be wished away we can at least still experience collective forms of insecurity. This is not a movement from class to individualism but the individualisation *of* class through commodified processes, since it is commodification that rips away at the social fabric and opens up the tears within which fears and anxieties appear to unite us around our separateness. As Bauman (1997: 193) has it, risk and freedom now accompany one another, but because this accompaniment is resented security can be maximised by exporting risk and insecurity to the least powerful (Bauman, 1998a).

What is distinctive about the new radicalist angle, then, is the use of 'commodification' and 'capitalism' as means of explaining the social changes that new social democrats attribute to something far more amorphous, 'modernity'. This does not imply that every facet of social change can be attributed to developments in capitalism but that the latter is far more important than new social democrats imagine. Two arguments will help to establish this point: (a) resisting an account which is heavily discursive and constructionist and (b) identifying free market inequalities as a crucial source of the new insecurities. We now look at these in the next two sections.

The discourse of risks

For some, because the social is what the self is always and everywhere immersed within, because we are social beings 'all the way down', because self and society form a mutual embeddedness, then it is conceited to imagine that we can in any way detach ourselves from ourselves (see Archer, 1995). Having dominated at least three centuries of thought that kind of Cartesian (subject-object) logic is, they insist, being overthrown. For those working within the Nietzschean tradition there can be no context-less spaces of experience and understanding, such that we are always inside horizons which can never be transcended (Laclau & Mouffe, 1985; Rorty, 1989). As such, the traditions of metaphysics, ontology and epistemology are at last being recognised as dead-ends that we can safely abandon for a radical sociological account, one that eschews all of the old dichotomies: materialist/idealist, realist/constructionist, subject/object, relative/absolute, knower/known, nature/culture. The term commonly utilised as an alternative to these various dualisms is that of 'discourse'. In the field of risk and insecurity this kind of approach is articulated by van Loon (2000: 178):

> It is not only impossible but also unnecessary to trace reality as an origin: this tracing itself is a fabrication of reality. In risk society, all we have are reality-effects and they are real enough!

We may speak of the reality of risks, therefore, but only if we remember that reality is itself a social discourse and not a condition prior to and independent of society.

The force of this argument derives from the thought that nothing can be untouched by the social. Even the most apparent physical risks that would seem to come from a place outside society (earthquakes, volcanic eruptions, etc.) are or are not hazardous depending upon the extent to which human communities have adapted to them. Nature is subject to processes that occasionally produce dramatic effects but whether those effects are risks or not depends upon the collective actions and perceptions of ourselves as social beings. The eco-system no longer exists in a pure state due to centuries of industrial activity on our part (McKibben, 1989). In its most extreme formulation some go as far as to insist that nature no longer exists, it is a cultural construct that has been discovered at the very moment of its disappearance (Beck, 1995: 38).

However, there are others who while acknowledging the pervasiveness of the social do not wish to collapse the dualisms of modern thought into a postmodernist mush. For example, in her work on time Adam (1990) has repeatedly stressed the situatedness of time, where time is socially and culturally mediated. Yet she nevertheless allows a place for natural reality as more than simply an occurrence within the social:

> ...we are locked into nature's silent pulse, that our activity and rest alternations, cyclical exchanges and transformations, seasonal and circadian sensitivities are tied to the rhythm of this earth and its solar system. (Adam, 1996: 92)

Therefore, risks and insecurities may be both social and extra-social, discursive and extra-discursive. On one level it may be true that the environment is a social product so that environmental risks (pollution, scarcities) are also social ones; yet rather than overturn modernist conceptions of the omniscient observer, to have 'social discourses' encompass all phenomena seems merely to shift the perspective of that observer from an 'outside' to an infinite and inescapable 'inside'; modernist thought is replicated by rejecting it wholeheartedly. Adam's approach therefore seems to suggest that risks can be both social and natural: the fact that nature is affected by the social *does not commit us to Beck et al's view that nature is nothing more than a social spasm*. As such we should not imagine that the traditional theoretical dualisms have simply collapsed, nor that we do have to rely upon a strong 'discursive constructionism' in order to resist philosophies of naturalism, essentialism and positivism.

This kind of approach may therefore be more productive than that which everywhere invokes 'the social'. Take Furedi's analysis of the culture of fear. In his discussion of Douglas and Wildavsky (1983) Furedi (2002: 8) insists that,

> This approach has the merit of interpreting the sense of risk as a social construct, relating to the prevailing subjective consciousness of society, rather than as a by-product of increased real dangers.

And later:

> ...the issue at stake is not whether perceptions of risk are real or not, but what is the basis for such responses .... In fact, there is no direct relationship between the process of problematization and the experience to which it refers. (Furedi: 2002: 59)

Furedi's attachment to a radical constructionism explains (or perhaps is explained by) his belief in the power of humans to determine their destinies by shaping the risks of which, according to Furedi, they are themselves the authors. He therefore reserves particular contempt for the Green movement which he regards as adopting a fatalistic and recidivist orientation that regards risks as something to be feared and exaggerates the dangerousness of the contemporary world.

Yet the tone of Furedi's analysis often imitates those whom he takes to task: his is a panic not about risks but about those whom he sees as fearing risks. The result is a flat, one dimensional reading whose God's-eye view refuses to recognise subtleties and nuances in those he would no doubt regard as realists and materialists. Environmentalists are caricatured as being anti-science (Furedi, 2002: 132), for instance, which is to conveniently ignore the intricacies of the Green critique (where some forms of genetic research are welcomed and some are not) and to collapse the Green critique of corporate power into the Green critique of science *per se*. But if we acknowledge the force of Adam's view, that nature should not be interpreted merely as a social effect, then Furedi's hostility is as naïve as it is unwarranted.

So what Furedi's (2002: 42, 103) constructionism pushes out of the picture is an ideological account of risk and insecurity, charging both Left and Right with inculcating people into a culture of fear. The problem is that he proposes no convincing alternative:

> The growth of risk aversion and regulation under free-market political regimes devoted to a different orientation points to the strength of the forces which brought them about. It indicates that despite the opposition of successive governments a new form of social regulation has successfully evolved. This must mean that there are powerful forces within the structures of society. (Furedi, 2002: 153)

But what if successive governments have not possessed a 'different orientation'? What if risk aversion was a forseeable consequence of their political strategy? If this is the case then Furedi's invocation of 'powerful forces' appears to be a convenient cop-out, and a peculiar one too in someone who is action-oriented when it comes to proposing solutions to contemporary problems but apparently less so when it comes to explaining those problems' origin. And although Furedi makes some reference to different nations his is an abstract analysis which ignores the extent to which risks may fluctuate from country to country – indeed, he has to ignore this comparative dimension if he truly believes that ideology lacks importance. It may be, then, that he is extrapolating from the Anglo-American experience and making unwarranted generalisations about 'society' as a whole.

The role of inequality

If this is the case then perhaps we should focus upon particular political regimes as exemplars of risk and insecurity. This is the insight to which Culpitt (1999: 112–3) is pushing when he observes that,

> The overwhelming nature of risk in society does exist; there is no escaping that. However, *some of the discourses about risk are socially constructed narratives*. Neo-liberalism constructed the discourses about welfare risk for its own hegemonic purposes ... . neo-liberalism has *used* the anxiety about risk society for its own political ends. (italics in original)

I agree with the thrust of this observation but would add that if ideology is important, and if Adam's approach is accepted, then ideologies are more than just social narratives which construct risk discourses but also means of configuring the interface between society and nature, without collapsing either term into the other. Ideologies may operate discursively whilst not necessarily being discursive 'through and through'. However, the more important point is that once ideology is readmitted to the picture then the recent influence of conservatism – particularly in some countries more than others – becomes central to our explanation of contemporary insecurities.

Therefore, while conservatism did not create contemporary those insecurities *ex nihilo* it may well account for the recent growth in riskiness and for the extent to which risk has permeated the social consciousness of particular societies. In short, where conservatives attribute insecurity to the lasting effects of the post-war settlement, new radicalists turn this interpretation around and cite the inability of that settlement to dispel the commodified fears upon which conservative capitalism feeds as much for its identity as for its electoral popularity.

What we are perhaps looking for, then, is a link between insecurity and inequality since social inequality has lain at the heart of the conservative project and the most unequal countries are those where conservative hegemony has most successfully taken hold. For Bauman the link consists of an inversion:

> Every type of social order produces some visions of the dangers which threaten its identity. But each society spawns visions made to its own measure … . threats are projections of a society's own inner ambivalence about its own ways and means … (Bauman, 1998a: 73)

Bauman argues repeatedly that insecurities prevail wherever individuation is overwhelmed by individualism (e.g. Bauman, 2000a: Ch. 2): that is, where the desire for freedom is translated politically into the desire for market and consumerist types of freedom, where the individual and the collective are regarded as zero sum, where merit is elevated above socioeconomic factors and where affluence and poverty are thought to be conceptually distinct. Individualism therefore seems to require inequality (so that stratifications in social circumstance can be interpreted moralistically as resulting either from nature or from differences in choice) and insecurity (as a spur to initiative in a dynamic, flexible and competitive market society where social mobility is [incorrectly] interpreted as fluid and volatile).

But individualism also fears itself, fears that it cannot deal with the quakes that it causes to surge across the social field. Individualism therefore breeds insecurities with which individualism itself cannot deal and so which are not necessarily part of the ideological plan. The point long made by Gray (1992) is that markets undermine the conditions of their own possibility by attacking the unarticulable codes and understandings that underpin social interaction and which sociologists refer to as the *lebenswelt*, the lifeworld (Habermas, 1987a). For instance, in endorsing a me-first ethic the free market may encourage the growth of a moral subjectivism where individuals measure society against nothing more than the immediacy of their own wants and so grow cynical about obeying the kind of authority upon which social order depends. What results, in those places where free markets let rip, are the kind of ontological insecurities for which a *laissez faire* morality seems inadequate. This is perhaps why the celebrations of contemporary conservatism for free market capitalism are more muted than they were in the

1970s and 1980s and why the neo-conservative stress upon obligation, punitiveness, compliance and tradition quickly came into fashion. Indeed, this evolution in conservative thinking is sometimes content to borrow from the solidaristic emphases of Right-leaning social democrats, propelling the recent craze for stakeholding, trust and social capital that, as we saw in the last chapter, have been promoted as mends for the fabric that unrestrained capitalism has torn.

So the solution to its own inadequacies for which free market societies reach is the scapegoat, the patsy. As inequalities generate insecurities so they make others appear alien and hostile, manufacturing a distinction between 'people like us' (those who aspire to better themselves) and 'the others' (those who want to waste the resources that we have laboured to create). So as they take hold insecurities can make inequality seem perversely like the remedy, rather than that which is to be cured, by creating a 'social distanciation' where people become more likely to misrecognise one another. This attempted reconciliation by conservatism of its self-contradictions is arguably most visible in the case of poverty and the underclass where instead of regarding the latter as both a product of and a threat to market forces conservatism must exorcise itself from the explanatory picture. Hence the underclass has to be seen to derive from anything other than conservative policies themselves – enter the seemingly endless panics about welfare dependency, the 1960s, cultural relativism, moral decline, bleeding-heart liberalism, etc. The underclass is therefore a construct, a '...safety-valve for collective tensions born of individual insecurity' (Bauman, 1998a: 72; 1998b):

> In demanding the terrorization of the underclass, the silent American majority attempts to terrorize away its own inner terrors .... Poverty turns then from the subject matter of social policy into a problem for penology and criminal law. (Bauman, 1998a: 76–7)

Conservatism needs the insecurities of inequality; it also needs the insecurities of the outsider, the excluded, to explain why social inequality has not delivered the capitalist utopia it once anticipated. So insecurity is both the rationale for, and the effect of, conservatism and conservative hegemony consists of keeping rationale and effect separate through a philosophy that relegates the influence of conservatism over the last few decades to a negligible position. Conservatives wield hegemony by claiming not to.

To summarise, the new radicalist account of insecurities incoporates the following:

1. New radicalism agrees with the NSD that it is now less easy to distinguish between security and insecurity than formerly
2. However, this has not necessarily rendered older theories and concepts redundant and we should understand insecurity in terms of a need for fear and anxiety that the most commodified, free market societies have engendered

3. To explain insecurity we must have recourse to 'ideology' which means resisting philosophies which explain everything in terms of discursive constructionism, since although ideologies are discursive they are also a means of understanding the society-nature interface where nature is more than just a social effect
4. As such, the conservative influence is central in a way that new social democrats, given their attraction to many aspects of the conservative agenda, ignore
5. Conservatism engenders a collective need for insecurity since it creates insecurities, by widening social inequalities, and reconfigures security as a need for the excluded outsider who is both a desired product of, and a threat to, individualist moralities and prosperity

Framing Social Policy

Having outlined three political narratives through which attempts are made to understand and explain insecurities I now wish to relate those narratives to two important contemporary debates: globalisation and time. This should arm us with a greater insight into what is at stake in the social policies of the twenty-first century.

Globalisation[3]

For conservatives *laissez faire* globalisation does not necessarily imply an absence of insecurity and may indeed offer a greater sense of security than economic management by states, whether local, regional or global (Friedman, 1998). Globalisation is both a recognition that the conservative prescriptions of the 1960s and 1970s were ahead of their time and the final stage in the victory of free market economics as capitalism finally ascends from the national level to a fully global one. The logic at work here is one with which we are already familiar: markets work best when unobstructed. This means that vestiges of protectionism and economic barriers (capital controls, tariffs on trade, restrictions on ownership and exchange, high rates of taxation and public expenditure) must be dismantled so that a single global market can finally emerge. One implication is that welfare states must be privatised and commercialised. However, this does not mean that all forms of management are ruled out since the market can sustain navigation by those who have the market's best interests at heart, i.e. corporate rather than political representatives. At the national level, as we saw above, this can imply nurturing the cultural underpinnings of market relations; at the global level, it means assisting nations less developed in either an economic or political sense to adapt to global market forces by accepting the lead of those nations where *laissez faire* capitalism is most advanced.

This is why conservatives see no contradiction between a *laissez faire* logic and a situation where the IMF, World Bank and WTO steer the global economy by using a combination of carrots and sticks against those who do not toe the line (usually less developed nations, but not always). Governance and even institution building are necessary if a global capitalism is to prevail in the long-term. Little distinction is therefore made between 'globalisation' and 'free market capitalism'. Take Legrain's (2002) insistence that the Left should abandon its anti-globalisation stance and embrace globalisation on the grounds that the latter can be shaped in directions that the Left might find desirable. This argument, though, does not sit well with Legrain's (2002: 281) description of the Tobin Tax (see below) as a 'non-starter' since it is unacceptable to the interests of the powerful. The globalisation that the Left is enjoined to embrace would therefore seem to be one in which there is little room for manoeuvre because its parameters have already been set by (predominantly) American corporations.

Not surprisingly, social democrats reject this 'there-is-no-alternative' account and a great deal of attention has been paid to the beneficial aspects of measures which conservatives interpret as obstructions, e.g. state welfare. Although some originally prophesied the end of state welfare and so of social democracy in a global context there is enough evidence now available to suggest this, these were wild exaggerations that are not being borne out (Pierson, 2001a) although some remain pessimistic (e.g. Svallfors & Taylor-Gooby, 2002) (see Chapter 9). Where social democratic principles and systems are already firmly entrenched they continue to thrive since the opportunity costs of abandoning them are potentially higher than the gains which would arrive from doing so. However, although the end is not yet nigh a consensus has emerged that the era of welfare state and public sector expansionism is now well and truly over and Pierson (2001b) insists that we have now entered a period of 'permanent austerity' where social democracies will have to adapt to relatively limited economic and political resources, with globalisation presenting particular challenges (Mishra, 1999).

As we would expect the NSD demonstrates a fair amount of ambivalence towards conservative globalisation, regretting the extent to which the chief global agencies are failing to steer global markets in a more humane direction while being mesmerised by the innovative dynamics that markets are alleged to bring and refusing to advocate much by way of reform to the agencies established at the end of WWII. In keeping with their general agent-centred prescriptions new social democrats sometimes insist that because it is actors which count then if only powerful actors can be persuaded to accept an ethical approach, within a new regulatory environment, then there is no need for anything more radical. (Even something as modest as the Tobin Tax – a proposed tax that would reduce short-termist financial speculation – fails to receive general assent.)

> Those on the old left always say 'regulate, regulate', and greater regulation of economic life, in some respects and some contexts, is necessary. But deregulation can be just as important, in areas where restrictions inhibit innovation, job creation and other economic goals. (Giddens, 2000: 84)

What this does is to portray the (old) left as dogmatic ('regulate, regulate') and the NSD as realistic and flexible. In truth, the issue over where and where not to regulate, whether at the global level or otherwise, cannot be reduced to simplified ideological formulae.

Stiglitz (2002) offers a more robust and devastating account. As a former Chief Economist at the World Bank (1997–2000) Stiglitz reports at first hand the attachment of the IMF etc. to a simplistic markets-know-best philosophy where government is always assumed to be corrupt and/or inefficient and there is nothing the public sector can do that the private sector cannot do better. The apparent sophistication of conservative arguments is little more than the patronising arrogance of the powerful condescending to the powerless and masks a crude, one-dimensional view of economies and societies. Stiglitz (2002: Ch. 9) therefore calls for a series of gradualist reforms in order save globalisation from conservatism: a shift away from presumptions that favour liberalisation and deregulation, the balancing of social interests with commercial ones, a change in governance so that there is greater equality and democracy within the IMF etc., greater openness and transparency in decision making. However, even these recommendations are modest in comparison with those who have called for a complete overhaul of the IMF, World Bank and WTO (see below).

Still, both old and new social democrats are united in calling for the globalisation of social democracy as a means of reclaiming the initiative from conservatism (Held & McGrew, 2002: Ch. 9). This involves not only fighting for social democracy on the global stage but ensuring that social democratic principles and objectives (especially those of social justice) are reoriented around global imperatives so that our conception of what that stage is is correspondingly altered. A global social democracy would be multilateral in its support for a global civil society based upon the common provision of basic public goods, greater regulation and accountability, inter-state forms of sovereignty and political representation (such as the EU), the attainment of environmental goals, common systems of defence and policing and the transnational control of flows of people and capital across borders. However, new and old social democrats are likely to disagree on the extent to which contemporary orthodoxies require substantial reform.

In any event, the NSD view is one that accepts the inevitability of globalisation and so of the insecurities that it brings but which attempts to steer the supply-side of economies and societies so that those global insecurities can be regarded as sources of opportunity rather than fear.

New radicalist critiques of globalisation are already multifaceted, so much so that some allege they are incoherent, contradictory and unrealistic. This is because those critiques have crystallised in recent years around the 'Global Justice Movement' (GJM) which first manifested itself at the meeting of the WTO in Seattle in 1999. Though initially travelling under the label of the 'anti-globalisation movement', a label more often imposed by its enemies in the media, the GJM is not and cannot be opposed to globalisation *per se* since it itself represents the *globalisation of resistance* to a particular type of globalisation: the conservative version which, it is alleged, subordinates the developing world to the developed, people to profits, states to markets and the public sector to the private (Klein, 2000, 2002; Hamel *et al*, 2001). Why this resistance?

Firstly, it is alleged that conservative globalisation implies a shift in power away from national forms of corporatist bargaining towards the hegemony of global (and especially financial) capital (Hertz, 2000). So although there is no such thing as a global labour market and although there is less of an international division of labour than some originally feared, labour frequently has to act as if it is or could be under competition from markets in other parts of the world. This is particularly the case where ICTs permit jobs and tasks to be easily relocated. Consequently, the kinds of wage and job insecurities that are anyway endemic to capitalist labour markets become multiplied by the global stage. Furthermore, while capital may sometimes accept high rates of taxation and strong regulation in those welfare states that offer various compensations (the selling-point of social democracies) the economic centre of gravity always tries to pull societies back towards low tax and deregulation, explaining why social democracies may have reached the limits of their expansion. What is worse, through recent initiatives such as the Multilateral Agreement on Investment and the General Agreement on Trade in Services the proselytisers for conservative globalisation have sought to undermine the public delivery of welfare services by regarding this as an unjustified monopoly and restriction on private ownership and trade. Conservative globalisation offers only the 'security' of global competition.

Secondly, conservative globalisation opens up a new spaces for colonisation by the ethics of profit and commerce due to its creed that there is potentially nothing that cannot be subject to private ownership and competition. As will be noted in Chapter 6 biotechnology corporations have taken partial control of the food chain, through the advent of genetically-modified organisms, and certain parts of the human genome, by patenting certain genes and so restricting others' access to them. Here, genetic security is held to lie in the externalisation and commodification of biological interiors. We might understand this as the copywriting of the genetic commons.

Finally, a point reiterated in Chapter 8, recent years have seen a shift away from legislation based upon civil liberties and towards greater surveillance, towards the idea that security can only be promoted if freedoms are surrendered. This tendency certainly took hold after the attacks of September 11th 2001, but was arguably in place beforehand (Fitzpatrick, 2001b). If, as I noted earlier, conservatism involves socio-cultural regulation as a condition of deregulated economies then this is as true at the global as at the national level. If markets never emerge *sui generis* but through the manipulation of society through states committed to them, as Polanyi (1944) argued long ago, then this must also be the case with global markets. Therefore, rather than being undermined by globalisation the competition state (Evans & Cerny, 2003) – or what I have called the 'security state' (Fitzpatrick, 2003: Ch. 2) – is that which nurtures global capitalism by disciplining localities into accepting their passification. This implies that the post-9/11 sprint towards authoritarianism represents an acceleration of already-existing trends rather than the emergence of anything radically new.

It is in opposition to these facets of globalisation that the GJM has grown but whether it possesses, or even should possess, a grand narrative is far from clear. Traditionally, opposition movements have corresponded to the model of a political party: strong consensus, determinate goals and 'top-down unity'; a model that has all too often encouraged the kind of intolerance, factionalism and heretic-seeking with which socialism and communism are still associated. By distributing itself along multiple lines of identity the GJM arguably represents a genuinely diverse popular front which avoids this danger: it is an umbrella term for a number of movements. However, the need to specify what they are for rather than against has motivated members of the GJM since at least 2001. Should the goal be a post-capitalist world or a different form of capitalism? To what extent can existing global institutions be reformed? To what extent do the needs of the developed and developing world conflict? The GJM has been struggling with the need to balance diversity with consensus in response to such questions (Monbiot, 2003).

And a recurring theme has involved support for greater democratisation. If *laissez faire* capitalism is held to represent an undesirable kind of insecurity then democracy is often valued as a much more positive alternative. But democracy is here dissociated from its conventional form – representative, centralised, infrequent – and theorised in terms that are more directly interactive, participatory and dialogical (Fitzpatrick, 2003: Ch. 9). So whereas capitalism and democracy have frequently conjoined the new radicalist case is that, because of conservatism's influence, the latter is more than ever a bulwark against the former. Such democracy offers the opportunity for greater justice without any absolute guarantees: democracy is never finalised and political battles always have to be won anew. However, its assumed superiority to *laissez faire* capitalism lies in the observation that whereas the latter can subsist without empowering the great mass of people (and may even require this) democracy cannot.

In terms of social policy the dilemma involves creating the required level of social equality, without which democracy may be no more than chimerical (Fitzpatrick, 2002a). There is, at least within the UK, a recent fashion for decentralising the public services. For the Right this is usually no more than a justification for sneaking privatised forms of competition into the public realm (Green, 1995) and so many on the Left worry that a decentralised welfare state militates against egalitarian goals (Walker, 2002) – though there is also a tradition of wishing to empower service users which also bears strong egalitarian credentials (Beresford, 2002). So if social equality and welfare democracy are to converge then abandoning traditional forms of equalisation (tax and spend) and management (top-down) may be premature, though it is far from clear whether such strategies are really consistent with the more ambitious and far-reaching demands of the GJM.

In sum, the GJM represents a potentially exciting development in radical politics whose influence and search for answers to the problems of conservative globalisation is likely to be ongoing. The basic message is that the conservative insecurities which prevail in the most commodified societies are not inevitable and can be replaced by democratising alternatives.

Time

For conservatives time can be considered as that which is under the control of individuals unless constrained by outside forces. The sovereign individual can choose how much time to spend earning a living, whether or not to do so by working for others, what type of work to pursue, and so forth. The conservative ideal is that of flexitime whereby employers and employees can fit around each other's needs: employers often want flexibility from their workforce, especially in a global market which is permanently open; employees want to juggle work time against family and leisure times and are increasingly able to do so as the office and the home merge through computers and other forms of remote technology. Security in and of time therefore derives from individuals having the greatest amount of control over when, where and how they work – hence the ugly neologism, 'flexicurity'. In a free market reason dictates that where either employers or employees are unwilling to be flexible then they will disadvantage themselves accordingly and so have to adapt or else continue to pay the consequences, but what is not warranted is outside interference, e.g. the imposition by government of maximum hours at work, since this can only distort the market and introduce rigidities and bottlenecks into market relations. A 'work-life balance' is more likely to result from the demands of market actors rather than from the nanny state imposing its will from the centre.

For those further to the Left the conservative account is problematic by ignoring the extent to which the nature of time is as much social as physical, i.e. woven into social relations, and so cannot simply be considered as being under the control of individuals (Adam, 1998). For instance, by bringing job insecurities in its wake *laissez faire* capitalism creates the kind of temporal insecurities that conservatives mistakenly interpret as signs of free choice.[4] Social inequalities therefore bear temporal characteristics and so time has become crucial to social scientific understandings of inclusion and exclusion. Take the following contributions to this idea.

Leisering and Leibfried (1999) observe that most life histories periodically demonstrate some degree of poverty: poverty is a permanent possibility for most people that we deal with using state welfare institutions. Socio-economic structures exist but within those hierarchies can be found a diversity of biographical trajectories. The aim, then, is to devise life-course policies which offer institutional supports that enable those periods of vulnerability and insecurity to be successfully bridged (Esping-Andersen, 1999).

Gershuny (2000) distinguishes between service economies based upon 'low-value' services from those based upon 'high-value' ones. High-value economies are usually to be found in social democratic countries where the satisfaction of basic needs has facilitated the emergence of more sophisticated tastes that drive a virtuous circle of high-value production and consumption. The implication is that high-value economies are inconsistent with large degrees of income inequality but also that, because economies now depend upon services rather than industrial production, inequalities can only be reduced by raising the productivity of human capital (see last chapter) rather than through tax-and-spend redistribution.

What the above research suggests is that insecurity manifests itself along the dimensions of time where the latter has to be understood in social rather than individualistic terms. Temporal insecurities are most prevalent in countries where inequalities are severe since inequality makes exclusion more prevalent and exclusion is not confined to a particular class of people but is a condition into which almost everyone can and will fall at some point in their lives. Therefore, and against the conservative reading, state welfare is a useful means of negotiating such periods of insecurity. However, if we are to devise the appropriate 'life course' or 'time use' policies we have to take the complexity of biographical trajectories into account rather than designing a one-size-fits-all kind of welfare reform. This is more likely to involve new forms of 'horizontal' insurance, e.g. endowment accounts upon which people can draw to tide them over, rather than vertical redistribution. This is a message more compatible with the new than the old social democracy.

A new radicalist account will agree about the social nature of time and regarding the temporal dimension of exclusion and inequality but will be more sceptical about the shift of attention away from structural hierarchies (Fitzpatrick, 2004a, 2004b; cf. Esping-Andersen, 2002: 23). While it may be true that most people can and will experience periods of low income and/or exclusion we should not be diverted from the greater risk to which certain social strata are prone. In other words, by concentrating too much upon the biographical dimensions what the social democratic account arguably ignores are the hegemonic conflicts through which social groups confront one another via the mobilisation of resources. This does not mean that 'horizontal' policies concerning time should not be emphasised, merely that these must supplement rather than replace the search for a 'vertical' equalisation of resources, i.e. a concern to flatten the social hierarchies rather than simply increase upward mobility within them.

Another dimension of time to which new radicalism draws attention is the environmental one (Fitzpatrick, 2003: Ch. 7). The expansion of capitalism in the nineteenth and twentieth centuries was dependent upon the colonisation of space, i.e. the search for new resources, workers and markets. While this expansion is still ongoing it has been coupled with a colonisation of time where in order to provide for the desires of the present we plunder resources upon which the future also depends: we buy security today by exporting insecurity into the future. This mortgaging of the future would be acceptable if the natural resources we use were converted into forms of capital that either enable nature to be renewed or else substitute for natural resources in ways that minimise environmental harm. However, environmentalists deny that this is presently the case and most regard contemporary capitalism as ecologically malign in its short-termism, its rampant consumerism and for the illusion it fosters that infinite wants can be infinitely supplied.

Temporal policies must therefore take intergenerational justice into account, meaning that questions of justice cannot be separated from those concerning sustainability. The dilemma for social policy lies in recognising that reducing poverty may often require forms of economic growth that are unsustainable in the long-run. For Dobson (2003) the circle is squared by emphasising the obligations and duties of humans to that over which they wield power: animals, future generations and the ecosystem in general. But unlike the NSD, where the concern with responsibilities is still centred upon an individualistic ethic of aspiration and consumption, Dobson's is much more of an other-directed ethic where the just distribution of resources is possible if and only if we consume fewer resources and consume them more responsibly.

Concluding Remarks

What, then, is at stake in the social policies of the twenty-first century? The first lesson from this chapter is that current debates should not be thought of as being between defenders of the old and pioneers of the new. Many politicians and columnists enjoy framing ideas in this way but it is a lazy impulse that we must resist. Welfare systems were never intended to be static and unchangeable and, so far as their future reform is concerned, there are many different versions of the 'new' on offer. Secondly, insecurity and risk is at the heart of those debates and we could retrospectively see the discussions of Chapter 3 in this light: arguments concerning agency, community and class are ways of understanding how we might reform welfare systems as a means of enhancing control of our selves, our environments and our circumstances. Finally, principles and objectives familiar to us across the modern period have undergone, and continue to undergo, development without substantial revolution, and I have here represented the latest stage of growth in terms of conservatism, social democracy and the new radicalism. So what is at stake in the twenty-first century is what has always been at stake: a battle for hearts and minds waged between those for whom free market capitalism is or must be triumphant, those who seek a social form of capitalism and those for whom capitalism must become subordinate to a series of just principles (which may or may not require the abolition of capitalism and I am deliberately leaving this question open). Social policy is one of the most important terrains upon which these battles are taking place.

In this chapter I have suggested that, far from disappearing, the collective need for insecurity has evolved into a need for forms of apprehension and anxiety through which we can still experience a collective sense of identity and fate. Yet uneasiness and risks are saturated with ambiguities and, no matter how prevalent, the very meaning of insecurity is uncertain and so subject to contestation and opposition. In short, the future is never closed and in social policy there is always more to play for.

I now intend to illustrate this thesis further by delving into two debates in which the temptation to adopt deterministic readings of social change is prevalent. In Chapter 5 we examine the social implications of ICTs and in Chapter 6 we likewise explore the new genetics. Although this focus upon technology may appear to be a boys-with-toys concern I hope to show how even these debates can remind us of the openness and possibilities residing within the social field.

5

Information and Society

Introduction

Information has always been central to social policy (Leonard, 2003).[1] In this chapter I am going to look at some contemporary developments and focus specifically upon two issues; the question of whether we now live in an information society and the relevance of the revolution in ICTs for social policy. One problem is that the literature on ICTs and welfare remains under-developed and tends to be highly fragmented in terms of its objectives and disciplinary orientations. The aim of this chapter, then, is not necessarily to join the dots but to suggest where some of the main dots are located. What are the main issues we should address?

Firstly, even if we do now live in an information society (and I will subject this thesis to critical examination) we have to spend a fair amount of time exploring the extent to which this society represents a rupture with 'pre-information societies' (for want of a better term). This issue is obviously crucial for our conceptions of the contemporary development and future possibilities of the welfare state. Secondly, we need to understand what is meant by the digital divide and therefore of what social inclusion in an information society might imply. Thirdly, I will suggest that in order to achieve such understanding we have to theorise the social contexts into which ICTs are being introduced and so I will design an hypothetical application of 'regime theory' to ICTs. Finally, we need to examine where the UK stands in relation to the preceding debates and questions.

94

Information Society

Do we or do we not now live in an information society? There are many who have asserted that we do, for what could be less controversial than the observation that information and computer-mediated communication (CMC), the circulation of patterns of data, have become central to social interaction? But to be significant the information society thesis must observe more than the centrality of information and CMC, it must establish that the organisational forms of industrial modernity have given way to a new social informatics. This is the assertion of two of the most important defenders of the information society thesis: for Manual Castells society has become profoundly networked, for Scott Lash physical things have dematerialised into the data streams of 'virtual objects'. It is these arguments which we concentrate upon below.

According to Castells (1996–98, 2000) we now live in a 'network society', the form taken by society in the 'information age'. The information age is organised primarily around the production and distribution of information and has replaced the paradigm of the Industrial Age, organised primarily around the production and distribution of energy. Castells describes the network society in terms of six main features which he relates to recent social, worldwide transformations.

Firstly, we have entered a new technological paradigm, centred around microelectronics, ICTs and genetic engineering. Castells insists that information technologies represent a greater change in the history of technology than those associated with the Industrial Revolution. Furthermore, we are only at the beginning of this technological revolution, as the Internet becomes a universal tool of mobile, interactive communication, as we shift from computer-centred technologies to network-diffused technologies, as we make progress in nanotechnology (and thus in the diffusion capacity of information devices) and as we unleash the revolution in genetics and bioinformatics.

Secondly, we live in a new economy characterised by three fundamental features. It is *informational* in that the capacity to generate knowledge and process or manage information determines the productivity and competitiveness of all kinds of economic units, be they firms, regions or countries. The new economy is *global* in the sense that its core, strategic activities, have the capacity to work as a unit on a planetary scale. By core activities he means financial markets, science and technology, international trade, business services, multinational production and communication media. But globalisation is highly selective. It proceeds by linking up everything that has value – as defined by the dominant nations and companies – and discarding anything which lacks value. And the new economy is *networked*. Castells identifies as the primary economic unit, not factories and workplaces, but informational networks of enterprises. Both large and small businesses increasingly work according to a strategy of changing alliances and partnerships – specific to a given product, process, time and space – which are based increasingly upon the sharing of information. This new economy is certainly capitalist but it is a new brand of capitalism in which the rules for investment, accumulation and reward have changed substantially.

It follows, thirdly, that there are new forms of work and employment based around the notion of flexibility: part-time work, temporary work, self-employment, work by contract, informal or semi-formal labour arrangements and relentless occupational mobility are the key features of the new labour market. This flexibility implies that work becomes 'feminised', in that it requires communicative competence, multi-tasking and inter-relational empathy, and 'self-programmable', such that the 'command and compliance' model of Fordism is replaced by one based upon autonomous self-organisation: creativity rather than simple obedience. The archetypical worker is no longer the 'organizational man' of the mass factory or office (Castells, 2001), but the 'flexible women' who is equipped with the ability to retrain herself, balance unpaid domestic work with paid work and adapt to new tasks, processes and sources of information.

Fourthly, culture is now organised primarily around an integrated system of electronic media, including but not limited to the Internet. But the new media system is not characterised by one-way messages from the elite to the masses. The new media are inclusive, establishing bridges from network TV to cable TV or satellite TV, radio, VCR, video, portable devices and the Internet. We are seeing the rise of an interactive audience, superseding the uniformity of the mass audience (see Chapter 9).

Fifthly, the emergence of a new social structure is linked to a reconfiguration of time and space. Time becomes 'timeless'. In contrast to biological time & clock time, timeless time is defined by the use of new ICTs. Time is compressed (as in split second global financial transactions) and past, present, and future occur in a random sequence (as in the blurring of life-cycle patterns, both in work and parenting). And space becomes dynamic. The space of flows refers to the technological and organisational reconfiguration where geographical territory & place begin to matter less. It is the flows between places that begins to matter.

Finally, the state is also undergoing a process of dramatic transformation. Its sovereignty is called into question by global flows of wealth, communication, and information and the state's legitimacy is undermined by its dependence on media politics. The weakening of its power and credibility induce people to build their own systems of representation around their identities. However, the state does not disappear: it adapts and transforms itself. It builds partnerships between nation-states and shares sovereignty in order to retain influence, e.g. the European Union. And the state in the information age is a network state, a state made out of a complex web of power-sharing, and negotiated decision-making between international, multinational, national, regional, local, and non-governmental political institutions.

The network society therefore consists of centreless webs which undermine the relevance of traditional sociological categories: individual/social, agency/structure, capital/labour. Yet Castells is by no means a naïve optimist who would have us sit back and enjoy the ride into a new informational utopia; instead, his analytical, non-prescriptive approach seems designed to draw attention to a number of potentially injurious ambiguities that are emerging.

As production is subsumed within informational networks the production-based social classes of the Industrial Age cease to exist, but this does not mean that social exclusion and stratification are thereby erased also, since the discarding of that which is deemed to lack value is more prevalent than ever. Beyond the realm of employable labour, legions of discarded, devalued people form what Castells terms the growing planet of the irrelevant. Because of this structural divide in terms of informational capacities and because of the individualisation of the reward system, in the absence of a determined public policy aimed at correcting structural trends, we have experienced a dramatic surge of inequality, social polarisation, and social exclusion over the last 20 years in most countries, but particularly in those that have fervently embraced the free market. Yet as well as widening social/digital divides the network society also makes it harder for those divides to be narrowed. In societies characterised by centres and peripheries, summits and plains, it was easier for policymakers to shape and engineer social material. But in the centreless webs of network societies there are no summits to which we can ascend in order to view and reorganise what lies beneath.

The injurious ambiguity therefore consists of a network society making social divisions wider while reducing our capacity to correct those divisions. The dilemma for social policy is obvious: state welfare is needed more than ever but, if it is to survive, the welfare state must be reformed into a flexible series of informational networks which abandon the search for the commanding heights of society and economy. Social justice becomes ever more necessary as the traditional tools of social justice become unavailable to us. Castells does not believe that all is lost, however, and we shall see why below.

Lash (1999, 2002) seems to agree with Castells that injustices have if anything become more virulent in an information society. The problem is that informationalism has destroyed the dualisms upon which the social critiques of industrial modernity were founded: whereas critique once reached for an 'outside' that transcended the object of its gaze, in a society of information networks everywhere is an inside of everywhere else. Since we cannot step away from the flows of global communication to construct a theory *of* information the critique of information always occurs within information streams themselves, implying that critique is irresolvable and of infinite duration. Such 'informationcritique' must be as reflexive (in Beck's sense of reflex) as the information society itself (Lash, 1999: 263). Here, the proliferation of ephemera, unintended consequences and side effects leave no time or space for reflection, perhaps implying that we can no longer have recourse to the concepts of public space and civil society. And although we may certainly still speak of 'spaces' these will consist of zones of inclusion or exclusion rather than relations of exploitation within a process of production. For what now counts is less the ownership of material assets as the ownership of patents, copyrights and prototypes.

So what Lash is doing is attempting to move beyond both the tradition of critical theory and its nemesis, post-structuralism. Both imply a linearity of, respectively, ideology and discourse whereas informationcritique is as non-linear as information society itself; both try to understand the *reproduction* of society while informationcritique recognises that society can only ever be *produced* due to information's fragmentation of meaning and signification.

Criticisms of Castells and Lash

But should we follow Lash in his haste to discard what he sees as the remnants of industrial modernity? There are two considerations which should make us pause.

Firstly, Lash is too quick to omit reference to that which does not quite fit his theoretical approach. Take one example. He talks about the ownership of prototypes having superseded that of assets but this seems to resurrect the kind of dualistic thinking that Lash condemns others for utilising. By contrast, although Rifkin (2000: Chs 3–5) is also certain that tectonic shifts are occurring in the nature of capitalism – where the buying and selling of property is being replaced by the renting of services – rather than proposing a wholesale theory of dematerialisation he finds that assets become subject to part-time forms of ownership. Yet in separating out assets from prototypes Lash (2002: 73) must also propose a simplistic distinction between the old and new media:

> Whereas all of the old media operate in a time of representation, the new media work in the register of presentation: presenting in a brutal manner, without interpretation, without even ideology – at least in the pure form of information. There are to be sure conventions and protocols for information production, whether for the nine o'clock news, a televised sports event or broadcast political meeting. But these are protocols, methods for presentation, not representation.

This not only risks underestimating the extent to which the old media were 'present' within the flow of events – e.g. the Nazi use of radio and representation (Burleigh, 2000: 206–15) – but overestimates the extent to which representative frameworks (aimed at objectivity) have faded. The problem for Lash is that he has to hold the information society as being radically new while describing it in terms that occasionally betray the opposite. He seems to believe that whereas transformation into a new social order was once based upon orientation to the previous order, now the social is in excess of itself as social change has itself altered according to the accelerative dynamics of information technology. But Lash can only maintain this reading by demonstrably ignoring (as in the case of corporatised media ownership) examples of the old which gatecrash the realm of the new.

The second consideration follows on from this. Even if ours is an information society this does not thereby render older versions of critical theory redundant. Ideology is certainly dated if it regarded as no more than a super-structural epiphenomena but there is a more recent school of thought – articulated by Eagleton (2003), for instance – which ties it into the forms of intimacy, emotional desire and libidinal affect that Lash regards as post-ideological and post-hegemonic. Again, Lash may be guilty of attributing to others the dualisms with which he himself works, e.g. that between the 'inside/outside' of critical theory and the 'always inside' of information critique. To propose an outside is not necessarily to fall back into quasi-Marxist essentialisms and reductionisms. Similarly, exploitation and exclusion are far from being opposing terms, even in an information society. The former is certainly redundant if it means nothing more than the extraction of surplus value but many have long denied that exploitation must be theorised in this way (Roemer, 1982; Elster, 1985: 167–204). Furthermore, to imagine that exclusion has superseded exploitation presents a one-dimensional picture of domination by ignoring the *complex degrees* of inclusion and exclusion which persist and so the hegemonic strategies through which the positional relations of power are maintained – see below.

Therefore despite the sophistication of Lash's ideas we do not have to accept either that the information society has arrived in its entirety or that familiar forms of social critique have been made redundant. Such considerations also reflect back upon the problem with Castells's approach, as we can now see by introducing social policy into the picture.

Castells and Himanen (2002) outline what they call the Finnish model of an information society, contrasting this with the Silicon Valley and Singapore models. For whereas the former is market-driven and the latter is authoritarian, the Finnish model shows how economic success in information technology can be combined with high levels of social justice and equality. To be sure, dominant functions and processes are everywhere being informatised but historical and cultural diversities ensure that such developments can take any number of paths and bear any number of social consequences. In the case of Finland the following characteristics seem crucial (Castells & Himanen, 2002: 74–5):

- High levels of investment in research and development;
- Public action to encourage and facilitate business innovation;
- Public systems encouraging individual and corporate creativity in designing and exploiting new innovations.

On the face of it the welfare state should be inconsistent with an information society since, according to the free market logic, the free flowing dynamism of information must undermine the economic and administrative rigidities of state welfare. Yet the Finnish experience points towards a virtuous circle whereby information-driven growth and productivity fund state welfare systems and those systems inspire growth and productivity in turn, partly by nullifying the insecurities that technological change brings and partly by facilitating the high levels of investment, creativity and education that informational economies require, with publicly provided, high quality schools and universities being of obvious importance. Therefore, an 'informational welfare state' is that in which information is infused with the principles and aims of welfarism (the virtues of collective security and social justice) and welfare systems adapt to the centreless networks of post-hierarchical information. The flexibilities and mobilities demanded by the information economy are enabled by capital and labour offering mutual security to one another rather than through the hire-and-fire ethic of Anglo-American inegalitarianism. The latter imagines that entrepreneurial innovation always and everywhere requires a monetary incentive but the lesson of European social democracy is that a publicly-spirited ethos of cooperation, something not driven by the profit motive, is equally important:

> ... it could be that, without a stronger welfare dimension, the informational economy may face such harsh opposition that its development will become extremely volatile or be unable to continue. This would make some type of welfare state a prerequisite for the global information economy. (Castells & Himanen, 2002: 88–9)

The importance of Castells and Himanen's work is that they show how and why the information age is characterised by social diversity such that any number of different social models are consistent with the advent of information networks. As has happened within the globalisation debate within recent years (as noted in the previous chapter) the basic message is 'social democracy is good for you'. However, what they do not to is to provide a typological framework – such as that explored below – which allows us to view the spectrum of 'info-welfare regimes', nor do they supply normative reasons as to why the Finnish model might be considered economically and socially superior to its alternatives.

One reason why they fail to provide the latter is because Castells and Himanen (2002: 87) fall into the cliché of contrasting the 'old' welfare state (passive, defensive, reactive) with the 'new' (active, enabling, dynamic), a distinction which overlooks the extent to which the welfare state has always 'activated' people into the labour market and ignores the fact that 'passive' policies will always be needed by certain groups. Consequently, many are attempting to supersede the passive/active distinction with one of prevention/non-prevention (e.g. Lister, 2003b), and although supporters of active welfare no doubt regard this as the primary means *of* prevention the overwhelming emphasis they give to labour market activation neglects the many other sources of prevention which exist – including, but not limited to, domestic labour and third sector work. So rather than making a sophisticated analysis less likely a normative stance which engages with such debates can potentially widen our understanding of the 'info-welfare regimes' which are in emergence and for which we might strive. Such a stance is offered below.

The essential problem might lie with the metaphor of the network. Unless it is theorised precisely the network can be easily perceived as consisting of 'nodes' in a continuous state of dynamic but basically egalitarian flux. This implies a rhizomatic social model where stabilisation gives way to flow and material power to cultural representation. Yet a network can also contain nodes which are more powerful than others and flows that are, paradoxically, flows of stability. In this second version, rhizomes have not superseded the arboreal hierarchies of modernity and what we are currently living within is an uneasy combination of 'vertical' structures and 'horizontal' networks that does not fully conform to either model. Castells seems to swing between these two versions. On the one hand, as we saw above, he is fully aware of exclusionary processes and the power of 'dominant interests'; yet Castells is also tempted to swing towards the former version of the metaphor in his rush to overturn traditional sociological theories. For instance:

> ... above a diversity of human-flesh capitalists and capitalist groups there is a faceless collective capitalist, made up of financial flows operated by electronic networks .... This network of networks of capital both unifies and commands specific centers of capitalist accumulation, structuring the behaviour of capitalists around their submission to the global network .... While capitalism still rules, capitalists are randomly incarnated ... (Castells 1996: 474)

So although power still exists it is the 'power of flows', the streams of informational codes to which even capitalist agents must submit.

Castells therefore works with two versions of the network: one which is in some degree hierarchical and one which is rhizomatic, and he seems unable to fully acknowledge his debt to both since this might require the acknowledgement that perhaps the features of the industrial age (bureaucracy, class, etc.) have not quite been superseded after all. This may explain why although he is content to identify contrasting models of the information society he has not (yet) offered prescriptions through which justice-enhancing interventions into that society can be made. By over-emphasising the importance of flows his foray (with Himanen) into the social policy arena is one that relies too heavily upon path dependency (see Chapter 9) and downplays our continued capacity to engineer social progress – and, indeed, social regression. For countries like the UK, which are poised between social democratic and conservative types of capitalism, this approach is ambiguous at best.

If we therefore conceive of the information society not simply as a post-industrial network of rhizomatic flows but as one which is being shaped by the lingering forms of industrial hierarchies – where much of the informational web has been woven by corporate governance – then we can retain many of Castells's insights without exaggerating the difficulties of achieving collective action. This suggests that an 'active' welfare state of informational networks is not quite the magic wand that Castells and Himanen seem to imply.

Where does this leave us? It presumably leaves us able to draw upon more older traditions of thought than either Castells or Lash would permit, traditions that do not abandon objectivist and emancipatory critiques of hierarchical inequalities of power, commodification, ideological struggles and capitalist hegemony. Certainly, these critiques have to acknowledge the extent to which socioeconomic relations are now mediated and therefore reconfigured by ICTs, but unless we have made a quantum jump into a new era then the purpose of these traditions is to establish how and why the information society dovetails with a society of industrial modernity whose remnants still punctuate our landscape. For Webster (1995: Chs 4–6) the relevant traditions have emerged within and around the school of critical theory, a central claim of which is that it is still possible for the knower to achieve critical distance from the known, even in an environment saturated by technologically-mediated information, and so to effect change upon the known according to rational principles of justice (Kellner, 1999; Fitzpatrick, 2000).

One implication of this is that online and offline spacetimes may be regarded as conceptually and ontologically distinct: we cannot dismiss the online realities of cyberspace as unimportant but nor can we convincingly claim that the offline has simply become a screen through which information circulates or, even more contentiously, that it is imploding into the singularities of technological networks. The 'meat' of human bodies still assumes physical and social shapes that have not dematerialised into codes and algorithms. So although we move rapidly and repeatedly between online and offline realms we have not thereby become post-human cyborgs, the hybrids supposed to emerge when nature and machine collapse into a boundless interface – a between-ness that is left with nothing to be between (Lash, 1999: 262; cf. Fitzpatrick, 1999b, 2002b; Dreyfus, 2001).

An additional inference is that the concepts central to social policy (distributive justice, wellbeing, etc.) do not have to be redefined out of all recognition. People in the offline world still suffer from harms and from hopes that need 'non-virtual' attention. However, nor is it the case that welfare systems merely have to adapt to ICTs through administrative reorganisation, for while they do not erase the reference points of industrial modernity ICTs potentially revolutionise them. One example. If social policy is concerned with the means by which we collectively ensure the just distribution of collective resources then what happens when resources become informatised? The field of education is now less about chalk-and-talk and more about teaching others how to teach themselves and learning how to learn (Dutton, 1996). It is less about knowledge as 'filling a deficit' (the accumulation of what was previously unknown) and more about 'protection against surplus' (filtering out extraneous information to prevent overload); it is both a science of technical skills and an art of critical appraisal and smart application. But what are the practical implications of this? Do we simply have to plug schools into networks and networks into schools? Should we embrace the language of human and social capital? Or do older, liberal notions of reflection and participative discourse come back to the fore? Whatever the solution, such questions cannot be addressed by treating social policy simply as a series of administrative fixes.

We return to these kinds of issues in the final section but in order to get from here to there we need at least a brief discussion of some key concepts within contemporary social policy debates.

Inclusion, Exclusion and Critical Theory

Massive attention has been given in recent years to the implications of ICTs for social inclusion and exclusion – and vice versa. Research into digital divides has multiplied to the point where it would take a Herculean effort to summarise it all. Fortunately, there are few people who have concluded that digital divides are of minor significance, with perhaps the most famous example being the pronouncements of Newt Gingrich (Gingrich & Armey, 1995), ex-future President of the USA, that social problems can be eliminated at a stroke by giving poor households a laptop. What happens when we dismiss such crude approaches?

It is easiest to define inclusion and exclusion in terms of access, for what could be clearer than that wealthier households will have greater access to ICTs than poorer ones? But while acknowledging that access differentials will persist Norris (2001: Ch. 4) is one of those insisting that as ICTs proliferate we will have to focus less on 'absolute inequalities of access' and more on 'relative inequalities of use': that is, ICTs are following the familiar consumerist logic. Unsurprisingly, all of the usual indicators appear when data on social stratifications relating to the Internet is gathered ICTs are accessed and used more by those with higher incomes than lower, more by the occupationally and educationally advantaged than the disadvantaged, more by men than by women, more by the young than the old (Selwyn *et al*, 2001). In short, broader patterns of social inequality inscribe themselves onto the virtual world. For those such as Norris, then, while inequalities of access can be expected to decline (though not disappear) – and are already doing so in the case of gender – relative inequalities of use are certain to persist. Why is this?

A full answer to this question would require a considerable diversion into longstanding theories of social reproduction. However, due to limited space available here, we can bypass this diversion by asking whether we have any evidence or reason to suppose that ICTs will alter the dynamics of social reproduction in such a way that exclusions will vanish and inequalities cease to be problematic, even on a relativist scale. The literature cited above suggests that no such evidence is yet forthcoming. Could this be because Lash is correct after all, i.e. that the old social rules have been torn up and society is no longer subject to reproducibility? But as I argued earlier this assertion depends both upon a very selective reading of recent developments and upon the unfounded injunction, common within much contemporary sociology, to shed traditional concepts and categories. So while bypassing this sociological diversion leaves us without a full account of relative inequalities of use in ICTs it does, at least from the critical theoretical perspective, suggest that we cannot avoid interpreting the spread of ICTs in terms of struggle and conflict, positionality and hegemony. Therefore, the hints of an alternative account can be suggested (cf. Schiller, 1996; Dyer-Witheford, 1999; Fitzpatrick, 2002b).

According to critical theory ICTs are not the passive recipients of social inscriptions but positional spaces occupied and shaped by those who 'got there first'. As such, exclusion means more than 'being outside' or 'being kept outside', it means continually having to chase what appear to be zones of inclusion to find, on eventual arrival, that their meanings have changed because they have already been evacuated by those further down the track of privilege, status and power. A simple distinction between inclusion and exclusion therefore proves to be a clumsy tool for the information age because it elides their mutual infusion. A zone is always and simultaneously a space of *both* inclusion *and* exclusion, a cascade of multiple effects for those who occupy different and competing timeframes: an interior for those who chase, an exterior for those who are chased. And while we might once have had a reasonable expectation of purchasing consumer goods that would last for decades goods are now so infused with interactive, computerised components that what we purchase is the promise of redundancy: self-terminating technologies. Therefore, the speed at which positional struggle takes place has accelerated in the information age without necessarily being replaced.

Yet this acceleration is not simply a 'speeding up' but also a contraction of the social distances across which we travel and are, in turn, travelled. Bauman (1998b), for instance, identifies profound ambiguities in the ontological spaces of our globalising, consumer societies: postmodernism certainly represents a speeding up but, even more than this, it also signifies the enfolding of modernist divisions.[2] A simple distinction between centre and margin into which agents can be neatly slotted (the centred and the marginalised) along socioeconomic lines has kaleidoscoped into multidimensional junctions where centres and margins relentlessly intersect one other. Therefore, while recognising the force of postmodernist accounts of self and society Bauman does not rush to discard all modernist reference points (e.g. Bauman, 1998b).

Each one of us occupies multiple zones of both inclusion and exclusion, transcending some and avoiding others, and so being always excluded at the moment of being included. However, this does not mean that older categories of hegemony, ideology and collective action should be abandoned: a critical remoteness is still achievable by facing the immediacy of the other. There are some zones from which it is better to be excluded than others and forms of power that can be said to rule. All social groupings transgress the lines of inclusion they find within and around themselves, but some groups find this transgression harder as a condition of others finding it easier. Therefore, relative inequalities are maintained through the ontological ambiguities of the information age's social dynamics. Positional struggle is struggle *between* selves but also struggle *within* selves, and so relative inequalities are maintained by inviting agents to become the source of their own exclusion by speeding up time and collapsing distance through the medium of technological information.

The main implication of this discussion is that an ideological framework cannot be abandoned after all since this framework is the means by which we understand the struggles over, and implications for, social inclusiveness which occur in and around ICTs. In itself this is hardly controversial and we have already seen its practical application in the work of Castells and Himanen. But whereas Castells and Himanen are content with an 'analytics of non-intervention' my view (see above) is that we have to appreciate the implicit drama of competing worldviews if we are to comprehend what is really at stake in constructing such a framework.

Info-Welfare Regimes

A starting-point that it would be difficult to avoid is the cross-national taxonomy of Esping-Andersen (1990). Although it has now been subjected to extensive critique, qualifications and to the additions of further classifications the basic model has proved remarkably resilient (see Chapter 9 also). Drawing upon the threefold distinction of Titmuss (1974) Esping-Andersen identifies three ideal-typical welfare states.

The liberal regime is highly individualistic, based upon the expectation that individuals should be self-reliant within a market environment where state assistance only provides minimal, residual help of the last resort. Social rights are barely in evidence and individuals are expected both to insure themselves against various risks (especially those related to employment and health) and to pay their own way through life. The liberal regime therefore has its roots in the nineteenth century Poor Laws where draconian entitlements based upon selectivist means-testing provide such undesirable levels of assistance that only the most abjectly destitute would apply for them. A strong distinction between the deserving and undeserving poor is maintained with each group assumed to occupy a different moral culture to the other, a distinction which cuts across any apparent similarity in material circumstances. Sticks rather than carrots are emphasised so that whereas the state is minimally present in one sense, in another sense it intervenes actively to regulate the behaviour of the poor through workfare and similar schemes, and some even maintain that its policies on incarceration are merely an extension of the same logic (see Chapter 8). However, some carrots do exist in the form of social insurance schemes. Even in the USA, for instance, 'social security' provides cover to middle-income families and so has proved generally immune to the kind of cuts inflicted upon residual 'welfare' benefits. However, taxes and social expenditure are comparatively low.

The conservative (or corporatist) regime aims at a degree of social integration that falls short of state collectivism. Based largely upon the traditions of nationalist (Bismarkian) conservatism, social Catholicism and Christian Democracy, corporatist welfare revolves around hierarchies of status and familialism. Here, compulsory social insurance is much more important but tends to be organised in terms of occupational divisions rather than upon the principles of egalitarianism and universalism. National state assistance is more generous but, as in the liberal regime, it is a provision of last resort since individuals are expected to first seek help at the 'lowest level' possible: from family, charity, church and local/regional forms of government. Some insurance systems are centralised and uniform but most are highly fragmented and complex, mirroring the divisions of occupational class. Private and commercial forms of provision play a relatively marginal role in comparison to that of not-for-profit (often church-based) associations which blur the boundaries between public and private. The strong emphasis upon employment accompanies a 'male breadwinner' model where the participation of women in the labour market is quite low. With the family assumed to be the main source of wellbeing (domestic welfare) it is women who are expected to provide for the needs of dependants.

Finally, the social democratic regime is strongly universal, with targeted means-testing being of minor importance, and 'decommodified' in that markets have little role to play. Benefit levels are high and levels of both inequality and poverty are correspondingly low, though levels of social expenditure and taxation are inevitably very high. The social rights of citizenship are therefore centre stage and familial responsibilities are assumed to belong as much to men as to women and so there are higher levels of gender equality than tend to be found elsewhere. The public sector is large, partly in order that high employment levels can be maintained, and so activation policies emphasise the duties of the state and of employers as much as the duties of individuals to find work.

Is it possible to take these ideal-types and apply them to the interaction of welfare systems and ICTs? The answer to this question obviously depends upon a host of assumptions. Principally, we have to assume that the worlds of welfare co-exist, and will continue to co-exist, with that of ICTs. We can follow the lead of Castells and Himanen in this respect. Furthermore, even if ICTs are enabling the reconfiguration of welfare systems – rather than depositing them in history's dustbin – we have to assume that this is happening at a pace which does not automatically render familiar concepts and debates redundant. Finally, we have to be content to remain at the level of hypothesis-building since this is still a very new area of research and, so far as I am aware, there is little data corresponding to the kind of cross-national taxonomy sketched above. If ideological maps are important, though, then it may be worth building a model, however speculatively. The following overview of what I shall call 'info-welfare regimes' is therefore offered cautiously and tentatively.[3]

We have already reviewed what Castells and Himanen (2002) denote as the Finnish model and, if it is reasonable to treat Finland as a social democratic archetype, as most commentators assume, then we can treat their account as an embryo of a social democratic info-welfare regime. This regime would continue to be based upon universalism such that the introduction of ICTs into welfare services is designed to enhance inclusivity rather than to reflect social divisions. It would be state-centred in that the role of the private sector – in introducing and running ICTs within the public sector – would remain modest. Care would be taken to monitor and address the emergence of digital divides (whether based upon class, gender, ethnicity, etc.), meaning social equality remains as a key goal of policy. ICTs would therefore represent a source of security rather than insecurity. And government would actively intervene to steer ICTs in the direction of employment generation, to sustain the high levels of productivity needed to fund generous social expenditure (especially through systems of education and training), to harness entrepreneurial creativity for social purposes, to maintain high levels of cooperation between capital and labour and so to enable forms of job flexibility that are family-friendly.

Part of the problem with this hypothetical sketch – notwithstanding the contribution of Castells and Himanen – is that the Scandinavian social democracies have been reducing benefit levels and tightening eligibility since the early 1990s. While usually being designed to defend rather than retrench the welfare state this period has coincided with the explosion in ICTs. Therefore, it is at present unclear from the Scandinavian experience whether ICTs represent a threat to traditional welfare (by facilitating the de-collectivisation and commodification of welfare practices) or whether their long-term effects are generally supportive.

A conservative info-welfare regime would demonstrate more ambivalence towards digital divides, resisting them wherever they threaten the cohesion of society or the competitive productivity of the economy but being less committed than social democratic regimes to overall levels of equality. Corporatist measures and concerns would therefore drive the research into,

and implementation of, new technologies in the belief that only full collaboration from the social partners can ensure their proper utilisation. ICTs
would nevertheless reflect the occupational complexities of the conservative
regime and would not necessarily engender an integration of insurance
systems and services. The private sector would therefore play a much greater
role in the research and management of ICTs, albeit in cooperation with the
state and public sector. In the early stages at least ICTs would be highly gendered with gender inequalities being more pronounced than in comparable
countries.

Finally, in the liberal info-welfare regime ICTs will be characterised by the
principles of market competition, economic individualism and social responsibility. Research and development will derive mainly from entrepreneurs
in the profit-hungry private sector with the state being concerned mainly
with hands-off regulation of business. However, away from such economic
imperatives state authorities will take much more of an interest in monitoring
and policing Internet activity for signs of criminality and anti-social behaviour. Beyond training in the basic skills for using ICTs digital divides will be
less of a concern than in conservative and social democratic regimes and a
technological determinism is more likely to prevail in the belief that low
incomes do not constitute a significant barrier to participative inclusion in
the use of ICTs. Strong divides will be in evidence, even so, mirroring the
ghettoisation of public and private, rich and poor.

Many countries demonstrate aspects of each of the above models. The UK
is one such hybrid – though arguably closest to the liberal system. Here,
there has been some concern demonstrated towards the forms of social
exclusion that ICTs might provoke, but this has been framed in highly productivist terms where exclusion primarily implies a lack of paid work in the
globalising 'knowledge economy' (PAT 15, 2000). Other dimensions of
exclusion and inclusion have been downplayed. A degree of technological
determinism has also been visible whereby inclusion has been promoted
through opportunities to access ICTs rather than through the vocabulary of
redistributive equality (HMSO, 1999). For example, in 1999 £15 million
was set aside to provide 100,000 computers under a Computers Within
Reach scheme where low income individuals and families would be provided
with cheap, secondhand computers, software and printers. Before being
quietly discontinued in 2002 the scheme was an immodest failure, partly due
to recipients lacking the financial resources that would enable them to exercise their intended role as consumers. The most successful examples of inclusionary policies have been at a local level where different sectors and agencies
have eschewed a deterministic approach (Nixon & Keeble, 2001; Hellawell,
2001; Leonard, 2003). New Labour has therefore been ambitious in its aim
to make the public sector fully accessible online by 2008 but its vision of a
'wired welfare state' has overestimated the extent to which online access
can alleviate offline exclusions (Selwyn, 2002; Nettleton & Burrows, 2003;

Hudson, 2003). And the boosterism it demonstrates towards some aspects of ICTs has accompanied a series of social panics about the 'outsiders' which an hysterical media obsesses about periodically: paedophiles, benefit fraudsters, asylum seekers, terrorists. ICTs have therefore been variously constructed both as entrances through which these outsiders can flood and as gates that we should therefore keep firmly locked. Consequently, issues of civil liberties and privacy have been under constant threat and a discourse of duty and security has predominated (Fitzpatrick, 2002b; see Chapter 8), a discourse that potentially threatens the demands for commercial freedom that New Labour otherwise supports.

We therefore have models of three info-welfare regimes, in outline, and at least some evidence that these descriptions capture the social realities of different countries, though let me reiterate my earlier warning that these thoughts are speculative, tentative and await a large-scale research project.

Education, Health and Social Technology

I now want to say something more about the UK experience by focusing upon particular welfare systems.[4] To what extent are the above features – hybridised but with a liberal bias – visible within recent welfare developments? For reasons of limited space I am going to review just two areas – education and health. It is worth noting, though, that Henman and Adler (2001: 41; cf. 2003) have recently speculated about the existence of ICTs regimes in relation to social security, characterising the liberal welfare state as that which is concerned to reduce administrative costs and make service delivery quicker and more accurate, in contrast to the social democratic state where the priorities are improvements in service delivery and transparency in decision-making. In other words, the liberal focuses upon efficiency, productivity and surveillance while the social democratic focuses upon quality, democracy and empowerment; characteristics that complement the principles outlined in the previous section. Are similar trends discernible within the education and health systems?

Education

ICTs obviously provide new implications and opportunities for education. Education is becoming more of a technique *and* more of an art (Dutton, 1996). The technique centres around the ability to channel through the technological archipelago with relative ease and speed, where skills become 'second-order', i.e. the skill to access other skills. Filing (the storing and retrieving of data) becomes a principal occupation and we have to learn how to manoeuvre the databases that pile on other databases in a seemingly endless labyrinth of hypertexts. The art consists of being able to distinguish, at a distance, relevant from irrelevant information: to skip across the surfaces of data so that you do not sink into the digital swamps that now surround us everywhere. As ICTs proliferate, then, education comes to mean more than simply 'learning how to learn'; it represents a site of ambiguity, a technical art for which critical faculties must be nurtured, the kind of faculties which are ironically undermined by the factory-farming methods that UK education has come to adopt (Kellner, 2000).

We therefore have to be sceptical about claims that new technologies will themselves revolutionise what pedagogues do and how they do it. For example, grand claims have been made in favour of distance learning where pupils can attend schools from home or students can take virtual degrees on a digital campus. But although it is undoubtedly the case that ICTs are changing and will continue to change the nature of education – not all of them for the better – the classroom is not about to be replaced by a library of CD-Roms and the campus is not about to dematerialise. Dreyfus (2001: 33–49) makes the point that education is a social exchange requiring face-to-face interaction where actual presence offers the kind of wisdom, inspiration and mutual learning which disembodied communication and remote viewing can supplement but never replace.

In short, we return to the point already made: the online enables the offline to be reconfigured such that society now has to be conceptualised as a technologically-mediated interface, but this does not mean that familiar problems, questions, concepts and debates have thereby been rendered redundant (Burbules & Callister, 1999). For example, Henwood *et al* (2000) find that although women and not formally excluded from education and training in computers, cultural representations continue to be such that women continue to be regarded, and regard themselves, as less competent, so allowing gender inequalities to be maintained.

So in terms of the UK we ought to be concerned about the extent to which socioeconomic divisions continue to drive educational opportunities. In 2003 it was reported that Britain still has one of the greatest class divides in education in the industrialised world, where the attainment gap between poor and better-off children is evident at less than two years of age and widens at primary and secondary school levels, by which time poorer children are one-third as likely to get five or more good GCSEs as their wealthier counterparts (End Child Poverty, 2003). Such divisions are consistent with a politics of market competition and economic individualism and suggests that the introduction of ICTs into schools and homes will have been strengthening digital divides rather than reducing them.

Furthermore, while the educational potential of ICTs are widely recognised, frequently accompanying this recognition is a fear about the misuses that access to new technologies can bring (Etzioni, 1999). Sometimes this consists of worries about children abandoning books and traditional social interactions in favour of video games and other frivolities; and media panics about the Internet have also been prevalent in the UK, with paedophiles and 'groomers' often assumed to be lurking around every virtual corner. Either way, these fears are usually out of all proportion to the actual risk, a possible reflection of the extent to which as a society organises itself around market relations so the insecurities and anxieties that this generates are sublimated into other areas, e.g. fears about the social order's vulnerability to new sources of social irresponsibility (see Chapter 4). The introduction of ICTs into UK education has therefore been riven with a profound ambivalence about their implications.

Health

Here, too, it can be difficult not to enthuse about the potential benefits of ICTs (Detmer, 2000; Fieschi, 2002; Patel & Rushefsky, 2002; Harlow & Webb, 2003; Hameed, 2003). ICTs improve the accuracy of medical information, allow it to be shared between authorised bodies more efficiently and, in the form of a smart card, makes information more portable; networks of health care, information and expertise can be formed within hospitals and between hospitals, surgeries, community services, pharmacies and homes (even when separated by great distance), so that health care becomes more of a continuum than before; telemedicine means that consultations, monitoring and operations can be performed even when practitioner and patient are not physically present to one another; the Internet erodes the formally sharp divisions between doctor and patient as people become more active in terms of their own healthcare by accessing data online and sharing experiences, e.g. in usegroups. Consequently, some are quite optimistic about the benefits of ICTs if only they can be harnessed effectively (Hudson, 2003).

However, many commentators caution against getting too carried away. As with education what matters is how, and why, technologically-mediated information is contextualised (Downing, 2001). Free-floating information can be dangerous even when it is accurate since what matters is not only the information's content but also the precision and strength of its application to specific health-related circumstances. For instance Nettleton and Burrows (2003) underline the significance of online self-help groups as means by which medical advice and social support can be provided in dispersed networks of care. However, a danger arises when such communities begin to replace rather than augment the practical, face-to-face types of advice and support that any well-functioning health care system should provide. One threat is that ICTs may facilitate a further shift towards a welfare pathologism in which individuals can be blamed for not acting responsibly on the preventive information provided by the state. Yet even if developments fall short of this scenario it is now clear that individuals are faced with an overwhelming amount of complex (and often contradictory) medical information to digest.

Digital citizenship therefore means becoming a specialist who lacks formal training, an expert without expertise, and some commentators therefore agree with Lash that we have become reflexive citizens who have no time and space left for considered reflection (Nettleton & Burrows, 2003). The state's role, then, is radically ambiguous. On the one hand it acts as a source of information overload and complexity; on the other, its job as a *welfare* state is to somehow tame and pacify these information streams, to identify and disseminate the essential themes and narratives, and to enable practitioners and citizens to apply the information intelligently and cooperatively. Over the last few years the NHS has embraced many aspects of this new health informatics but with an emphasis upon reducing service costs and the *provision* of information rather than upon a more *interactive* conception of digital healthcare (Cullen, 2003).

Yet the ultimate worry, as with education, is that the massive inequalities which have arisen in the UK since the 1980s will significantly reduce the potential benefits of ICTs. Though researchers continue to argue over the details it is clear that inequality and poverty are not only bad for a deprived person's health but are bad for everyone's health (Wilkinson, 1996)! Therefore ICTs have come along at a time when, in the UK, their introduction into a context of massive social and health inequalities does not bode well for all but the most bleary-eyed technological determinist. So while the less well-off are dependent upon a public sector starved of resources for decades the more affluent can cherry-pick the best of what the state has to offer while also accessing and utilising healthcare through the commercial and voluntary sectors. ICTs are therefore another means by which the middle-classes can be first in the queue.

So, once more we are perhaps left with a sense of critical ambivalence towards ICTs: a huge potential for empowerment, collaboration, democratisation and improved efficacy which, in the UK, is combined with massive social inequalities and the prevalence of market individualist priorities and ideas.

Social technology

We might provisionally conclude, then, that the kind of trends identified by Henman and Adler are identifiable within the education and health systems also, with the main problem being less a reluctance to exploit ICTs and more a series of offline realities that construct the offline/online interface around values, assumptions and objectives that presently restrict the realisation of their full potential. This does not imply that the UK can be simply treated as an example of a liberal info-welfare regime since the UK is a country traditionally hard to classify and, certainly in comparison with the USA, social democratic principles and constituencies continue to influence. Yet it may suggest that to realise this potential the UK has a further political and intellectual distance to travel than some of its neighbours.

In particular, it indicates that technological and administrative fixes cannot repair the social tears that several decades of political failure have ripped and shredded. There are two main reasons for this. Firstly, because administration itself has to be reinvented as a means and not an end. If in the information age we have to conceive not of public space but of a dynamic kaleidoscope of public *spaces* then rather than undermining the purpose of the public sector – where we all retreat into our privatised enclaves – it may imply an enhanced role whereby the public sector becomes less an managerial and technocratic machine and more an open *agora* upon which these publics encounter and talk to one another. Here, the state becomes not just another network, a modular intersection within an informatic web, but a search engine that can weave together other networks in response to changing circumstances but always according to the enduring themes of social justice. In so far as ICTs are interpreted merely as more efficient means of welfare delivery, therefore, then they may only serve to take us farther away from this conception and consolidate rather than overturn the Weberian bureaucracies of industrial modernity.

Secondly, because technological fixes cannot guarantee the forms of solidarity that contemporary individuations require. We have become used to the thesis that collective and communal sorts of identification and association can no longer be treated as given (Etzioni, 1994). But while conservatives have interpreted this as a green light for *laissez faire* capitalism the value of NSD is that it goes one step further and recognises that individuality can no longer be treated as given either (Giddens, 1991). In other words, consumerist and competitive forms of individuality are one element of the self (one 'subject-position') but by no means the self's essence. ICTs are therefore the technological expression of a network society in which connecting and reconnecting become the principal activities (Mulgan, 1998), suggesting that, while the autonomous self is here to stay, because autonomy does not necessarily imply atomisation, and because my sense of self is dependent upon yours, then mutuality is also an unavoidable feature of social networks. But where new social democrats potentially err is in imagining that this 'mutual autonomy' renders older conceptions of equality and social justice redundant. For unless we agree with those information society theorists who believe the social formations of industrial modernity have melted into thin air (Leadbetter, 1999) then solidarity and equality have not separated. In short, a technological fix is no substitute for, and may even be a political diversion from, the mutuality of social equals.

Conclusion

In this chapter I began by questioning at some length the arguments of Castells and Lash to the effect that the network or information society represents a profound rupture in human affairs. I suggested that such theses have more to do with the obsessions of the theorists than the object of theorisation and that it is premature to imagine that older forms of social theory and critique have been left redundant. I then reviewed the debate concerning digital inclusion and exclusion, proposing that an ideological framework is still relevant, and used this framework to outline – albeit tentatively – three info-welfare regimes: the liberal, conservative and social democratic. I went on to indicate that while it would be reductive to characterise the UK solely in terms of market liberalism it does exhibit significant features of the latter, particularly in the degree of socioeconomic inequality which now prevails. I finished by arguing that while applying technological fixes appears to be the easiest and most fashionable approach it actually takes us farther away from the forms of interactive (and egalitarian) solidarity that a network society may require. What this suggests is that the contemporary prospects for progressive social change in the UK are not encouraging until and unless more inroads into socioeconomic inequalities have been made.

I now want to see whether similar conclusions can be drawn vis-à-vis another new technology.

6

Genes and Environments

Introduction

A gene is a sequence of DNA, the self-replicating molecular strands which form the biological basis of life, that are contained in the 23 paired chromosomes each of us inherits from our parents. Genes are coded to produce the amino acids out of which proteins, and eventually cells, are produced. Interpreting the code therefore enables you to understand something of the biological characteristics of the organism in question.

What the hell has this got to do with social policy? Well, a great deal (Nelkin, 1999). The history of social policy is strewn with battles between those who interpret human biology this way or that way. And because the natural order, especially when viewed as the work of God, is widely assumed to be *the* moral arbiter ('that shouldn't be permitted, it's not natural') then disagreements over biology have both inspired and masked arguments over how society should be organised. In the nineteenth century, social Darwinism was driven by the idea that because there are natural superiors and inferiors then society should ruthlessly expel those who cannot or will not help themselves. Its fondness for philanthropy, charity and public works has to be viewed in terms of the mellifluous ease with which the Victorian era was able to weld together biological discoveries and *laissez faire* economics.

And so wars over biology are visible within the discourse of many early designers of the welfare state (Thomson, 1998). Indeed, because some of the latter were also supporters of eugenics it is not outlandish to read the early history of state welfare as a social branch of eugenic engineering (Fitzpatrick, 2001c). Such an interpretation would be easier to dismiss were it not for the fact that eugenically-inspired experiments were only discontinued in the social democratic welfare states as recently as the 1970s (Broberg & Roll-Hansen, 1996). Therefore, when we peruse what geneticists enjoy calling the 'book of life' we are gazing at the biological architecture of modern social policies.

For some within the 'new genetics' the human body and the social environment should be understood as the accumulated inheritance of genetic evolution: they are 'gene machines', the carriers of genetic information from generation to generation. The first aim of this chapter is to consider such claims. Yet an even more considerable declaration is that we can and should make these organic and social machines more effective through the application of biotechnology. If genetic engineering enables us to eliminate disease and so reduce suffering then what's wrong with that? The second aim of this chapter is therefore to review some of the key arguments for and against biotechnology and then apply such considerations to several key areas of social policy.

Darwin vs. Darwin

Disputes within (rather than against) evolutionism have occupied centre stage for many years now. The standoff between different schools of Darwinism is largely (cf. Sterelny, 2001) a disagreement about the role and importance of genes to the human subject and so ultimately to society. Radcliffe Richards (2000) is no doubt correct to observe that the main schools agree about much more than their sound and fury towards each other would suggest. Yet there are important differences between them nevertheless, even if these are often differences of emphasis. Those we hear term 'genetic Darwinists' insist that gene lineage represents the explanatory key which unlocks the secrets of human interaction and social cultures – they include Dawkins (1976, 1982, 1996), Pinker (1995), Dennett (1996), E. O. Wilson (1975, 1978) and Ridley (1996). The 'organic Darwinists' believe that this is too simplistic and we should instead adopt a more holistic focus which treats organisms as the unit of selection and which does not seek to explain everything according to natural selection in any case – they include Gould (1997), Rose (1997), Lewontin (2000), Jones (1994) and Midgely (1995). Let's look at these schools in turn.

Perhaps the key text of genetic Darwinism remains *The Selfish Gene* published in 1976. Here, Dawkins argues that lifeforms are primary characterised by the drive for self-replication and reproduction. The term 'selfish gene' has obvious rhetorical strength, so much so that Dawkins (e.g. 1976: 36) has sometimes allowed himself to go beyond metaphor and talk of genes as if they really are agents, or egotistic little actors. Organisms, or phenotypes, therefore have to be understood as evolutionary effects of the underlying genotype and so Dawkins characterises them as vehicles, or survival machines, through which genes survive by making descendants of themselves through reproduction. It follows that organic processes consist of endless adaptation to their environment, as those features of the phenotype that are environmentally redundant are jettisoned through natural selection. Genes therefore supply the mechanisms of natural selection that Darwin was not able to fathom.

The 1970s also saw the birth of sociobiology under the influence of Wilson, to whom Dawkins acknowledges a considerable debt. Put simply, sociobiologists contend that all forms of individual and social activity can ultimately be explained by reference to the biological need for survival and perpetuation. If you want to explain differences between the sexes, for instance, then you need to appreciate that because men are biologically suited to father numerous children then they are more likely to be aggressive, competitive and promiscuous, in contrast to women who, because they can only give birth to a limited number of children, are more likely to be compassionate, co-operative and thorough in their choice of sexual partners. Sociobiology also inspired the more recent emergence of evolutionary psychology (Cronin, 1991) which applies biological explanations to human language and intelligence. If you want to understand what it is to be human, e.g. our facility with tools, then you have to explore the struggles for survival that took place in the pre-human stages of history.

So genetic Darwinists believe that human nature is fundamentally genetic and that this nature is the ultimate source of all socio-cultural forms of relation and behaviour. This is not necessarily to reject the existence of social constructions or the importance of nurture, but it is to observe that what we call the social is ultimately a manifestation of the biological. For Pinker (2002) those who deny its genetic foundations are guilty of propagating a 'blank slate' interpretation of humanity in which nothing can be said to precede the constructions of the social. This is to advance an incorporeal and so inadequate view of the self, he insists. Ridley (2003) concurs, pointing to what he sees as the genetic basis of instinct, heritability and intelligence; though this is not to propose that the social environment is unimportant. Wilson goes as far as anticipating that the humanities and social sciences will eventually abolish themselves once their failings, due to the denial of biological and psychological causation, are honestly admitted, for never,

> ... have social scientists been able to embed their narratives in the physical realities of human biology and psychology, even though it is surely there and not some astral plane from which culture has arisen. (Wilson, 1998: 202)

For social policy the lessons of genetic Darwinism seem obvious: those social policies which reflect and work with the grain of human nature will probably succeed, but those which ignore or contradict our biological inheritances will fail and generate potentially disastrous consequences (Wilson, 1998: 156). As such, one of the key questions that genetic Darwinists have sought to answer is, 'if our biologies are essentially self-interested then what gives rise to altruism?' Several answers to this question have been proposed – and see Chapter 3 also.

The first answer is to observe that despite their biological selfishness organisms have an obvious interest in cooperating since everyone gains if everyone works together. Unfortunately, self-interest also leaves the individual organism with the knowledge that if everyone else cooperates, while they refuse to do so, i.e. defects, then they will benefit as a result. Yet because this knowledge is common everyone has an interest in defecting and so cooperative systems are likely to collapse very quickly. Cooperation is therefore threatened by the free rider but defection is efficacious so long as only a few free riders exist, a situation unlikely to prevail since the more organisms see the benefits of free riding, and defect as a result, the more those benefits reduce in value: free riding undermines the condition of its own effectiveness. What we call altruism is therefore a chimera, a misnomer that misconstrues the facts of evolutionary adaptation.

The second answer is to interpret the group as the unit of selection and suppose that groups which prosper the most are those in which the organisms demonstrate the greatest amount of altruism and cooperation, i.e. selfless commitment to the whole. At present, though, group selection attracts relatively little support amongst evolutionists (cf. Sober & Wilson, 1998).

The third answer, the one for which most genetic Darwinists express support, is to treat altruism as enlightened self-interest, as a qualified form of selfishness that is most likely to emerge when societies of cooperative reciprocity are in place. Cooperation is a form of trade that occurs when organisms realise that they can gain more from working together than they would separately. However, because most acts of social exchange do not occur simultaneously an understanding between organisms has to prevail. What Axelrod (1984; Ridley, 1996: Chs 3–4) referred to as 'tit-for-tat' strategies inspire organisms to copy the behaviour of others: if you scratch my back then I will scratch yours, but if I scratch yours and you refuse to reciprocate then the next time you come to me asking for a back scratch I will tell you to get lost. Therefore, a system of mutual monitoring can preserve the cooperative group while minimising the risk of defection.

Interestingly, though, computer experiments with game theory suggest that a variant on tit-for-tat is more successful for group preservation. Let us say that you refuse to reciprocate my scratching of your back. If I then tell you to get lost the next time you ask for my help then the cooperative scheme will collapse more quickly than if I allow you some leeway, i.e. treat your defection as a rectifiable mistake and allow you to defect once or twice in the expectation that you will be shamed into seeing the benefits of cooperation rather than those of free riding. In short, when a certain amount of generosity and forgiveness is built into tit-for-tat then it offers a more robust basis for social cooperation than mutual monitoring alone. And since those characteristics are more likely to be demonstrated towards kin then altruism resembles a form of biological and emotional attachment.

It is here that direct connections with social policy can be made. As noted in Chapter 3 Titmuss has been lambasted for imagining that state welfare can be based upon altruism and that it can encourage the spread of altruism amongst the population. Altruism, it has been argued (Field, 1996), is too rare and fragile a property upon which to base a social order and we are better off regarding individuals as potential knaves so that we build into our social institutions forms of protection against knavish behaviour (LeGrand, 2003). An ethic of duty, desert and reciprocity is therefore superior to one based solely upon rights, needs and altruism. Yet even if tit-for-tat strategies are more vigorous than those based upon pure selflessness the superiority of 'generous tit-for-tat' might suggest that we should not be as obsessed with knavery and free riding as the critics of Titmuss have been. This is to reiterate a point made in Chapter 3 to the effect that an ethic of reciprocity supplements, but does not necessarily dispel, the broader choice between an ethic of altruism and one of self-interest.

So this may be the point at which those committed to egalitarian and radical social policies should be sceptical of the more extreme claims of the genetic Darwinists given their premise of biological self-interest. Genetic Darwinists on the political Right are certainly hostile towards state welfare systems (e.g. Ridley, 1996: 264), though even those on the Left demonstrate support which incorporates anti-welfarist prejudices:

> The welfare state is perhaps the greatest altruistic system the animal kingdom has ever known. But any altruistic system is inherently unstable, because it is open to abuse by selfish individuals, ready to exploit it. Individual humans who have more children than they are capable of rearing are probably too ignorant in most cases to be accused of conscious malevolent exploitation. Powerful institutions and leaders who deliberately encourage them to do so seem to me less free from suspicion. (Dawkins, 1976: 117–8)

So, might the *organic* Darwinists offer a more palatable approach (Rose & Rose, 2000)? The central charge they make is that the genetic Darwinists are guilty of biological reductionism and genetic determinism. In so far as the accusation lambasts Dawkins *et al* for reducing everything to gene sequences it is unfair: the idea that every characteristic of humans can be traced, on a one-to-one basis, to a particular gene is scientifically untenable and the genetic Darwinists are (usually) perfectly aware of this. They may nevertheless be describable as 'weak determinists' in so far as they ultimately explain the phenotype as an assemblage of the genotype such that selectionist processes in the latter give rise, after complex interactions, to the former. For organic Darwinists, then, even weak determinism is crude because it under-emphasises the importance of context (Rose, 1997).

Firstly, genes have contexts, namely the organisms within which they are embedded and from which they cannot be detached without reducing them to abstract bits of information without meaning: the equivalent of Wittgenstein's imaginary lion, one that can talk but whom we cannot understand because the lion's cultural frame is totally alien. Secondly, organisms have contexts, namely the physical and social worlds external to it. Therefore the organic Darwinists identify a dialectical interdependency between genes, organisms and environment where each evolves in response to the others so that, rather than talking about simple adaptation, we have to appreciate the existence of multiscalar adaptation at many levels of selection, the implication being that organisms are not the passive receptors (the survival machines) of genetic influence.

Like the genetic Darwinists, then, the organic Darwinists argue that we have to overcome the nature/nurture distinction, but they accuse the former of being conceptually unable to transcend the distinction at all. For organic Darwinists the dialectical interdependency of gene, organism and environment means that we should talk less of nature/nurture and more of levels of potential for *self*-evolution, since if organisms are active then they can transcend their genetic origins. But by favouring a weak determinism in which gene lineage plays the central role, the genetic Darwinists are committed to treating later stages of evolution as if they can be easily traced back to the earlier stages. So while Pinker may be correct to criticise 'blank slate' interpretations of human nature, by supposing that the only alternative is to imagine the slate being filled with genetic wiring he only succeeds in pushing nurture (particularly parenting) away from nature, retaining the very distinction he claims to be transcending.[1]

The disagreement comes to a head over competing interpretations of culture (see Chapter 9 also). For genetic Darwinists 'genes hold culture on a leash' (Wilson, 1978: 172), meaning that culture has to be understood (almost in Marxist terms) as possessing only a relative autonomy from the genotype. The leash in question is said to consist of 'memes', the cultural equivalent of the gene, a further means by which replication occurs and adaptive selection proceeds (Dawkins, 1976: 192; Dennett, 1996; Blackmore, 1999). We therefore have a biological explanation for cultural conservatism in which culture is something we inherit rather than something we both originate and transform. But for organic Darwinists all of this is, quite simply, nonsense (Midgley, 2000): arguments from analogy, or another example of scientists getting carried away with their metaphors. For example, while genes might be said to bear dominant and recessive properties where are the equivalent properties for memes? Does the fashionable resurgence of something long held to be unfashionable signify an evolutionary process? In other words, the meme is another example of geneticists reducing everything to biologism. The genetic Darwinists resist this accusation by pointing out that we can choose to rebel against our genes and memes by telling them to go jump in a lake (Pinker, 1995), but if genes really do hold us on a leash then this leads to one of three possibilities: (1) the rebellion is illusory, (2) the rebellion against our genes is something they themselves permit – and how meaningful is that tenet? – or (3) the 'leash theory' of relative autonomy is wrong and a central proposition of genetic Darwinism falters.

The alternative is to conceive of culture (and human nature) as consisting of 'emergent properties'. Gould and Lewontin's (1979) famous illustration of the idea is that of the spandrel, an architectural feature which was not part of the original blueprint but which emerges during the actual construction. The purpose of the example is to make the point that something can be more than the sum of its parts and that the later stages of growth are not the simple consequents of the earlier stages. Emergent properties are therefore the means by which an organism transcends itself, escapes the determinations of its origins and develops the potential to self-evolve. So while it may be true that culture did not drop out of the sky from some 'astral plane', the fact that culture, society and self had biological origins does not mean that we are on the leash that held us thousands of generations ago: the cultural cannot be seen as simply the latest chapter in the book of natural selection (Gould, 2000: 103–5).

It then follows that altruism does not have to be reduced to interactions of self-interest since the latter do not encompass the full complexity of human identity and association (Rose, 1997: 199–203). To extrapolate conclusions about cooperation in human societies from the behaviour of animal tribes or computer simulations provides work for those fascinated by anthropology, computer algorithms and prisoners' dilemmas but, as I indicated in Fitzpatrick (2001a: 15–16), game theories are better treated as guides of how to bring about the social futures we find desirable rather than as metonyms for an immutable present.

So by providing a more rounded account of organisms and their environments, and a more convincing account of the potential for change, organic Darwinists offer social policy a more productive route for thinking about the interactions of genetics, biology and social welfare. You can still interpret individuals as tending towards selfishness and knavery if you want, because while culture might transcend its materialist origins this does not commit us to a rosy view of social cooperation – we might have so far failed to realise our potential. But the point to remember is that such failures do not have to determine future developments. This leads us onto the more prescriptive aspects of the debate and the possible role of biotechnology in helping us to shape our social futures.

For and Against Biotechnology

So where might support for organic Darwinism get us in terms of policy on the new genetics? Should we support population screening or not? How does genetic testing alter our conceptions of health, privacy and autonomy? Can and should a distinction be maintained between therapeutic and reproductive cloning? Who should have access to genetic information and why? It is these questions we now go on to consider. Of course, we should always be wary of the hyperbole surrounding the subject, e.g. fears that the human self is about to be defined predominantly as a genetic being (cf. Novas & Rose, 2000), and of speculating idly about things that scientists cannot actually deliver (Martin & Frost, 2003). However, the fact that something – full human cloning perhaps – is scientifically improbable does not make it worth ignoring. Because scientific illiteracy has sadly given rise to flawed public policies many times in the past, we cannot simply leave these issues to scientists.

In attempting to decide the best position from which to assess recent and proposed innovation in the new genetics we can review those offered by some of the key political and social scientific authorities on the subject. In keeping with the overall approach of the book I am going to assume a broad Left-Right distinction and sketch some of the key ideas, both for and against biotechnology, which have emerged in both camps. Please note that this distinction does not correspond exactly to that between, respectively, organic and genetic Darwinists, although there is a fairly close correspondence.

Human nature and the free market

Those on the Right who have highlighted the dangers of the new genetics include Fukuyama – though see O'Hear (1997) also. Fukuyama (2002: 99–100) wishes to resist a drift towards what he refers to as the post-human condition – the way in which human nature is coming to be defined by technology – and so to defend an international regulation of biotechnology. In its hostility to free market libertarianism there is much in Fukuyama's stance with which the Left would agree. There are two main problems with it, however.

Firstly, Fukuyama's default position lies always with the deregulationists such that the burden of proof rests upon those who would regulate. So although he himself supports regulation of biotechnology it is a reluctant support which emphasises costs and underestimates the benefits of regulation. Secondly, Fukuyama (2002: 97) is a philosophical naturalist who believes we should always defer to the natural order of things and avoid imagining that human beings can improve upon it through intervention. He therefore, *inter alia*, exaggerates the extent to which there are essential natural characteristics set by genetic factors. For instance, Fukuyama (2002: 136–8) is content to follow the lead of those psychologists who attribute 50% of our IQ to genetics and brushes aside those who have queried this figure and those who challenge the idea that intelligence is quantifiable along a single dimension at all (Gould, 1997; Kaplan, 2000: Ch. 4). In short, Fukuyama is opposed to biotechnological intervention but not necessarily to genetic determinism, a regulationist position that would ignore forms of genetic intervention that could be of social benefit and that would ground legislation upon an essentialist view of natural inequalities.

There are also those on the Right for whom biotechnology is a potential force for good if it is left to the implementation of market actors. For Silver (1998: 264),

> If it is within the rights of parents to spend $100,000 for an exclusive private school education, why is it not also within their rights to spend the same amount of money to make sure that a child inherits a particular set of their genes?

Unfortunately, Silver never gets to grips with the argument that perhaps parents should not have the right to spend $100,000 on a private school education either!

Among those who have attempted a more thoughtful defence of *laissez faire* markets are Ridley and Murray. Ridley (1999: 312–3) contends that we can never escape from genetic and 'external' determinisms but we can distinguish between good determinisms (those which enhance free choice) and bad ones (those which don't):

> Freedom lies in expressing your own determinism, not somebody else's. It is not the determinism that makes a difference, but the ownership.

And this has to imply private ownership since it is here that the greatest amount of control can be wielded: 'genetic screening is about giving private individuals private choices on private criteria' (Ridley, 1999: 299). Therefore, because genetic good fortune is blind to social privilege then existing laws on discrimination are sufficient and there is certainly no need for the state to tell you what you should and shouldn't do with genetic information about yourself (1999: 268–70).

What we have here, then, is basically a familiar tale where the power of the state is bad but the power of the firm (the biotechnology corporation, the insurance company, the employer) is good because in a market environment they respond to our needs and demands. Don't they? Ridley does not even get as far as considering the possibility that there may be ambiguities within our notion of 'the private', where because the sum of private decisions may lead to collective consequences that rebound upon and undermine the spaces of individual liberty, so that we cannot glorify private choice if we are to defend it effectively. Ultimately, Ridley's supposition that considerations of 'the public', the common good, the state and equality are external to those of 'the private', individualism, the market and liberty resembles Nozick's defence of 'full self-ownership' that was critiqued in Chapter 2.

Murray's contribution is rather more eccentric. Murray (2000) believes that the new genetics is beginning to prove that the Right's view of human nature (as innate, competitive and self-interested) is the correct one.

Therefore, because it imposes upon nature and society an artificial equality the egalitarianism of the Left is sure to be undermined. As a kind of death rattle, though, Murray anticipates a revival of eugenics on the Left as it attempts to achieve through genetic engineering what social engineering has been unable to deliver. The solution to this threat is to leave genetic innovations to market forces.

There are many grounds upon which Murray can be criticised (Fitzpatrick, 2001c) but at heart his is a prime example of the danger of reading social prejudices onto the genetic code.[2] For instance, he states that although genetic differences exist between men and women, poor and rich, white people and black people, and people of different nationalities, so what? 'Vive la différence', according to Murray. But this remarkable concession to pluralism does not quite square with his other pronouncements. If the poor are genetically different from the affluent then how can we celebrate this difference when Murray (1984) has repeatedly highlighted the supposed dependencies and inadequacies of the poor as a threat to society? And his celebration of racial differences translates into a kind of benign apartheid given Murray's insistence elsewhere that black people are inherently less intelligent that whites (Herrnstein & Murray, 1994; Pilnick, 2002: 48–55).

The Right is therefore characterised by three interpretations of the new genetics. Those conservatives like Fukuyama who would regulate biotechnology but are suspicious of any suggestion that human nature is profoundly social; those libertarians like Silver and Ridley for whom private (and no doubt corporate) decision-making is sacrosanct; and those like Murray for whom the new genetics is another excuse to propound a dangerous agenda.

The return of society

There are many on the Left who are hostile to biotechnology (Rifkin, 1998). Habermas (2003: 61–5) argues that a genetically engineered child is one whose autonomy has been adversely affected, *even if that child has otherwise benefited as a result*. This is because biotechnology introduces something new into human affairs. Whereas all parents shape their children's development it has hitherto been possible for the child to take control of such socialisation through a critical reappraisal of themselves and their circumstances. But the genetically engineered child would be a programme who would owe its sense of self to a programmer. The dependency thus created here would be so unilateral that any critical reappraisal would always be partial and the child always an effect of another's wishes. This kind of 'asymmetrical paternalism' would be so strong that it could undermine our understanding of our selves as social, ethical and communicative beings. That said, Habermas admits that some engineering might be warranted in order to prevent extreme, medically-related harm; though he does not specify where harm-preventing interventions end and illegitimate ones begin.

Bowring (2003) also provides an extremely powerful critique of biotechnology. His essential complaint is that biotechnology represents another form of disenchantment, another way in which we alienate ourselves from nature in appearing to achieve mastery over it, another means of forgetting the meaning, wonder and creativity of our embeddedness in the natural environment. Technology is an instrument by which we turn ourselves into soulless technicians, appendages to the machine and machinic logics, distracted by the ease of technological solutions to surrender control to the corporate agendas of profit and the privatisation of life. By regarding nature as a mechanical apparatus we are transforming it as such and so transforming ourselves into cyborgs: 'The mechanisation of nature will lead to the mechanisation of ourselves ...' (Bowring, 2003: 143).

Bowring sits squarely within the traditions of critical theory and existentialism. The problem is that his is an all-or-nothing critique which views us as being on a slippery slope where there are no intervening stages between the top and bottom of the incline (Bowring, 2003: Ch. 8). He may be correct to lambast those who would leap without hesitation into the deep-end of genetic engineering but identifies little difference between them and those who see reasons to paddle in the shallow end to discover what the benefits might be. Bowring sets up an ideal (of natural embodiment) against which *any* form of technological application is going to be found wanting. The possibility that the shallow-enders may share the moral sensibility he lauds remains unconsidered since technology must, he believes, derive from an abstract rationality. But this sharp division between the embodied and the abstract contradicts the very faith in humanity to which he appeals; since if our sensibilities are being gradually eroded then is there much point in appealing to a space beyond the corporate, technocratic prison which, for Bowring, surrounds us everywhere? Perversely, Bowring shares the same premise as the deep-enders he abhors: once we start down this road there is no turning back.

At the opposite extreme to Habermas and Bowring are those on the Left who demonstrate varying degrees of enthusiasm for the new genetics (Singer, 1998; Dawkins, 1999). Buchanan *et al* argue that the state has to regulate the new genetics in some way or another:

> ... just as the state is the principal agent acting in the interests of future generations in such fields as land and resource management, so too does a eugenic role for the state, if needed, fit into the standard categories of legitimate areas of concern for government. (Buchanan *et al*, 2000: 337)

Does this mean that Murray was right to anticipate the revival of a eugenic Left after all? Not if eugenics implies something akin to totalitarian coercion vis-à-vis sterilisation, selective breeding and involuntary euthanasia. However, to limit our definition of eugenics to this extreme case is to hide away from the extent to which the new genetics can have eugenic outcomes even with the best of medically-inspired motives. If eugenics is defined as a population policy which is exercised through reproductive technology then, far from dying in a Berlin bunker in 1945, it has been evolving throughout the last century (Kevles, 1985; Broberg & Roll-Hansen, 1996; King, 1999), from the birth control advances of Marie Stopes, to *in vitro fertilisation* in the 1970s, to the new genetics that we are now considering. And even where we do not have an explicit population policy the interactions of millions of daily decisions have potential eugenic implications and so may be said to constitute a *de facto* policy (Duster, 1990; Glover, 1999). Eugenics may therefore be an ineliminable aspect of the new genetics (Kitcher, 1996) and in drawing attention to this Buchanan *et al* are proposing an alternative to the kind of *laissez faire* eugenics favoured by those such as Murray.

But what kind of interest should the state take? Buchanan *et al* (2000) insist that where we can prevent avoidable suffering then we should do so, such that banning genetic engineering as a preventive measure makes no more sense than banning other forms of prevention. After all, if social justice requires the redistribution of undeserved *social advantages* then does it not also demand the elimination of undeserved *genetic disadvantages*? And they maintain that parents should have the right to know the genetic characteristics of their children and to make appropriate decisions. What all of this implies is that embryos with a predisposition to a genetic disability or condition are more likely to be aborted, but this is acceptable in order to prevent avoidable suffering and if society can value its disabled people (whether their disability is genetic or not) (Harris, 1998: 92).

But is it reasonable to imagine that we can operate a policy of screening for, testing for and in many cases terminating such embryos while also valuing those of differential ability? Does the former not undermine the latter? Where birth is a matter of chance then disability can be regarded as a contingency to be encountered and accepted; but where birth becomes increasingly a matter of choice then 'deviations' become mistakes that can or (as in the case of wrongful birth and life suits) should have been rectified. Here, Bowring's allegation of a disembodied rationality has force. Buchanan *et al*'s (2000: 272–6) counterargument, that a women would be justified in terminating an embryo where the child will 'suffer a serious impairment', slides quickly from (a) those conditions that seriously limit opportunities to (b) those which involve suffering. In the first place a limitation may not involve suffering and, in the second, what the able-bodied interpret as a limitation may be nothing of the sort.

Such is the position of Kerr and Shakespeare (2002) for whom genetic policies must have far more safety-measures built into them than Buchanan *et al* envisage. They propose that most disabilities be interpreted in terms of the social model (Fitzpatrick, 2001a: 149–52) and a politics of difference, meaning that the source of most limitations and 'suffering' lies in social obstructions (physical, ethical and cultural) rather than in biology of the disabled person. To treat parental decision-making as sovereign is to risk turning disabled people into members of the much-anticipated genetic underclass. Parents' right to information does not necessarily imply a right to *all* information since, if it were possible, we would presumably want to deny their right to know about predispositions to conditions, e.g. homosexuality, which attract other forms of prejudice.

However, while rejecting the position of genetic enthusiasts Kerr and Shakespeare do not retreat into the enclaves of Habermas and Bowring. Theirs is an intermediate position which acknowledges the desirability of termination, albeit it in a minority of cases. Disability is a minority status that shares many characteristics with other minorities *but not all of them*: in some cases it can involve real limitations and suffering that the social model *per se* does not capture. Therefore:

> In these extreme cases of impairment, it would seem inhumane not to allow women to have access to this information and to have the right to terminate pregnancy on the basis of the characteristics of the foetus. (Kerr & Shakespeare, 2002: 139)

Kerr and Shakespeare do not go into detail about which impairments are extreme but they do indicate that social polices have to be far more complex than those which follow from the respective positions of genetic cynics and enthusiasts (Glover, 2001).

Social Policies and Genetics

The problem is that while this intervening position sidesteps the purities of technological 'antis' and 'pros' it means that we cannot devise a simple blueprint for those social policies which interact with the new genetics. Even if we alight upon one kind of model, e.g. based upon fundamental rights (Andrews, 2001: 175–6), no easy answers are forthcoming. What follows is therefore a series of dialogues designed to illustrate the thinking of those who agree that we have to commit ourselves to an open-ended complexity rather than go searching for a single, all-purpose map for policy-making. To this end, we will review the following three areas: insurance and employment, screening and testing, therapy and engineering.

Insurance and employment

Insurance systems enable individuals to pool risks and so to live more fulfilling lives because they can anticipate that the effects of the slings and arrows which hit us all occasionally will be mitigated. With social insurance you share the scheme with most adults in the country; with private insurance the scheme's membership is much more selective. In private schemes deciding where the burden of risk should fall is a delicate balancing act: if it falls too heavily on the insurer then premiums will be high and payouts will be low; but if it then falls too heavily on the membership those most in need of insurance may be effectively excluded. It all depends upon the distribution of information. Where the insurer possesses information that you do not have then the burden is more likely to fall on you; where you possess information that the insurer does not have then the burden will fall on them. Many insurance firms in the health and health-related fields there-fore argue that they should have a high (and perhaps a full) degree of access to genetic information on the insured since otherwise they are open to exploitation. Those who know they are due to develop a crippling or a fatal condition may, unless the firm has access to the same information, be able to take out huge policies in the knowledge that either they or their families will soon be in a position to benefit. The consequence would be costly for the firm but ultimately, in a process of adverse selection, also costly for other insurees: to recoup its losses the insurer will hike up premiums and so risk excluding some on low incomes most in need of cover (Pokorski, 1997).

But while such access to genetic information seems reasonable on the face of it there are potentially consequences which should make us pause (Kass, 1997). Firstly, it might be that armed with the foreknowledge that they may have to disclose the results many people will elect not to take a genetic test at all, a decision that could have serious ramifications for their health. One solu-tion would be to force people to be tested and force them to disclose the results subsequently, but this degree of coercion seems out of proportion to the problem we are trying to address. Secondly, it is possible that the in-formation can be misused or misinterpreted by actuaries. In a commercial environment the inclination to exaggerate the risk of a predisposition actually developing into the relevant condition may well be considerable. In attempt-ing to deflect the burden of risk-taking away from itself the insurance firm may adopt a motto of 'better safe than sorry'. This might also be true in the case of conditions where the genetic link is either indirect or largely unknown. Thirdly, and more generally, many worry that the more genetic information about ourselves is out there in the world then the more difficult it is to control and the more likely to trickle between interested third (and fourth and fifth) parties. This has implications for privacy and consent that we consider below. Finally, basing risk assessment more and more upon genetics contributes to a culture where we are defined, and come to define ourselves, in terms of our biologies, ignoring the extent to which we are social beings and the extent to which disease is caused by social factors for which we no longer seek social solutions because we have been distracted by a 'genetic-technological individualism'.

So what might the solutions be to problems of adverse selection? One solution is to deny that there is a problem such that insurers are exaggerating the risk for commercial reasons: because they fear not having access to information available to competitors and because they wish to maintain a position of superiority vis-à-vis their membership. Since the risks of adverse selection are minor compared to the profits the insurance industry makes then they are simply going to have to absorb the costs. Another solution, one which has attracted both the industry and policy commentators, is to require disclosure only in the event of expensive policies being taken out or to render policies above a certain limit void when disclosure of relevant information has been withheld (Association of British Insurers, 1997). The problem with this solution is that it may discriminate against those who genuinely need expensive policies and it may be that, even in the event of less expensive ones, insurers can acquire the information they want in other, less direct ways.

The final proposal is to socialise the private insurance industry (McGleenan & Wiesing, 1999). One way of doing this is for the state to construct insurance schemes for more and more areas of social life, including not only health but things such as home ownership. Additionally, the state could require the private insurance industry to follow regulatory codes designed to protect the most vulnerable and disadvantaged in particular. The problem with this solution is that it implies the kind of collectivism for which many electorates have demonstrated an antipathy in recent years. Nevertheless, because insurance schemes have a social impact and can carry potentially deleterious consequences then it is socially just ends against which they must be judged. If, for practical reasons, this does not engender out and out socialisation it certainly suggests that the state should direct the burden of risk away from the relatively powerless and upon those who, in the long term, make considerable profits.

What of employment? If there is a risk of some becoming excluded from insurance protection is there also a risk of some people being excluded from the labour market because of their genetic predispositions? In some industries there are certain conditions which render workers more susceptible to ill-health and so increase the costs to their employer of providing sick pay, replacement cover, etc. as well as rendering them more vulnerable to litigation. And in the workplace generally employers may want to identify those who are 'genetically fit' and so likely to impose less of a financial 'burden'. Should employers therefore have a right to see genetic information and even a right to require a genetic test where one has not been carried out? Does this place too much power in their hands and threaten discrimination against those with a higher risk of occupational hazard and/or ill-health? Does it take the emphasis away from employers' responsibilities to ensure safe working environments? Or is it perfectly reasonable to utilise a technology which can match workers to those environmental circumstances for which they are best suited?

In the USA the debate has been pre-empted because employers have been taking advantage of biotechnology for years with many now using genetic information for one purpose or another and critics warn that, in most cases, this represents a worrying escalation of intrusion into employees' privacy (Hubbard & Wald, 1998; cf. Reilly, 1999). Yet should we completely outlaw the use of genetic information, even when it can be potentially beneficial? The Nuffield Council on Bioethics (1999) acknowledges situations where the existence of certain genetic predispositions should be taken into account, especially where the welfare of relevant third parties is concerned. For this reason, limited and carefully proscribed forms of screening and testing may be permissible. However, the benefit of the doubt is always given to the employee and the employer would not be allowed to fire, coerce or refuse employment on the grounds of genetics. The BMA (1998: 171) argues similarly that individuals '... should be free to accept certain risks, providing they are informed of the implications and the decision does not put others, who have not consented, at risk.' This also offers some protection to the employer whose liability is reduced in those circumstances where genetic screening would have benefited the individual who refused to be screened, or where individuals accepted the risks associated with a revealed genetic condition.

Kelly (2002) argues, on the basis of research in Kentucky, that there is little evidence to date of the emergence of a genetic underclass due to insurance-based and employment-based forms of exclusion and discrimination. The possibility that such an underclass will appear in the future cannot be ruled out, however. Luck in the genetic lottery is not stratified according to social hierarchy but where inequalities and disadvantages exist then bad luck in the lottery may add another dimension that it is difficult for individuals to surmount alone. This is where social policies can make an important difference and I have suggested above that this means utilising genetic information for the purposes of insurance and employment on a very selective basis.

Screening and testing

The dilemmas presented by screening programmes predate the new genetics but it is certainly the case that genetic screening illustrates the ethical predicament of advanced medical technology (Lenaghan, 1998: Ch. 2; Pilnick, 2002: Ch. 4). Screening is used to reveal whether a foetus is at risk of developing a genetic disorder, thus provoking a decision about whether the pregnancy should be discontinued or not. This is precisely what has the disability movement so worried since the fear is that, where a disability is predicted the mother will want to terminate in most cases, especially when either conscious or unconscious pressure is applied by the medical profession. Screening therefore legitimises bias against disabled people and medicalises their conditions as deviations from a 'healthy' norm. It could represent a new form of eugenics.

The counter-arguments are those which we reviewed in the previous section: namely that people have a right to genetic information about themselves and their impending offspring, that all parents wish their children to have as high a quality of life as possible and that abortion in the event of a revealed disability does not necessarily engender discrimination. The disability movement responds in turn that the information revealed is partial and so likely to encourage biased decision-making; and since there are many examples of actions being limited or even prohibited entirely, wherever they may have deleterious social consequences, then screening ought to be outlawed on the same basis (Kerr & Shakespeare, 2002: 123–5).

Further objections to screening concern the subtle ways in which it may undermine choice whilst appearing to improve its quality. As the technology has disseminated so the use of screening is routinised, becoming a standard, common sense and unquestionable part of the process of pregnancy from which few women see the need to dissent. Pregnancy therefore becomes a technology-driven maze through which women are guided by experts whose views and assumptions are difficult to challenge at the time: the distinction between consent and non-consent therefore becomes blurred.

Current health policies reveal a worrying ambivalence, then. On the one hand they appear to improve quality of life and aid choice; yet they may also be appealing to prejudice and irrational fears, while actually undermining the control which women have over their bodies.

Unlike screening genetic *testing* is carried out where the risk of a genetic disorder is already known or suspected (Lenaghan, 1998: Ch. 2; Long, 1999). Here, too, it is easiest to believe that that only benefits can result from improved medical technology. The field of pharmacogenetics, for example, promises to make drugs more effective by tailoring them to the specific genetic makeup of the individual concerned. But it is not necessarily the case that knowledge leads to better control. Knowing that you are likely to develop a late-onset disorder may mean that you alter your lifestyle for the better but it is possible that you will also develop a kind of *genetic fatalism* where your quality of life is reduced rather than enhanced. In other words, the diversity and complexity of human psychology cannot be easily slotted into medical categories designed to reflect a technocratic rationale. The proliferation of genetic tests means that counselling becomes more important than ever but many have expressed fears that, due to the complexity of genetics, that counselling is always directive, i.e. people are subtly steered towards decisions that the professional 'knows' to be the right one (Pilnick, 2002: 91–4).[3]

Genetic testing also alters the meaning of privacy and confidentiality. In addition to insurance companies and employers, other third parties with an interest in your genetic information may include family members (Andrews, 1997). Knowing that you have a genetic condition do you have a responsibility to reveal this to family members and, if you choose not to, should health professionals do so? Where maintaining confidentiality places others at risk then what is the right course of action? An additional problem arises when we remember that family members not only have a right to know about relevant genetic information they also have *a right not to know*, perhaps out of fear of succumbing to genetic fatalism. But how can the wishes of family members be respected when finding out what those wishes are may itself disclose the fact that relevant genetic information is already available to them? As before, consent is potentially undermined by a technology that, on the surface at least, appears to improve choice.

At present the British Medical Association (BMA) (1998) favours the maintenance of confidentiality, although it acknowledges that there may be a few cases where confidentiality can be legitimately breached. However, it also supports professionals encouraging individuals to share information with family members voluntarily, another possible example of directive counselling:

> The BMA believes that, as with other areas of health care, the doctor's duty of confidentiality to the individual patient is of fundamental importance and should only be breached when there is a legal requirement or an overriding public interest ... however, individuals should be encouraged to consider the implications of their decisions for other people. (BMA, 1998: 69)

Though because our notions of public interest and legal protection are subject to change then such adherence to confidentiality may evolve in the future.

Screening and testing therefore bear implications that go way beyond the immediacies of a particular programme or procedure. The very meaning of health begins to alter. Increasingly, we no longer see ourselves as either healthy or unhealthy but as caught in a twilight region between the two. As biotechnology peers further into human genomics so the body becomes a site of risk, a zone within which potential conditions and diseases are always lurking. One argument is that the more we stare into the technological mirror the more we see a technological construct being reflected back. The more health and health-prevention is fetishised then, paradoxically, the more we catch sight of actual or potential signs of ill-health; the more we attempt to wipe the mirror clean of impairment then the more dirty it can appear to be and the more obsessed we become with pursuit of an unobtainable ideal. As we act according to a medicalised norm then differences that arise due to chance begin to appear as defects that could and should have been prevented.

As indicated in the previous section such considerations do not necessarily prescribe policies in which screening and testing are banned, even assuming that this was possible, but it does mean focusing more clearly than we have managed to so far on the social lenses through which we view health and technology.

Therapy and engineering

For the most part, commentators have regarded somatic cell therapy as acceptable and germ cell therapy as unacceptable (Suzuki & Knudtson,

1990: 183–191). This is because somatic cells are the body's ordinary cells, in which case any alterations bear implications for that individual alone, while germ cells are the sperm and egg cells so that any changes effected here will be passed on to the individual's descendants. Precaution has therefore dictated that gene therapies be limited to the former, where consent can be given, rather than to the latter.

But even somatic cell therapy is still very much in its infancy, though the completion of the Human Genome Project, announced in 2003, may mean that important advances will be made over the next few years. The apparent benignity of somatic cell therapy has been called into question, however, not only by those who fear we are playing God or violating nature but by some in the profession who point to the inherent dangers and the fact that experiments have led to more fatalities than researchers have admitted – the death of Jesse Glesinger in 1999 being the most prominent. Furthermore, would gene therapy be available to all (in which case what are the cost implications for public health care systems?) or would it exacerbate health and social inequalities as a process which only the affluent can afford?

Bowring (2003: 180–2) also worries that gene therapy is the first stage of a slippery slope in two senses. Firstly, because the distinction between medical cures and cosmetic enhancement is thinner than we like to tell ourselves so that the technique can easily evolve into a commercial business by which, in a pattern all too familiar, our insecurities are exploited as we desperately buy the products to correct the imperfections that the market suppliers tell us we possess. Secondly, he observes that gene therapy opens the door to cloning. That door is already opening slightly in the form of therapeutic cloning where cells are cloned for purposes of transplantation (including that of cloned human and animal organs in the future, perhaps) and in order to treat diseases such as Alzheimer's. Bowring (2003: 201–4) argues that as embryos cloned for medical research becomes more widely accepted then either the pressure will mount for a cloned embryo to be implanted in a women's uterus or an accident will occur with the same outcome. And once the first cloned human has been born then the moral rubicon, facilitating the birth of more clones, will have been crossed.

Arguments for such reproductive cloning are in fact not difficult to come by (Stock, 2002; Harris, 2002) and generally consist of scenarios where full human cloning can be imagined to be desirable, for example:

1. to save the life of a dying child by cloning him or her a genetically identical sibling,
2. to allow a lesbian couple to bear a biological child,
3. to allow a single women to have a child without donor insemination.

However, critics (Putnam, 1999) allege that even such apparently benign examples are problematic. In scenario (1) the cloned sibling is being treated as a means rather than as an end and while parents usually have children for instrumentalist reasons of one form or another, this does not mean that cloning should be permitted for the same reasons. In scenario (2) the child may experience considerable identity problems in having two biological mothers (a genetic mother and an egg/womb mother) and no biological father. In scenario (3) the identity problem may stem from the child being *both* the offspring of the mother *and* her genetically identical twin, both daughter and sister. And such problems occur long before the prospect for designer babies.

The additional form of genetic engineering with considerable health implications is that of Genetically Modified (GM) foods (Shiva, 2000a, 2000b). The controversy has raged since the late 1990s when the introduction of GM foods through the backdoor was suddenly exposed to public light. The possible advantages of GM foods (Pilnick, 2002: 126–33) are that,

a) they are basically no different from traditional forms of agricultural cross-breeding,
b) they represent a more efficient and precise form of cross-breeding in which produce can be engineered with or without particular properties,
c) with a rising world population hunger and malnutrition requires that we take advantage of biotechnology to increase yields.

Critics (Tokar, 2001: Chs 1–8), though, point out that,

d) traditional cross-breeding could not have violated the natural barriers between species that genetic modification is able to transgress,
e) once released into the social and natural environment GM organisms cannot be recalled so that the unintended, long-term consequences are unpredictable and potentially dangerous,
f) world hunger is due to problems of social distribution, allied to greed and profligacy on the part of developed nations, and not to problems of agricultural production,
g) through processes such as terminator technology, GM foods place the food chain in the hands of the same biotech industry that is busy patenting the human genome and undermining biodiversity by expropriating, through 'biopiracy', plants and crops in the developing world.

Of course, it may be that the debate should not be seen in all-or-nothing terms, that stepping onto a new path does not turn the path into a slippery slope. Yet if, as I argued in the previous section, we ought to be cautious without being over-cautious then there is a heavy burden of proof upon those who would take us into a world of reproductive cloning and GM foods. To date, though, many advocates fall back on the deterministic claim that because we *can* do something then we *ought* to do it, a position which is arguably less compelling than the precautionary approach I am advocating here.

Conclusion

I have argued that organic Darwinism is superior to genetic Darwinism because it leaves room for a non-reducible conception of the social which identifies multiple levels of life and culture where gene sequences are just one of a number of contexts. This organic Darwinism is more conducive to a politics of social justice. I reviewed the arguments of various conservatives and free market libertarians and have gone on to sketch the contrasting positions of those on the Left who reject biotechnology, those who embrace it and those who hold an intervening stance. I argued that a precautionary approach, one that is open to the use of biotechnology so long as issues of social justice (and not simply individuals' choice) are at the fore is the reasonable one to adopt. It also implies that we cannot design a simple blueprint for social policy but, in reviewing the above debates, I have proposed that we proceed much more slowly than various enthusiasts would like.

So, no, we are not gene machines and, more importantly, we ought to resist those who would use biotechnology to engineer us as such. Social policy occupies a position vis-à-vis the new genetics that is somehow both peripheral and central: peripheral in the sense that the world of chromosomes, nucleotides, gametes and DNA splicing seems far removed from that of social policy; yet central in that we view this world through a social lens and argue over its implications depending upon disagreement over what is and is not a desirable society in which to live.

In the last two chapters I have indulged my boys-with-toys interest in new technologies. In doing so I have hopefully revealed that the label is fairly misleading since a wide series of ideas and perspectives must be applied if we are to understand and utilise intelligently the new powers we have at our control. As stressed at the end of Chapter 4: the social field can never be corralled entirely, there are always gaps and opportunities in the fencing. In the remaining three chapters I want to continue to identify where some of the key openings and closures are. We begin by exploring spaces that while they may appear intimate are in fact grounded within the very social field we are gradually roaming around.

7

Social Psychologies, Emotions, Bodies

Introduction

The previous two chapters have dealt with subjects where some wish to detach technologies from their social embeddedness. In this chapter we turn towards subjects where the social framework is more obvious but still highly contested. We are going to deal with three principal dimensions of the self (psyche, emotions and the body) by first outlining the contours of some recent debates and exploring the connections with social policy as we proceed. The intention here is not to integrate the three dimensions closely but to underline the point being made throughout these later chapters, that contestation and debate revolves around disagreement over the nature of the social.

Social Psychology

So far as I am aware there is no theory of social psychology that has been applied, at a definitive and generic level, to social policy. Specific interventions have been made. Zigler *et al* (2002) draw upon a range of literature from neurophysiology, child psychology, social science and public policy to underscore the importance of infant and toddler care to the efficacy of welfare services – a theme dear to the heart of social democrats. From the Right, the 'dependency culture' thesis bears some resemblance to social psychological theories of learned helplessness where circumstances from which no escape seems possible can induce passivity and submissiveness (Peterson *et al*, 1993). If dependency therefore derives from people feeling they have no control over their fate then surely the solution is to induce an alternative set of learning patterns by removing the welfare crutches: being cruel to be kind. Unlike its psychological counterpart, however, such prescriptions derive from very narrow interpretations of 'dependency' and 'control' (see Chapter 1).

Yet by and large, although policy-makers and recipients possess a wide and complex range of motivations, values, moods, attitudes and ways of perceiving and interpreting the world, the field has preferred to view these through the lens of economics (as was the case with LeGrand in Chapter 3), sociology and politics. What these disciplines tend to do is suggest that social problems are ultimately amenable to rational solution through forms of systematic intervention. But unless, as Thorngate (2001) argues, we take account of the non-rational, as well as the downright irrational, then policy-making will lack the full range of conceptual tools needed to intervene effectively. Here, it is perhaps politicians who are way ahead of academics and practitioners (for a change) since they know the importance of communicating with gut instinct, sentiment and sheer prejudice. Psychology therefore draws attention to the role played by the psyche, while *social* psychology reminds us that the psyche is always interactive and inter-relational, enmeshed within communal contexts.

The connection between social policy and social psychology was hinted at in *Welfare Theory* when I suggested that any definition of welfare has to take account of a subjectivist sense of well-being (Fitzpatrick, 2001a: 9–10; see Kahn & Juster, 2002). My intention below is not to provide a comprehensive account of the 'social psychology of social policy' but to say a bit more about well-being by reviewing two areas that tap into important themes within social policy.

Strangers and outsiders

Quality of life depends to a large extent upon how and why we relate to 'insignificant others'. To what extent do we acknowledge strangers and outsiders as resembling ourselves and to what extent should we alter our lives to accommodate theirs? A certain amount of the literature in social psychology offers a rather pessimistic response to this question. We do not have to look far to find theories and experiments which suggest that humans desire conformity to such an extent that they can be easily manipulated by those who wield authority and power.

In the years following WWII a number of influential experiments were performed to aid understanding of how a kind of collective insanity and hysteria can sometimes emerge, whether this be in Nazi Germany, Stalinist Russia or McCarthyite America (Brown, 2000). Milgram's famous experiments in the 1950s revealed that the desire to obey authority is so strong that 65% of participants were prepared to administer a potentially lethal electric shock to a person in the next room whom they couldn't see, and 100% were prepared to administer a 'very strong' shock. The shocks were all an act *but the participants did not know this!* Also in the 1950s Asch found that, due to fear of social disapproval and isolation, over 50% of people will conform to majority opinion even when that opinion, e.g. about the length of a drawn line, is palpably false. And in the late 1960s Zimbardo found that in a simulated prison environment student volunteers who were assigned the role of guards quickly began to brutalise and degrade those who played the role of prisoners. Indeed, much research has confirmed that when randomly assigned to teams the team identity will rapidly subsume the personal identities of its members, usually in terms of conflict and rivalry with the other team(s).

So what is going one here? How can people who would no doubt proclaim themselves as being decent, thoughtful and autonomous act in this way? And would we, as participants in those experiments, behave any differently? One possibility is that an individual's ability to understand and act upon the world is so limited that they have to join with others for reasons of ontological security, even when this might involve inflicting harm on others. Group membership and compliance to institutionalised norms is therefore the *sine qua non* of social action and understanding. A more disturbing (Freudian) possibility is that there really are destructive drives within the human psyche that can surface under the wrong conditions. In the Milgram and Zimbardo experiments the proximity of authority figures combined with a physical, symbolic and moral distancing from the victims to produce disturbing results.

Either way, the implications for social policy are pessimistic because if the latter is concerned with social justice then we may always be fighting an uphill battle against the human tendency to obey those who hold power, i.e. those who benefit from structural inequalities, and to punish those identified as non-compliers. Of course, it may be that the desire to conform to authority can sometimes be used in favour of social justice. During the era of the classic welfare state levels of well-being (arguably higher than those we have experienced since) derived partly from a sense that because experts know best we could trust them to lead us in the correct direction. The problem is that social conditions conducive to beneficial cooperation seem rarer than their converse, and if they depend upon a high degree of conformity to what extent can those conditions be regarded as justice-enhancing anyway?

I will shortly propose why we are not necessarily committed to such pessimism but before doing so let me review some of the main explanations of why mere strangers can be converted into outsiders to be feared and hated.

Prejudice is the quintessential instance of defining an 'out-group' as negative (Jones, 1996; Augoustinos & Reynolds, 2001). Overt forms of prejudice are increasingly rare but the value of social psychology is that it reveals how close to the surface are more subtle forms, e.g. the tendency to view black people as lazy or prone to violence. So how do social psychologists explain the persistence of prejudice? One possibility is that prejudice is innate or hard-wired into the human psyche. The problem with this explanation is that it treats psychological factors as the cause of social ones, when it is clear that the scale and intensity of prejudice is dependent upon social influences. Nevertheless, many have sought to make personality central to their theoretical accounts. Even the Marxist-inspired Frankfurt School, to take one example, identified an 'authoritarian personality' as that which emerges when a person is brought up by disciplinarian parents, whom they both love and hate, to defer to authority and hierarchies of status. The problem with this research was that it seemed designed to condemn a particular group (white, bourgeois males) as potentially fascist (Duckitt, 2000).

If we move beyond personality-centred explanations might prejudice therefore be a form of socialisation, a kind of learned behaviour passed from generation to generation, or a type of displaced aggression where one group blames another group for circumstances, e.g. economic depression, that are beyond the control of either? The focus in such explanations is upon inter-group relations. Sidanius and Pratto (1999), for instance, associate prejudice with those groups who possess what they call a 'high social dominance orientation'. This orientation exists because the group wishes to defend the relations of inequality and dominance from which they benefit. Doing so requires discrimination against other groups they somehow hold to be inferior as well as blaming the latter for the negative consequences of those very relations. The hypocrisy this involves is somehow sublimated beneath the psychological surface: the equivalent of blaming immigrants for the prejudice one feels towards them.

Another theory of inter-group processes which has been popular for decades is that of 'relative deprivation'. Relative deprivation occurs when one reference group compares itself to another and finds that reality fails to live up to its expectations so that the resulting disappointment can trigger social tension and aggression. In his influential account Runciman (1966: 26–7) refers to research that had been conducted in a tornado-hit community. Those hardest hit were, unsurprisingly, those who felt the greatest sense of deprivation. However, those whose houses are sustained only minimal damage experienced the next highest sense of deprivation because they were comparing themselves to those whose houses had remained completely undamaged. By contrast, those who had experienced much more damage considered themselves to be lucky because they were comparing themselves to the hardest hit. The point is that a sense of relative deprivation *may* reflect an objective reality, then again it may not (Schwartz, 2004: 58–60, 150–1). A group that has little to complain about may nevertheless complain a lot if (a) it misreads social realities and its own location within them, and (b) it blames another reference group for its grievances. Prejudice may therefore be characterised as an objectively false sense of relative deprivation and may also explain why there has been such a backlash in recent years against the movement towards equalities of gender, ethnicity, sexuality, etc. and why some white, middle-class men identify themselves as the new victims. Few people feel as victimised as those who have the most to lose from attacks upon privilege.

We therefore have a range of explanations of prejudice, ranging from the pathological to those that look at inter-group processes. Of course, what is distinctive about contemporary prejudice is that it bumps up against the egalitarian notions of respect and fairness that are now proclaimed almost everywhere. As well as pushing prejudice below the surface this also leads people to search for out-groups which are so 'negative' that they are immune to an egalitarian ethic. In the UK in recent years these new out-groups have included 'bogus asylum seekers' (Berry, 2001) and paedophiles, for who could support those who invade our neighbourhoods to steal our taxes or murder our children? Bauman (1999: Ch. 1) characterises protests against these hate figures as an expression of the kind of collective action which is rare in our fragmented, consumerist societies unless it is innocuous (as in the death of Princess Diana), accords with views of the political mainstream or occurs as a media-sanctioned event. So perhaps prejudice is not so far below the social-psychological surface that it cannot erupt again in sublimated forms under particular circumstances.

Traditional social psychology therefore offers a rather bleak picture of social interaction since we seem to be presented with harsh realities into which it is difficult to intervene, intervention being the *leitmotif* of social policy. However, a more critical school of social psychology has emerged since the 1970s that accuses older traditions of being theoretically and methodologically conservative. In the Milgram experiment, for example, different results might obtain when the polarities are reversed, i.e. when it is the 'victim' who is present and the authority figure who is absent. As with the prisoners' dilemma (Fitzpatrick, 2001a: 16) the outcome of the game all depends upon the rules you set up to begin with. That people are capable of immense cruelty is a mundane observation; that such cruelty is taken to define the human condition is a theoretical construction with political overtones and so different implications for social policy.

Critical social psychologists are therefore concerned not only with explanation but also with social reconstruction. Two examples will illustrate the point. Like Fromm and Reich in the 1930s, Parker (1997) accuses psychoanalysis of underestimating the importance of capitalist economics, of treating *homo economicus* as the archetypal individual and so of pathologising social problems and interactions. He therefore calls for a 'critical psychology' that is committed to social change rather than regarding change as a by-product of other factors. In contrast to Parker's Marxist background,

Wetherell and Potter (1992) are much more inspired by Foucault (see Chapter 2). Here, prejudice (specifically racism) is interpreted as a discursive construction where, rather than attributing negative attitudes to stereotypical others, prejudice is understood as being assembled from the available repertoires that circulate within and around the self. Prejudice is not the result of some demonic presence in the psyche or in the social field but emerges from very commonplace and mundane maxims: it is not the opposite of what we hold to be common sense, but its *effect*. The implication might be that to question and challenge commonly-held assumptions is much more politically radical than you imagine.

These examples hardly constitute an introduction to critical social psychology but they do illustrate the point that the subject can be highly reflective and political. If society is interpreted as the product of immutable psychological forces then this might lead us to support social policies of 'containment', i.e. where the job is to confine and restrain the destructive impact of these forces. This corresponds to some of the neoconservative ideas we reviewed in Chapter 1. Introducing more of a social perspective into the explanatory picture means that room can be made for justice-enhancing policies. Runciman (1966: Ch. 13) felt that while we cannot stop people from experiencing a sense of relative deprivation we can employ a Rawlsian framework to reduce unjust inequalities and so to distinguish between legitimate and illegitimate feelings of deprivation. Critical social psychologists go further and locate social change at the heart of their approach, though this engenders a much broader notion of intervention than implied by traditional understandings of social policy. Some hint of what this might mean is given in the next section.

Badges and hierarchies

Let me now say something more about social policy by briefly exploring two areas (cf. *Journal of Social Issues*, 2000): perceptions of income distribution and attitudes towards the welfare state.

How important is it that people regularly overestimate levels of average income? Surveys (Taylor-Gooby *et al*, 2003: 10; H. Dean, 1999a: 124–6) reveal that most individuals from all educational and professional backgrounds think that the average (mean) income is much higher than it is and express some surprise when told the actual level (£24,600 before tax in the UK in 2003). As a result, and despite the fact that 65% of the UK population were below the mean in 2003, people tend to underestimate where they themselves are located in the income hierarchy, with middle-income earners usually underestimating how relatively well off they are. Ordinarily this would be an unremarkable fact but one consequence is that when people perceive themselves to be less prosperous than they really are they are less likely to support policies which are seen to 'impoverish' them further. So while overestimating the number of the relatively affluent might give rise to a generalised support for redistribution (because it is thought that lots of other people can afford to pay more) when many apply redistributive measures to their own circumstances (as people who do not see themselves as relatively affluent) support begins to melt away. This is one reason why people frequently say they want to see more redistribution but are much less willing to vote for it. It is other people who should pay more, not me.

Middle-income earners, in particular, may be reluctant to vote for redistributive measures since they see themselves as having contributed enough to society already. Analogous to the householders whose property has received only minimal tornado damage, because their preferred reference group is those even more fortunate than themselves, a defensive sense of grievance can emerge and a preference for forming political alliances with the more rather than the less affluent, i.e. the groups they aspire to join rather than the groups they aspire to leave behind. The tornado analogy breaks down, though, at lower-income levels. Since the very poorest are often thought to have 'brought it on themselves' (see below) the tendency of each group to seek similarities between itself and its more affluent neighbour extends across the income spectrum – though this does certainly not rule out the possibility of hostility towards members of the 'undeserving rich', e.g. 'fat cats'. As Schwartz (2004: 154) notes, people in an individualist and consumerist society are encouraged to feel unlucky that things are not better than feel fortunate that things are not worse. And these 'upward counterfactuals' all too easily translate into a sense of grievance towards those below us who are thought to be holding us back. In this respect, then, the badge of social membership is desert and being an insider means always staying ahead of those who are thought to deserve less because they earn less.

It presumably follows that if social democrats *et al* are to introduce redistributive policies then some attention must be paid to the social psychology of income distribution. It is not enough to stress either social rights or social duties (or both) if people possess distorted ideas about the distribution of benefits and burdens across society.

What of attitudes towards the welfare state? Repeated research has shown that state welfare has remained far more popular than its detractors would wish (Park, 2003). A slightly more complex picture emerges when people are asked about particular services, however. By and large, a popular distinction is made between 'good welfare' and 'bad welfare'. Good welfare includes health, education, pensions and care services; bad welfare includes unemployment benefit, means-tested benefits and various aspects of social work and criminal justice. The difference lies in the client-group to which each service applies and the nature of the problem. Pensions are popular because the elderly are seen as deserving, as having paid their taxes and made their social contribution; health is popular because bad health is something that might strike any one of us at any time. Bad welfare, though, is that which goes or risks going to those seen as feckless and irresponsible.

This league table of popularity leads to some curious views on the cost of welfare (Taylor-Gooby *et al*, 2003: 7–8). When asked to estimate how much various benefits cost lay people vastly overestimate the expensiveness of unemployment benefit and benefits for single mums (groups popularly represented as a drain on the economy) and underestimate the cost of pensions (sweet old gran deserves support after a lifetime of work). In fact, in 2001–02 Job Seekers Allowance accounted for just over 3% of UK social security expenditure, single parent benefits for 0.1% while the state pension accounted for over 36%.

Some strange anomalies therefore appear when people are asked about welfare reform. Dwyer (2000: Ch. 5) reports that his interviewees were willing to support an unconditional right to healthcare, despite recognition that people may act irresponsibly towards their own health. They were far more supportive, though, of attaching conditions to the receipt of benefits, despite the fact that socio-structural factors presumably play as large a role here as they do in determining health. One anomaly is that people may be willing to deprive you of an income but offer unconditional treatment for the ill-health that this is likely to cause! And many have long commented on the greater amount of disapproval reserved for benefit fraudsters in comparison to tax defrauders (Cook, 1989). The inconsistency in attitude might be explained by the difference between in-kind and in-cash services: the specific nature of the former is held to offer some safety-net against irresponsibility whereas the latter may encourage irresponsibility (moral hazard) by granting claimants more freedom than they are thought to deserve.

This reiterates the point that desert is a common badge of citizenship: the category of 'need' is certainly valued but often struggles to break through the perception that some social groups are more deserving than others – and so their needs more worthy of recognition (van Oorschot, 2000). Just as people often treat those who are doing slightly better than themselves as the appropriate reference group, so they make judgements about the activities and lifestyles of others according to prevailing norms as filtered through their subjective interests. The tendency is for people to represent society to themselves through a hierarchy of desert, even if groups within that scale are arranged in partial accordance with their own experiences and impression of self-worth. A sense of economic and moral proximity therefore provides the framework through which people are defined as insiders and outsiders; and it is all too easy to caricature social equality as a threat to that sense of proximity (of identity and belongingness): as if closeness is dissipated once everyone is near by. In social policy terms this means that those who are materially and culturally disadvantaged are frequently suspected of being morally deviant and so calls to prove oneself as deserving are thrown more often in their direction than in that of the affluent and privileged.[1] Citizenship is skewed. To be included I must demonstrate that my badge is bigger and brighter than those of the others over there.

An understanding of social inequality must therefore incorporate social psychological insights into what people see – and how and why they see it – when they look higher and lower than themselves. It also follows that the pursuit of social justice may require forms of cultural and psychological 'intervention' that go far beyond the usual range of political and economic prescriptions. If this seems like an impractical conclusion at which to arrive it may at least draw inspiration from someone who rejected the concept of social justice. Margaret Thatcher was correct when she portrayed economics as merely an instrument, the ultimate aim being to reconstruct people's souls. To alter the pattern of incentives and disincentives is not only to affect behaviour but also the motivations, expectations, values and perceptual-cognitive frames out of which our identities are woven. Indeed, far from being impractical this is what social policies do anyway every single day.

Emotions

Sociological theories

The message of the previous section was that if social policy has got something to do with quality of life then it can hardly afford to ignore the insights provided by social psychology since our perceptions and interpretations of ourselves and others are intimately bound up with our sense of well-being. In this section we pursue this theme further by looking specifically at emotions.

Discussions about emotions and related concepts have made occasional appearances in the history of ideas, usually with reference to reason and rationality. Key Enlightenment thinkers sought to supplant what they saw as religious dependence upon faith and superstition with knowledge based upon the rigorous application of reason. As Spinoza (1986: 158) said in the *Ethics*, published in 1677:

> To act absolutely according to virtue is nothing else in us than to act under the guidance of reason...

while for Kant (2001) the 'moral law within' could be illuminated by the light of reason. So although humans may be characterised by passions they can and do become virtuous in so far as they tame and transcend them through rationality. As a result the age of scientific materialism often seemed to devalue emotion as much as the pre-modern era had devalued reason.

Those who reacted against this Enlightenment bias included conservatives like Hume and Burke. As the 'slave to the passions',

> ...reason alone can never be a motive to any action of the will; and ... it can never oppose passion in the direction of the will. (Hume, 1969: 460–1)

Reason is itself the passion to reach judgements dispassionately. For Burke (1968: 151–6), by leading 'away from the heart' reason cannot replace respect for tradition as the means by which the passions are quelled and made less destructive. Romantics from Rousseau onwards also rejected the ascendancy of rationality over feeling and emotional attachment: 'emotion recollected in tranquillity' was Wordsworth's famous definition of the origin of poetry. And all counter-Enlightenment thinkers sought justification for their suspicion of the attempt to elevate reason above emotion, by imposing abstract systems of thought upon social and natural complexity, in the horrific aftermath of the French revolution. Hume's (1969: 463) observation that,

> 'Tis not contrary to reason to prefer the destruction of the whole world to the scratching of my finger.

might be taken as a chilling forewarning of what happens when we attempt to create secular and rationalistic versions of heaven.[2]

This traditional view of reason and emotion as conflictual has been challenged for a number of years now by those who reject a simple dichotomy between Enlightenment and counter-Enlightenment thought (see S. Williams, 2001). Part of the inspiration for this challenge has derived from a sociological vogue for studying emotions that dates from at least the late 1970s (Kemper, 1978). As one of the principal influences here Hochschild (1983: 7) coined the term 'emotional labour' to describe a change in modern economies from the production of objects to the production of sensations, reactions, dispositions and feelings:

> This labor requires one to induce or suppress feeling in order to sustain the outward countenance that produces the proper state of mind in others...

The main example of emotional labour she uses is the work performed by flight attendants, whose job is not simply to serve the stale turkey but to convey a sense of security, homeliness and even sexual allure. So in the post-industrial service economy emotional labour has become ever more common: feeling has become something to manufacture and manage, the means of establishing bonds between organisations and lifestyle-oriented consumers in the expectation that customers will return for the same experience again and again. But this commercialisation of emotion comes at a price since when feelings are bought and sold it is the simulation of authenticity which becomes important; and if the key to success is to 'sell oneself' then subjectivity risks becoming colonised with forged copies of its former self, replicas of feeling and relating where we no longer know or care about the distinction between what is and is not sincere (see below).

Since Hochschild interest in the 'sociology of the emotions' has blossomed. For example, Elster (1999a, 1999b) has sought to explore emotion through the perspective of 'methodological individualism' which maintains that the elementary units of social life are the actions and interactions of individuals. Any social force, relation or structure which *seems* to transcend the individual realm can actually be explained as the product of individuals' actions. But if this is the case, wonders Elster, then how can we account for those factors (drives, cravings, addictions) over which the individual seems to have limited control? Elster sets out to explore emotion as an intersection of neurobiology, choice and culture. Emotions originate from neuropsychological mechanisms (and so are universal in character rather than being social constructions) which are then shaped by the choices of the agent as well as by the beliefs, norms and values of the agent's environment. In fact, since methodological individualism interprets culture as the effect of individuals' actions Elster is being a little disingenuous here; for if culture is the product of choice then we are left with two basic variables (neurobiology and choice) rather than three. For Elster, then, although we cannot choose emotions we can shape the circumstances through which emotions are experienced. Methodological individualism therefore offers one way of reconciling reason and emotion.

The cost, though, may be an over-emphasis upon the importance of agency. Can social phenomena really be so strongly attributed to individual choice? Barbalet (1998) takes a different approach in attempting to understand how emotions reside within the social-structural relations of power and status: they are the link between social structure and action rather than, as for Elster, between neurobiology and choice. Take class, for instance. Traditional approaches have treated class as referring to the systemic inequalities inhering in material conditions within capitalist society. This has led many Marxists to a devaluation of the subjective (epitomised by the lazy term 'false consciousness') where class mobilisation has been understood in terms of objective interests and movement either away from or towards the 'for itself' of class action and consciousness. But according to Barbalet (1998: 68) if we wish to understand the conjunctions and disjunctions of the objective and subjective then we cannot afford to ignore the role played by emotions:

> What converts structural contradiction to class antagonism significantly includes the feeling of resentment which leads the members of social classes to action. Such action derives from or is directed toward unfair advantages, which are implicit in class inequalities.

Rather than being an individualised pathology – the residue of objective interests – resentment is a resource through which some of us appreciate that we share interests that are in conflict with the interests of others. What Barbalet's approach risks doing, however, is diverting attention away from the central claim of the oppressed, namely that their interests are *inherently* superior to the oppressor's interests instead of just deriving from an alternative form of resentment.

What we have, then, are some ongoing attempts to make the emotions a key reference point for social theory and, if the above accounts are somewhat incomplete, they certainly help to reconceptualise our understanding of self and society.

Another popular theory of recent years has been that of postemotionalism. Popularised by Meštrović (1997) this proposes that we now live in an age where emotional responses have ceased to be authentic and genuine. The emotional labourer is often called upon to fake sincerity in order to maintain the spectacle, the performance, of making expressive connections with the consumers of emotional surfaces. The 'authenticity industry' sells goods and services by affecting to care about us, by empathising with our lifestyle choices, by manufacturing our emotions and selling them back to us: 'we understand your passion because we share it too'. Emotions become a kind of psychological fast-food to be consumed as quickly and cheaply as possible. Politicians emote compassion with one eye on focus groups and leader columns; an enormous amount of TV now shows people confessing their darkest secrets in order to receive some kind of therapeutic reward from their (hopefully) sympathetic audience. And where self-regarding materialism has become rampant each of us connects with others only in order to promote our own needs and interests. Our culture has become a glorified self-help manual.

Meštrović's thesis seems to fly in the face of contemporary society's self-image where emotional maturity is thought to have become an indispensable asset, i.e. where EQ (Emotional Quotient) now accompanies IQ. In the UK the widespread public mourning that heralded the death of Diana was interpreted by some as an evolution in the national psyche beyond the imperialistic fondness for a 'stiff upper lip' (Blackman & Walkerdine, 2001). But for Meštrović these displays are only Disneyesque features of a fragmented society yearning for what it suspects it has lost: collective experiences in a post-collectivist era. Such collective events, e.g. the support for national sporting figures or the occasional craze for some TV programme, may, indeed, simply represent a more positive manifestation of the same impulse that Bauman noted in respect of paedophile-hunting (see above). In effect, our so-called emotional maturity is little more than an inauthentic form of compassion suited to a consumerist society where, so long as we convince ourselves that others are helped as a consequence, we can pursue egotistic activity with abandon. We express horror at famine and feel good from contributing to the relief fund because this allows the horror to be dispelled. The common term 'compassion fatigue' may even reflect this idea that concern for others is a form of exchange through which the ego receives a profit, though only up to a point of diminishing marginal utility.

Meštrović (1997: 66–8) posits a gloomy and pessimistic reading of social change that may embody no more than his own sense of Orwellian despair. He is so desperate to paint our socio-culture as postemotional that some of his examples are bizarre and drawn from narrow American experiences. It would be difficult to argue that he is wrong in identifying postemotional tendencies within contemporary society but can that society be characterised primarily as postemotional? Feminists would certainly want to argue that much of the care offered in the home and the public sector is not characterisable as simply another form of postemotional inauthenticity (see Chapter 2). We may have to struggle against the inclination to filter emotions through the sieves of a McDonaldised culture, but we may often *succeed* in doing so. Perhaps ours is more a society where postemotionalism is in conflict with forms of care, nurture and attachment that remain genuinely authentic.

Social policy and the emotions

While the ideas of those such as Hochschild, Elster, Barbalet and Meštrović constitute the sociological boundaries of recent debates, work within social policy has begun to develop some distinctive paths of its own. On the face of it the subject should be well-placed since welfare services deal with people after all. Here, though, it has been something of a laggard, perhaps out of fear that analysis of emotions harks back to the kind of moralistic interventions into the subject that characterised nineteenth century charity.

Curiously, the heirs to nineteenth century conservatism have practically overturned those earlier assumptions. Whereas the poor and destitute were once regarded as flesh and blood beings possessing a range of feelings, sentiments and commitments that needed to be 'corrected', the Right are now more likely to see the disadvantaged as devoid of emotional complexity and all it involves (the right to make mistakes, to have non-employment attachments, etc.). While they disdain the post-war settlement they inherited its tendency to hollow emotions out, albeit according to different assumptions; rather than seeing clients who can be slotted into the categories designed by distant, paternalistic experts the Right has seen either rational calculators who take advantage of the rest of us or a helpless underclass less capable of experiencing social empathy. Implicit within the new paternalism (see Chapter 1) is a distinction between 'our' normal emotions and 'their' deviant ones.

As a possible reaction to these tendencies some authors have sought a new way of looking at emotions. Of central importance here, as I have just observed, is the work on care since authentic caring has to involve emotional bonding on some level, even when a wage contract is involved. However, since we dealt with care in Chapter 2 I am not going to deal with it at length here (but see below and the next section).

Hoggett (2000) provides a series of impressive attempts to relate theories of psychology and the emotions to ongoing debates in social policy. His complaint is that the subject shares with the Left a tendency to over-rationalise social actors and interaction, and to fall into a simplistic form of social constructionism. If the aim of social policy and any progressive politics should be what he calls 'generative welfare', i.e. concerned to create the social environment most conducive to the realisation of human powers, then we have to appreciate the extent to which we are not agents who are or can be in full control of ourselves or our surroundings, i.e. the social and psychological forces in the face of which agency falters and occasionally collapses. Drawing upon the work of those such as Melanie Klein (1932) – who identified the origins of the psyche in the 'split' which young children undergo in their consciousness of self and not-self – Hoggett explores the myths and fictions through which people come to an always imperfect view of themselves and others. But rather than being a cause for despair this realisation should motivate us to evolve non-institutional forms of interdependency in which an ethic of non-oppressive care is perpetually expressed.

Froggett (2002) (no relation) has also offered an interesting and ambitious approach. Drawing also upon the work of Klein, Froggett introduces psychosocial insights into the basic welfare regimes of cross-national research. Firstly, she regards the market-led regime of possessive individualism as the least mature, as characterised by paranoid-schizoid anxieties where internal badness is projected onto the external environment. But whereas in a baby this leads to the kind of inexplicable crying that frustrates parents, in some adults (presumably those who never managed to reconcile the internal and external worlds) it creates a desire to exorcise all signs of vulnerability and dependency by treating those less powerful than oneself as the authors of their own fate. Secondly, the mixed economy of welfare (which includes the Third Way) represents a more moderate form of the same impulse: the same obsessions with dependency, irresponsibility and rational aspirations, though now allied to an ethic of solidarity and mutual fate. Finally, in the social democratic regime there is much more emphasis upon the collective good and responsibility for the less advantaged; in Kleinian terms this embodies a nascent kind of 'depressive love' where, rather than placing the object of love on a pedestal that inevitably leads to disappointment when they tumble off, others are accepted with all their faults and imperfections.

Finally, Rodger (2000: 154–63; 2003) links social policy to postemotionalism by attributing the latter to the era of the 'classic' welfare state when, because of the state taking over most of the functions previously reserved by philanthropists and charities, welfare professionals became characterised by a sense of pragmatic detachment from those they served. But this period may now be coming to an end and,

> As the idea of welfare pluralism becomes the new orthodoxy, can we expect a return to
> ... inner-directed drives in a post-modern world in which the idea of the welfare state is
> now viewed as being counter to the individualism of the era? (Rodger, 2000: 154)

For Rodger this all depends upon whether commercialism comes to prevail over the informal sector of care that represents another alternative to the post-war centralised state. The shape of the coming 'welfare society' therefore depends upon how we react to the present conjunction of two forces. The *individualisation of the social* refers to the way in which choice and personal responsibility have come to replace forms of state-sponsored collectivism, but also to a freedom based upon greater social inequality and social control of undesirables, i.e. those unable or unwilling to fend for themselves within the bounds of social norms. Additionally, an *amoral familism* denotes the tendency to view communal participation in terms of self-interest and self-advancement. What these forces add up to is an emotional withdrawal from society combined with an inward-looking gaze where the social becomes interpreted as little more than an instrument for the promotion of oneself and one's family.

Recent years have therefore witnessed a curious reversal. Whereas it was the Right that once stressed emotion (passion, patriotism, instinct, love of tradition) and the Left that emphasised the value of rational abstraction in creating a new Jerusalem, today it is the Right which is more likely to reach for abstract models of human behaviour and the Left that has begun to reintegrate an appreciation of emotional life into its social critiques (Hoggett & Thompson, 2002).

So let me then reiterate the point of this chapter: we cannot fully understand psychology or the emotions unless we understand the social contexts within which they are embedded. It is this understanding which leads us on to a discussion of the body.

Bodies

Theories of the body

The importance of the body to recent social thought (Featherstone *et al*, 1991; Howson & Inglis, 2001; Barbalet, 2002) arguably signifies a rejection of the mind-body dualism that distinguished the modern age and the long turn towards a post-Cartesian philosophy which eschews the impulse to understand the world by dichotomising it (Merleau-Ponty, 1962). At the same time, the body has become a conscious site of economic and political struggle, partly because of the feminist injunction to regard the personal as political – so that challenging patriarchy means resisting the subtle controls that are exerted over women's bodies (their appearance, their demeanour, their behaviour) – and partly because of the capitalist urge to make a profit out of whatever can be sold.

This simultaneous politicisation and commercialisation of the body has led to a rather schizophrenic culture. For instance, men have become increasingly targeted as potential consumers of beauty products. Does this represent a feminisation of the male body (a softening of machismo in the form of the 'new man'), its commercialisation (where men are subject to the same pressures as women by being expected to conform to idealised images) or both? And on 'lifestyle' television programmes people are frequently counselled to be happy with themselves, while also being advised that if they did after all want to lose weight, or wrinkles or grey hairs or whatever, then here's the way to do it...

Amid all this confusion, then, what do we mean by the body? To some extent the lay response is not a bad starting point. The body is that saggy thing you see in the mirror every morning: the epidermal package of flesh and bone which separates us off from others, the visible Lacanian 'I/me' of self-recognition. Yet implicit within this common sense view is a sociological understanding that the body is about image and that image implies a social relation. Even as they submit to its seductions many consumers are aware of how and why advertising reflects back to us perfect images of what we could be if we only tried harder and purchased more. This has facilitated bodily obsessions that, at the extreme, leads to eating disorders (to which children are increasingly susceptible) such as bulimia and anorexia. And if the body is a social relation then it is also a screen for symbols and signs: a text upon which the social order inscribes itself. In religious societies it is expected to 'embody' the word of God and so is mapped according to the appropriate taboos – what can or cannot be touched or shown publicly; in modern totalitarian societies the body was to keep itself in a state of permanent readiness, a movement of pure will capable of freely obeying the injunctions of authority. These three categories (the corporeal/separate body, the constructed/ intersubjective body, the body as social text) reflect the broad parameters of recent social theorising (Shilling, 2003). Let's review each in turn.

Naturalism is the idea that the body is primarily a natural, biological entity characterised by various drives and needs. This corresponds to a lay position where the body is treated as an immediate presence that frames the rhythms of daily life in its need for sustenance, hygiene, evacuation and emotional/sexual attachment. Social practices are therefore to be understood as consequent upon the material physicality of natural habits and instincts. The genetic Darwinism that we reviewed in the previous chapter offers a version of this thesis in which the body, as phenotype, is traced back to the organic codes of DNA.[3] But the obvious danger with any naturalistic view is that it individualises the social and then reduces individuals to bodily attributes (whether real or imagined): hence the widely-held beliefs that ethnicity is about skin-colour, disability is about physical handicap or that women are natural carers due to their reproductive capacities. In short, the natural body becomes a means of trapping the victims of social injustice, of attributing their disadvantage to biological properties that are supposedly immutable.

Yet does this mean, conversely, that the body ought to be regarded primarily as a social construct? Shilling (2003: Ch. 4) associates such views with Foucault and Goffman in particular. Foucault (1975, 1977) was dealt with throughout *Welfare Theory* and in Chapter 2, so I will not repeat myself here except to observe that he saw the body as the discursive self-production of power, as a social space in which we struggle with the disciplines out of which we are made. Goffman, meanwhile, understood the body as a social performance through which we interact with others via a spectrum of subliminal motions and signs. To be recognised as such the body must read and speak a non-verbal language of conventional behaviour by which we both open and close ourselves to others through self-classification. The body therefore transmits the exchange of identities within social settings: bodies are the conduits of society.

> The self, then, as a preformed character, is not an organic thing that has a specific location, whose fundamental fate is to be born, to mature, and to die; it is a dramatic effect arising diffusely from a scene that is presented ... (Goffman, 1969: 245)

So theories of the constructed body take us beyond the corporeal to the ways in which the body is made intersubjectively through social systems and discourses of one form or another. What we see is not simply the epidermis but an historical effect of social, political and cultural relations.

What of the body as social text? If metaphors signify changes within social structures (Lopez, 2003) then perhaps the key metaphors of the contemporary period relate to the way in which advanced technologies facilitate the re-mediation of social relations and practices. Chapter 5 noted the proliferation of a new vocabulary of networks, webs, grids, meshes and flows that some use to capture the advent of informationalism, but I also deplored the tendency of certain cheerleaders to get carried away with such terms and so ignore the enduring features of social power. Metaphors are therefore concerned with social boundaries and the changes they undergo. In this respect, a key metaphor has been that of the 'cyborg', used by Haraway (1991) to capture developments in the interface of nature and culture – and so implicitly of women and men – and used by others to look at the humanisation of technology and the technologisation of humanity (Fitzpatrick, 1999b).[4] The figure of the cyborg therefore is a way of articulating the 'boundary problems' to which contemporary bodies are subject.

One example. Since technologies can now explore the internal body at greater depths than ever before, and can increasingly accompany the body's mobility, our inherited notions of self and privacy begin to falter. The concepts of refuge and withdrawal begin to fade; we become isolated from distance. If there is nothing that cannot be seen and fewer places of social disconnection then in one sense everything becomes public but, in another sense, the category of the public also dissolves because there is no private realm to which it can be contrasted. So in a technological age the body is not fixed and embodiment always involves a process of acceleration away from its previous forms: like a cyborg it forever transcends given boundaries. There are those who are excited by the prospect of further technological advance, heralding the posthuman ability to transcend the limitations of modernity (Gray, 2001), and those who are deeply concerned that the new possibilities will be appropriated for some very old fashioned human vices (Andrews & Nelkin, 2001).

Understanding the body as a social text, though, has perhaps been less important in the recent literature than the attempt to overcome the dichotomy between natural and constructed bodies. For instance, Turner (1996: Ch. 4) initially adopted an approach that was constructionist, locating the body as a means by which social systems reproduce themselves. He therefore identified four categories of 'bodily order. Firstly, the reproduction of bodies across time through forms of restraint and exchange, e.g. in the prescribed forms of fertility offered by the exchange of daughters in marriage. Secondly, the control of desire (the internal body) through modes of self-discipline that impacted upon women's sexuality in particular, i.e. its subordination to child-bearing. Thirdly, populations have been regulated through space via systems of surveillance and social control (see Chapter 8). Finally, the external body has been represented in social space in ways that reflect hierarchical structures. Turner (1996: 33–4), though, came to believe that his initial ideas swung too much towards the constructionist side of the debate and one, moreover, that was highly structuralist and functionalist in its approach.

For while the body is undoubtedly a social construction we cannot thereby eliminate reference to its pure physicality, to its corporeal and existential presence in the world. Most obviously, the body is subject to processes of birth, decay and death whose meaning may be socially contextual but whose sheer facticity is ineliminable. Turner therefore proposes that greater account be made of the body's physical and phenomenological embodiment in particular cultural conjunctures (Turner, 1992; Richardson & Turner, 2001). Shilling (2003, 2004), too, is attempting to develop a synthesised narrative in which the body is conceived as both biological and social, shaped by but irreducible to the social relations and structures within which it is located – though he is less concerned than Turner with technological influences. This means seeing the body in terms of its natural evolution, its transformation by social factors and the way in which it constructs itself through social interaction.

Social policy and the body

These are the same kind of parameters with which social policy researchers have also begun to wrestle. Given its empirical bias it has been easier for the subject to comprehend the import of naturalistic bodies that veers away from too much abstraction (Nettleton & Watson, 1998; Ellis & Dean, 1999; Twigg, 2000). We might think of the alarm which the underfed and ailing bodies of young working class men generated amongst the British political elite during the Boer War, a dramatic demonstration of a public health crisis that, in its implications for imperial ambitions and national defence, contributed to the establishment of the post-1905 welfare state. Yet some interesting work has also been performed recently in an attempt to capture the theoretical complexities of the debate. For instance, Dean (1999b) sketches what he considers to be the moral repertoires which have underpinned the evolution of modern social welfare. These repertoires are distinguishable from each other by means of the metaphors which inhabit them, metaphors which he refers to the symbolic characteristics of the body.

The first of these repertoires is based upon the metaphorisation of the body as *machine*, as a Benthamite object of social engineering. This vocabulary says that the body is no more than the sum of its parts and because the body is simply an assemblage of components the 'parts' are unstable, tending towards chaos and anarchy, a tendency which is stabilised by the parts being subjected to supervision by 'disciplinary technologies'.

The second repertoire is puritanical: the body is that which must be purged of impurity and imperfection by being assimilated into the collective. This *reviled* body is the source of corruption and contamination. Like the machinic body, the reviled body is materialistic but is divided between 'relevant matter' and the 'irrelevant matter' which anchors it to the earth, to the converse of the spiritual which is the puritan's ideal.

The third repertoire concerns the *vulnerable* body which, because it is subject to invasion and pollution, requires protection and nurturing through paternalistic care. The vulnerable body speaks the morality of conservatism in that it is associated not only with growth and replenishment but with mortality and finitude. Like the reviled body, the vulnerable body is both the cause and the victim of disease; but whereas the former is cured through a 'proactive disposal' of impurity, the latter is more defensive, more concerned with a kind of 'coercive inaction'.

The final repertoire articulates the holism of the *organic* body, the flow and mutuality of circulatory systems. This is the morality of humanist collectivism: the endless convergence of freedom and order, of equivalence and hierarchy. With the organic body the cure for vulnerability is *active* control; but, unlike the reviled body, control is exercised through cohesion and *inclusion* and, unlike the machinic body, its functionalism is holistic rather than incidental (the parts of the machinic body can be replicated and replaced but the organs of the organic body are constitutive of the whole).

Dean goes on to suggest that these four moral repertoires, with their attendant bodily metaphors, correspond to the four social welfare regimes which have dominated the last two centuries of the modern era (see the description of Esping-Andersen's categories in Chapter 5). To the utilitarian, mechanistic body corresponds the regime of 'market individualism'. This regime is dominated by the market sector but these are markets which, rather than flowing freely, are subtly directed through specific channels towards particular socio-moral destinations, i.e. to the commodification of individuality and the identification of freedom with wage-earning and consumption. This, then, is the residualist regime of the liberal, nightwatchman state. To the puritanical body corresponds an authoritarian, fundamentalist welfare regime. Here, the state dominates in order that a narrowly prescribed range of social interactions may serve collectivist ends, purified of irrelevant matter. Around the conservative, vulnerable body is organised the corporatist regime: 'corporatist' because it emphasises the security and stability which is offered by the taut alliance of state and corporation, with strict (gendered) divisions between occupations and between workplace and home. The organic body of humanist collectivism corresponds to the social democratic welfare regime. This regime is managerially interventionist, preserving hierarchies of economic power by effecting a limited distribution of resources: more concerned with mobility between classes than with the goal of classlessness.

Like the above sociologists, then, social policy commentators have begun the search for an integrated approach that can encompass naturalistic and constructionist approaches to the body. The following four areas arguably constitute the main areas for future research and thought (cf. Twigg, 2002).

The first is that of health and medicine (Twigg, 2002: 425–8). For the most part the body is here treated atomistically and passively: atomistically because mainstream medicine finds it easier to scrutinise the individual body separated off from its social environment; passively, because the body is still expected to receive expert attention, techno-chemical invasion and paternalistic advice with acquiescence and gratitude. For example, the medical profession feels able to recommend that patients change lifestyles and work patterns but avoids much political commentary upon the economic and cultural origins of stress and anxiety. Alternative approaches to medicine – stressing the holisms of body, mind and society whose symbiosis necessitates a politicised dialogue between different forms of expertise – exist at the margins of public discussion.

The second area is that of care conceived more broadly (cf. Twigg, 2002: 427–30). Here the task for carers is to reconcile the body's need for hands-on intimacy, in which particular aspects of the body (the baby's need for feeding, the limb's need for redressing, the elderly person's need for bathing) are ultimately inseparable from other aspects, with the professional distancing that carers must maintain in order to complete their tasks effectively. As we saw above, emotional labour requires the performance of both surface and depth forms of attention, so lending itself to postemotional appropriation under certain circumstances – for instance, we might characterise examples of

inauthentic compassion within contemporary welfare states as survival strategies that compensate for a lack of needed resources while attempting to preserve a public service ethos.

The third area concerns distributive and normative inequalities. That
health inequalities relate strongly to social inequalities has become well established (Wilkinson, 1996), yet we cannot appreciate why such distributive patterns persist unless we appreciate the moral regimes that underpin them.
Bacchi and Beasley (2002) observe how full citizenship is identified with
those subjects who are said to have their bodies under control while those
who are deemed to be controlled *by* their bodies (due to addiction, natural
indolence, etc.) are regarded as second-class citizens at best. This distinction
corresponds to that between self-reliant independence and state-induced
dependency that, as simple as it is, reinforces injustice (Dwyer, 2000) and
elides the realities of social intersubjectivities and interdependencies. So,
here, we revisit the crudities of naturalism where social disadvantage is mis-
leadingly attributed to the physical properties of disadvantaged bodies. Take
one example.

The ageing body is frequently an object of 'desirable horror'. As longevity
has increased so youth has become a fetishised act of persistent recreation
though financial, cosmetic and dietary attempts to defer what is constructed
as a decline into loss of productivity and usefulness (Gilleard & Higgs,
1998). The naturalistic body therefore splits between the inner sense of a
still-youthful self and the increasing betrayals of the mirror image, a split that
requires endless reconciliation. Ironically, then, youth is preserved as
'natural' by forever recreating it through the very social mechanisms (the
commodifications of youth) that help to make old age appear horrifying in
the first place. Contemporary ageing therefore involves a struggle between
the attempt to control a body that is trying to control you; the alienation
implied here – between 'you' and 'your body' – provides another indication
of why purely naturalistic arguments falter and of why solutions to the
inequalities of ageing are as much cultural as they are economic.

The final area concerns spatial discipline and ways in which the body is
trained to train itself to observe the unsignposted borders of social interaction; instinctive behaviour into which we become patterned and habituated.
Education is primarily a form of socialisation in which we learn how to obey
rules without having them spelt out (Shilling, 2003: 18–19; and see Chapter
9). The co-policing of schools by families and families by schools provides an
environment within which children are monitored and taught to become the
subjects of monitoring. Through the disciplines of the clock, of game/role
playing, of story-telling, of fashion and of the authoritative voice the body
learns instinctive forms of compliance that cannot be as easily imbued into
the thinking, critical mind.[5] Indeed, unless children are to be turned into
automatons, a degree of disjuncture between bodily obedience and mental
estrangement is socially necessary if people are to feel free while consenting

to social rules. So long as it is not taken to extremes (extremes requiring other forms of discipline) youthful rebellion is the first means by which we learn to accept necessity as freedom, acts of rebellion that are carried into adulthood in work and in emotional relationships. Therefore, it is the body which is the archive of 'memory' and the means, following Bourdieu (1984), by which we constantly reinsert ourselves through the exchange of social and cultural capital into the grid of social habits that we first encounter when young. We will return to some of these themes in the next two chapters.

Conclusion

Let me now draw out some similarities in the above analyses and relate these to the ideologies with which this book is concerned.

Modern conservatism tends to view psychological, emotional and bodily qualities as fixed and static, for if the self is organised around essential, immutable properties then the job of society is presumably to reflect those essences. The Right is therefore more likely to support the idea of a psyche whose irrationalities require institutions of strong social control, of an emotional deficit on the part of those dependent upon the state, and of a naturalistic body which is asocial and apolitical. What this adds up to is a vision of the self that needs anchoring in a society based upon respect for authority, personal responsibility and natural inequalities.

But the sections above have also reviewed the challenges to such ideas that have come from across a range of disciplines. According to many of the above authors, the psyche has to be understood in terms that are profoundly social and even political, an appreciation of emotion is incomplete without reference to the social settings through which they are channelled and expressed, and the body is a construction, albeit one with a physical, ontological grounding. The social democrats and new radicals to whom I drew attention in Chapters 1 and 2 will no doubt derive different lessons from such theories, but they surely both agree that if the self is a *social* self then the implications for social reform are not as conservatives would wish.

As with Chapters 5 and 6, then, we can see that debates which can often appear distanced from the familiar agendas of social policy can, on closer examination, bear more than a family resemblance. Theories of social psychology, emotions and the body are arguably another stage upon which the ideological battles of the twenty-first century will be fought. They are three of the most important spaces of openness and closure residing within the social field.

8

Governance, Crime and Surveillance

Introduction

The same is arguably true of the three subjects to be covered below, though it has to be acknowledged that the potential for detrimental interventions by policy-makers is here more obvious and direct. It is part of my aim to show why. Even more than in other chapters the themes dealt with here are so vast that, to make things manageable, the principal aim is to distinguish those threads which connect all three. The literature on governance is recent and multiplies in ever new directions with every wave of public sector reform and so what I do below is identify the two features of contemporary society to which I think it most usefully draws attention. The first of these is then illustrated by reviewing the key theoretical debates about crime and social policy; the second feature is discernible in ongoing discussions of the surveillance society.

Governance

Deriving from a number of diverse yet complementary sources the debate about governance has been gathering pace since the early 1990s (Osbourne & Gaebler, 1992; Rhodes, 1996). It denotes processes of socio-political development that revolve around changes (1) between states and other global actors, (2) in the configuration of civil society and the relations between it and the state, and (3) in the 'internal' mechanics of the state. 'Governance' therefore refers to the administrative apparatus of government while signifying that there are now multiple modes of governing within which the state is no longer necessarily the dominant actor. The concept resonates with social policy because, in its concern to trace the minutiae of policy processes and their social effects, the subject has long sought to appreciate how society is administered at both the 'top' and the 'bottom' (Daly, 2003).

What follows is not intended to be a comprehensive introduction to the debate (for a reason to be explained shortly) but an attempt to identify its main foci, i.e. the principal ways in which state and society are thought to have been evolving (Powell & Hewitt, 2002: Ch. 8). Those themes will then be used to inform much longer analyses of crime and surveillance in the following two sections so that we can view in outline some of the most important welfare-related aspects of the debate.

Following Newman (2001; cf. Clarke & Newman, 1997; Ling, 1998) the literature has defined governance as follows:

- The term conveys a shift away from large, vertical, Weberian bureaucratic hierarchies towards more 'horizontal' models of service delivery, which can imply a role for either market competition, networks of agencies or some combination of the two.
- It refers to a blurring of administrative boundaries formally thought to be less permeable.
- This kind of blurring means that the 'mixed economy' becomes a dated misnomer for the ways in which governance intersects the public, private, voluntary and domestic sectors.
- Since many believe there are no longer any 'commanding heights' through which society can be manipulated governance indicates that the state has to recognise, coordinate and integrate itself into a wider spectrum of inter-agency partnerships through which it governs 'at a distance'.
- The state therefore becomes a steerer rather than a rower, a facilitator and regulator rather than a controller, in which its job is to detect changes in the social currents and effect slight movements on the 'rudder' by the use of reflexive policy instruments that themselves learn and adapt over time. This signals a shift from ideology (struggles over social ends) to management (technical debate over means).
- Participation and dialogue across civil society are therefore crucial since the implementation of policy initiatives becomes a negotiated process dependent upon popular support from both experts and non-experts; centres of authority therefore become more democratic in terms of both input and output.
- The effectiveness of policies therefore becomes dependent upon cultural intangibles such as trust and mutuality (see Chapter 3) that government can encourage (and can certainly undermine) but cannot directly engineer.

There are two reasons why we ought to be wary of the governance debate. Firstly, the literature is replete with wishful thinking in which a particular version of governance is sometimes proposed as the only possible version in order to advance the very changes that the proposer wishes to see. This is a trick new social democrats might be accused of performing, so that opposition to the kind of modernisation they prefer, e.g. a greater role for private firms in the public sector, is condemned as an ignorance of a new social environment whose basic contours they take to be immutable (Giddens, 2000). So we have to beware of the many hidden prescriptions that lurk within the debate.

Yet even more good faith approaches to governance are problematic. I have already indicated why in Chapter 2 when we looked at governmentality. The term is post-structuralist in origin and so is in one sense more limited in its application than 'governance'; yet both concepts depict a social world in which the identity of objects and agents has become less determinant than previously and where management of the self by the self is more crucial. Both terms convey the idea that we are always on the inside of the social world and have lost access to an 'outside' from which definitive explanations can be offered. So just as the governmentality literature does not allow us recourse to yardsticks against which changes to human subjectivity can be measured (see page 40) governance shies away from identifying the main origins of change.

Globalisation and the individualisation of society are certainly two dimensions that some have latched on to (Bauman, 1998b); the former implying that the state no longer has a given territory to dominate, the latter indicating that people have to be treated as active consumers rather than passive pawns. Yet these are 'triggers' rather then social origins *per se*, in that their usefulness as explanans depends upon the very theoretical generalisations that the governance literature loathes to develop. Even a commentator as knowledgeable and politically committed as Jessop (2003; see next chapter) shies away from the grand narrative needed to explain why a Keynesian welfare state gave way to a Schumpeterian workfare state.

So the reason why I have avoided providing a comprehensive introduction to the governance debate is because, for all its current influence, I feel uncomfortable with it unless (a) it overcomes the tendency to camouflage prescriptions, and (b) it can weave the many micro-narratives it has evolved into grand narratives of social change. That said it would be equally stupid to have ignored the kind of insights which the literature has provided into evolutions in social administration. We can see why by exploring the recent restructuring of UK welfare systems, drawing out the themes that I want to review throughout the rest of this chapter.

Managerialism and welfare

The subject of social policy has in some respects been ahead of the literature on governance since it has long been aware of how administrative practices flow through the capillaries of social life. This awareness took on a new urgency in the 1980s with the advent of radical Right attacks on public monopolies and collective provision. As market competition and the profit motive entered the lexicon of public policy the public sector gradually had to adopt many of the habits of the private. For example, 'tendering' and 'contracting out' is now such a ubiquitous practice that it is easy to forget how contentious the reform was initially. A politics of collective action therefore gave way to one of devolved and individualised responsibility, the state became less of a service provider and the growth of markets and quasi-markets led to a blurring of the distinction between public and private. The rationale here was to empower as consumers those whom the corporatist state was accused of ignoring.

Yet at the same time as the UK conservative government was delegating responsibility it was also centralising power. Schools had the option of becoming self-managing but this meant that they answered directly to the relevant secretary of state whose control over what schools taught (through a national curriculum) and, increasingly, *how* they taught it continued to expand. It might be said that this tension within modern conservatism – a movement both away from and towards the centre, perhaps as a recognition that free markets require protection from the explosive tendencies to which they give rise – mirrors and no doubt impelled similar patterns within post-Weberian systems of governance (see below).

By the early 1990s it was clear that the welfare state was not going to be dismantled, but equally clear that conservative reforms were here to stay for the time being. As New Labour came on the scene it became apparent that they would use much of the new model of governing to advance a more progressive agenda. So while it has introduced some reforms that were anathema to its predecessors (the emphasis upon social inclusion, devolution to regional assemblies, etc.) the period since 1997 has been characterised more by continuity than discontinuity with what came before (Newman, 2001: Ch. 4).

This has enabled analysts to offer some broad characterisations of how welfare administration has taken on many of the features of governance that were outlined above. In particular, we might stress the following as being crucial (Clarke *et al*, 2000).

- The emphasis has shifted from inputs (expenditure and social structures) to outputs (performance and efficiency). With the limits to social spending taken to have been reached policy-makers have sought ways of increasing productivity ('best value') from within existing resources. Outputs have been increasingly subject to quantification with accompanying rewards and penalties, e.g. through the growth of performance-related pay.

   Crucial to the measurement of outputs is the setting of specific targets that can sometimes reflect a skewed impression of what a welfare institution does. Indeed, as this shift in emphasis has taken hold those things which are not easily measurable have been excluded from categorisation as an output, e.g. the help that a teacher gives a pupil which is pastoral rather than exam-related. One consequence may be that these non-output activities begin to fade because there are no rewards attached to them and, by absorbing time and resources that could be used elsewhere, they may even attract penalties.

- A public service ethos oriented to social needs has been partly replaced with a set of formal, contractual relationships thought to be more responsive and accountable to the expressed preferences of welfare consumers. With its preponderance of producer-interests the assumption has been that the public sector must be periodically monitored, scolded and prodded back into line. Welfare consumers (LeGrand's queens) are thought as potentially able to assess the quality of public services as easily as they can assess the quality of toothpaste. Therefore, governments have increased the number of doors through which consumers can exit, either into the private sector or into another, more successful part of the public sector.

- Competition within and between public sector organisations has become more prevalent. Public sector agencies are expected to be more entrepreneurial and less risk-averse, to copy the examples of the private sector, to work with the private sector in partnership or to make way for private firms as and when they fail to do so.

  This had led to a fragmentation for which the constant development of joined-up strategies is thought necessary. League-tables are now routinely used as indicators of quality assurance and as a stick *pour l'encouragement d'autres*. Such measures have led to an uneasy coexistence of competition and collaboration within the public sector – the continued need for cooperation plus a reluctance to assist in the measurable performance of potential competitors.

- Power has shifted towards managers, though many are now supposed to internalise the technologies (the vocabularies and practices) of management. Professional autonomy has either been reduced or incorporated into those technologies. Regimes of auditing and inspection have become perpetual and it is these external evaluations and reviews which facilitate the internalisation of managerial regimes in which public sector agents play the game without always having to be formally reminded of the rules. This can mean that they transform what they do into the kind of information that the regime recognises as useful and through which the social world renders itself up for measurement. Play-acting and simulation become more common, either as ends-in-themselves or as means of keeping the auditors and troubleshooters at bay.

- Modernisation is never complete but is in a state of permanent revolution. The competence of individuals and of institutions is calculated in terms of their ability and willingness to accept and drive this volatility ever forward. Modernisation is never ending. Endless reforms, directives and acts of legislation are proof of the virility of government and that public services are in dynamic state of readiness, always in 'response mode' to social change and consumer preference.

We can therefore see how this kind of welfare managerialism corresponds to the components of governance outlined earlier. Both identify as important (a) the flattening out of the state into a complex series of associative networks and partnerships, (b) processes of negotiation and contractualisation that transverse multiple sectors and lines of responsibility, (c) techniques of information gathering that feed back into output-measurable activities, and (d) an emphasis upon stakeholding, though whereas the governance literature has stressed relations of trust and participation (see Chapter 3) the experience of UK welfare reform suggests stakeholding may also be a surrogate for the voices and exit-capacities of individualised consumers. Both therefore identify forms of governing at a distance.

It would take too long to run through the general advantages and disadvantages of the literature and of the changes in state-society interactions it identifies, but there are two particular themes that I want to highlight and use to inform the rest of this chapter (cf. Newman, 2001: 38). Governance and managerialism are frequently regarded as pragmatic, evidence-led philosophies concerned only with 'what works' in a complex society. Yet notions of what works are never ideologically neutral. Indeed, a sociologically-informed critique insists that discursive techniques of governance and managerialism create the very social world to which they offer themselves as the solution (Finlayson, 2003). It was noted above that as survival within a competitive environment becomes more important so the various actors have an interest in simulating the very information for external inspection that will ensure their survival. So rather than responding pragmatically to the world 'out there' technologies of governance may do nothing more than create a fog of simulacra in which statistics substitute for reality, and quantity for quality, where evidence-led policy becomes policy-led evidence and where hitting targets becomes, of itself, a sign of progress. This then is our first theme: social reforms may focus more upon the *representations* of social reality than the reality itself.

The second theme is more straightforward and, again as noted above, relates to a paradox of governance, i.e. the concurrent loosening and strengthening of power. As already argued this relates to the tensions within conservative thought and yet (partly through the social impact of conservatism) also expresses something interesting about our contemporary environment: a dual movement of centralisation and decentralisation. One the one hand, western society has never been as populated with individualised selves and yet this 'triumph of the person' is accompanied with a host of panics about moral irresponsibility and imminent social breakdown. As the state is assumed to have waned in power, so the individual has become sovereign, whether in the form of queens/consumers or knaves/defectors. The state therefore has to be brought back in as a means of suppressing some aspects of the very individualism that is heralded in other respects. The governance debate is useful in tracking this paradoxical movement throughout the machinery of administration. It is as if the freer we become the narrower the circles within which we can orbit to ensure that freedom does not lead to disorder and instability. This is our second theme.

I now propose to unpack these two themes with, respectively, closer reference to two related areas that have occupied a great deal of attention in recent years: crime and surveillance.

Crime

Principal social theories

The field of criminology is vast (Tierney, 1996; Maguire *et al*, 2002) and the interfaces between it and social policy too multiple to be adequately summarised here. Over the last half century criminology has flourished, absorbing and adapting the principal influences of modern social science. Most criminologists continue to maintain that crime and the responses to it are social constructions that have to be located in their environmental contexts. Yet within politics and government 'law and order' is widely perceived as the natural territory of the Right with sociological ideas regularly dismissed as an attempt to 'blame society' and excuse wrongdoing.

Many on the Right advance pathological explanations to crime (Wilson & Herrnstein, 1985) and so punitive solutions that revolve ultimately around imprisonment. Murray (1997) exemplifies this approach. On the one hand he interprets criminals as rational calculators who consciously weigh rewards against penalties; yet they are concurrently the products of the institutional and cultural dependencies induced by welfare liberalism and manifest in the criminal propensities of the underclass. As post-war social democracy gained influence with its politics of entitlement, and the emphasis taken away from a common sense morality by which individuals' attitudes and behaviour can be judged and modified when necessary, so crime rates began to soar (Hitchens, 2003). The Right's preferred solution is to scale back on state welfare and 're-moralise' the poorest by stressing their responsibility to be independent, transferring resources towards systems of discipline (in schools and homes) and incarceration.

The fact that Murray's formula (more welfare + less imprisonment = more crime) is not confirmed by the evidence (see Young, 1999: 143–7) does not reduce the appeal of this and similar critiques to political and media populists. The reality is actually more complex. Sometimes there is a negative correlation between crime and imprisonment, sometimes a positive one and sometimes no inferable correlation at all (Mauer, 2001). In some but not necessarily all countries increased affluence seems to have been accompanied by a rise in fears and insecurities (see Chapter 4), symbolised most potently during high-profile cases of child abduction and murder, e.g. the Bulger homicide in the UK and the Columbine massacre in the US. That most children are killed by their parents rather than by strangers and that rates of child murder remain constant year after year does not seem to reduce widely-held suspicions that the streets are not safe, courts are too soft and children out of control – young people being depicted alternately as victims *and* villains.

If anything, the Right's approach has been consolidated through its partial adoption by social democrats (Dennis, 1997; Field, 2003). Traditionally, social democrats have treated criminal justice as a sub-set of social justice whereas for new social democrats the concepts are equally important and neither can be subservient to the other. In the UK their advocacy of 'zero tolerance' has enabled them to set the recent agenda. Deriving originally from the 'broken windows' thesis, that by cracking down on minor incidents of incivility you deter the bigger ones before they have a chance to develop (J. Q. Wilson, 1975), zero tolerance demands that social order be maintained at the civic level through rapid and well-publicised interventions at any hint of community breakdown. Such policies potentially give rise to hard-line actions by the authorities against those, e.g. beggars, who are not committing any obvious signs of disorder. Its appeal is in marrying familiar social democratic concerns – targeting the causes of crime (though these are held to lie with drug use, a lack of skills and qualifications, and dysfunctional families, rather than anything deeper) – with a populist demand to 'get tough' on the criminal. Under New Labour (Mathews & Young, 2003) this would lead to a punitive drive against undesirables that resonated with tabloid instincts, involving support for curfews, more surveillance and imprisonment, a crackdown on raves and demonstrations, anti-social behaviour orders, on-the-spot fines and less patience towards the homeless (increasingly portrayed as drug addicts). Yet away from the headlines elements of a 'softer', more imaginative and community-safety approach have also been in evidence at the local level.

The efficacy of zero tolerance has been repeatedly questioned (Young, 1999: 121–8). UK crime rates have declined during the period of its popularity (since the early 1990s) but they have also declined where such policies have not been implemented. If this decline is attributable to a period of sustained economic growth and better security in and around homes then zero tolerance is at best a misuse of resources and at worst a politics of victim blaming.

Yet it is difficult to deny that those aspects of zero tolerance concerned with social conditions do resonate with some of the more intelligent schools of Left criminology. Take restorative justice, for instance. Restorative justice is inspired by the belief that rather than treating punishment as an administrative system where the voice of the victim is unwanted, a more relational dialogue between police, judges, victims and offenders should occur (McLaughlin *et al*, 2003). In the case of rape victims this means deploying a far greater sensitivity at all stages of the process than that which still frequently prevails in the masculine, interrogatory cultures of police stations and courts. Restorative justice therefore encourages a recognition between criminal and community, an emotional restitution that Braithwaite (1989) terms 'reintegrative shaming', e.g. when victims and offenders are brought face to face in joint counselling sessions the intention is to reintroduce the human face into what had been an impersonal act of harm. However, there is also the danger that 'restoration' can act as a mask for emotionalist retribution, as in some US states, where the intention is to humiliate and degrade the offender (Pratt, 2002), the modern equivalent of medieval stocks and pillories. From there we are not very far away from the vigilante instinct for reprisal.

Agreeing with aspects of zero tolerance, 'Left Realists' are those who, while supporting the essentials of the Left's critique, regard crime as a social problem affecting quality of life – especially of the poor (cf. Pantazis, 2000a) – and not merely as the surface manifestation of social structures. Fear of crime cannot simply be dismissed as an irrational effect of political and media manipulations: that people are subject to moral panics does not mean that they are simply the dupes of tabloid editors and would-be demagogues:

> ...we must pinpoint who actually suffers from crime, in this present period, and what are the social consequences of an endemic criminality. (Young, 1999: 50)

Nevertheless, Left Realists are undoubtedly more concerned than the NSD with the deleterious effects of inequality and possessive individualism. For Jock Young social inclusiveness has now given way to a society of exclusions centring upon an incongruity between what consumer culture promises (wealth and fulfilment for all) and what post-Fordist economies can actually deliver (labour market polarisation). The securities provided by work and community in an earlier period of modernity are swept away by market forces. Left Realism therefore treats material equalities seriously (Young & Mathews, 2003); policies of integration and inclusion are incoherent and possibly counter-productive without redistribution: 'Zero tolerance of crime must mean zero tolerance of inequality if it is to mean anything' (Young, 1999: 140).

Left Realism therefore shades into the more pragmatic aspects of the 'new' or 'critical criminology' from which it originally emerged. Critical criminology dates from the late 1960s and roots itself in a radical (often Marxist) critique of socioeconomic dominations and oppressions where much of the criminology practiced by academic and government researchers was condemned as serving power rather than challenging it (Taylor *et al*, 1973, 1975; Mathiesen, 1974; Cohen, 1985; Walton & Young, 1998; Ruggiero *et al*, 1998; Taylor, 1999; Carrington & Hogg, 2002). Critical criminology is less concerned with systems of punishment than with questioning orthodox views of crime, crime rates and judicial systems (Currie, 1998). Think of the way in which attention to crimes committed by the poorest is far higher than that given to white-collar and corporate crime, as well as the broader social and ecological harms produced by the endless pursuit of material wealth. Is fear of crime caused by crime or by social inequality (Pantazis, 2000b), especially in an environment where crime has become highly politicised? So what we call crime has to be understood in the context of social order and the systems of discipline and control through which it is maintained. Critical criminologists attribute crime to social inequality, and challenge the way in which it is pathologised, or attributed to the moral failings of (usually poor and socially excluded) individuals.

It therefore encompasses a diverse, interdisciplinary field. Of crucial importance is the work of those such as Christie (2000) and Reiman (1998) for whom crime control is a symptom of the disease rather than its cure. Instead of regarding crime and crime control as opposites we should see both as manufactured by unjust social conditions. As evidence of this Christie cites the trend towards increased rates of incarceration, a 'western gulag', especially in America. If mainstream views are correct then this should lead to less fear and apprehension but, if anything, the more people are shut away the more electorates have their anxieties and phobias confirmed; for when the imprisoned are predominantly males from poor, uneducated and frequently ethnic minority backgrounds then the threats allegedly posed by such groups only magnify in the popular imagination. And the more social democratic governments pander to moral panics the greater the fear they engender and the more they find themselves in an unresolvable 'arms race' with conservatives to feed those fears with promises of yet more punitiveness. And on it goes. Money spent on jail cells becomes electorally more acceptable than having it spent on benefits.

Crime control should therefore be understood as a public and private industry that, as well as offering jobs and investment (and so a source of economic growth), fuses with other systems, such as the welfare state, in a new mode of social control termed by some the 'prison-industrial complex' (Parenti, 1999; cf. Fitzpatrick, 2001b). One reason why Clinton was able to champion such low rates of unemployment – in contrast to the apparent sclerosis of European markets – was because during his presidency 2 million men were incarcerated and a further 3–4 million were incorporated into the criminal justice system at some level (Western & Beckett, 1999) – security has been one of the fastest growing industries of recent years. For Wacquant (2001, 2003) this is evidence of a 'carceral continuum' where the most disadvantaged are constantly recycled between prison, welfare benefits and low-waged work in a deregulated labour market. Prisons and ghettos come to resemble each other more and more in a continuum that particularly affects African Americans.

While he distances himself from critical criminology (by downgrading the significance of ideology) there are important similarities between it and the work of David Garland (1985, 1990, 2001a: 72, 2001b). According to Garland the Victorian enthusiasm for the minimal state in fact masked a desire to pacify and control the 'dangerous classes' whom the minimal state had abandoned to the vicissitudes of *laissez faire*. This was succeeded by the 'penal-welfare state' in which socioeconomic hierarchies were maintained but engineered through a series of integrative institutions into a system of disciplinary inclusion. Characterising this period was the expectation that the state could and eventually would solve the main social problems, including crime. But as the state's competence has been questioned and eroded from a number of perspectives so its sovereignty has transformed, leaving the state more of a steerer than a rower (see above). The communal is now the locus of social action (Rose, 1996) meaning that since the causes of crime cannot be solved more control than ever is directed towards the spaces within which crimes can occur. What Garland calls the new 'culture of control', a new punitiveness, has now superseded the penal-welfare state. Here, state, semi-state and non-state agencies complement and augment one another and control proceeds through the fragmentation of social spaces rather than their homogenisation. Governance occurs 'at a distance' on the supply-side of social action and so helps reinforce the view that those excluded have chosen to be so, i.e. by not taking advantage of the educational and employment opportunities available to all:

> If we are to see ourselves as the uncaused causes of our own actions and choices, as the moral individualism of market society teaches us to do, then those not fully in control of their own conduct must appear different in some extra-social sense. (Garland, 2001a: 198)

This critique accords with those who identify a form of 'actuarial justice' at work where interventions are aimed less at individuals and more at the physical and social spaces (the supply-side) within which individuals move and act (Feeley & Simon, 1994). Rather than reacting to crime after the event the rationale here is one of 'anticipatory deterrence' where behaviour is circumscribed before it can occur, e.g. through systems of surveillance, in order to reduce risks and manipulate the perception of risks. Crime control therefore adopts the techniques of the insurance industry in its risk assessments and calculation of probabilities (Ericson & Haggerty, 1997). Conversely, architecture and urban policies take on the characteristics of crime control so that crime is 'designed out' of the environment (see the comments on spatial surveillance, next section); or, rather, out of middle-class environments usually, so that thieves are even more likely to target those in their own neighbourhoods. The concept of actuarial justice itself accords with the governmentality literature's focus upon governing through freedom (M. Dean, 2003). The thesis here is that communities translate systems of discipline into technologies of self-control as a means of preserving the security which is the *sine qua non* of freedom. The public is encouraged to take responsibility for civic order, to become its own police force, and prisoners become active in their own rehabilitation. Control therefore comes to be experienced as choice and self-determination by autonomous risk-takers.

Finally, the contribution of feminist criminology should not be ignored (Mooney, 2000; Carrington, 2002; Carlen, 2002). On the one hand, feminists regretted the initial focus within critical criminology upon economic structures and the consequent tendency to overlook the more prosaic realities of crime. What this risked doing was ignoring crimes against women, especially acts of sexual aggression, since these are not easily reducible to economistic models.[1] That said many feminists have been content to situate themselves in proximity to criticalist ideas given the extent and depth of patriarchal attitudes and practices throughout the criminal justice system. Women who offend are more likely than men to attract punitive sentences, perhaps as revenge for having transgressed the boundaries of a stereotypical femininity (Rafter, 2000). At the same time, unless they are firmly locatable within those boundaries then women are also more likely than men to be blamed for attracting unwanted attention (Stanko, 1990). In short, feminist criminology has sought to raise awareness of gender and propose both realist and radical critiques of crime and criminal justice accordingly.

The review given above stresses the continuities which prevail among a series of disparate ideas but also the ultimate incommensurability that exists at opposite ends of the spectrum. On the one hand we have a pathological tendency either to treat individuals as if they popped into existence in a social vacuum or which attempts a 'catholic' reading of human nature – because humans are inherently flawed and corrupt they require strong institutional norms to prevent them from giving in to their immoral impulses. On the other hand we have a constructionist perspective that roots subjectivity in its social environment.

Social policy & governance revisited

I have already hinted at the role played in all of this by social policies. Welfare systems are and always have been closely associated with the conceptualisation and resolution of crime. Let's take poverty as a kind of case study.

For many on the Right the poor have not achieved the obligation to achieve financial independence and acceptable moral standards, so must be made to observe the economic and cultural norms they have rejected. Although not all crime is committed by people in poverty, crime derives from the lack of norms produced by a liberalism of permissive welfare of which the dependencies of the poor are the most symbolic manifestation. Yet poverty and crime are also the means by which we can recognise those norms as damaged and seek to rebuild them around the examples offered by decent and virtuous citizens. According to this line of thinking, shifting expenditure from welfare to punishment makes perfect sense since the former encourages social depravity (and exclusion) while the latter brings people back to an acknowledgement of their responsibilities.

For those towards the Left poverty is a structural injustice committed by the powerful against the relatively powerless, a sign of the inability or unwillingness to correct the circumstances into which people are born and through which they are distributed across a multiplicity of social hierarchies. While crime should not necessarily be excused, since some degree of choice and deliberation is usually detectible, we cannot ignore its social meaning: much of it being an effect of desperation, anomie and insecurity. Our task should be to detect the extent to which these experiences do and do not relate to unfair distributions of material and cultural resources and so use at least some of them to reengage with the struggle for social justice. The desire to hurt those who hurt, through punitive policies and institutions, is understandable but overestimates the amount of control that individuals *qua* individuals possess over the circumstances which make us what we are.

Obviously, these contrasting descriptions simplify and risk caricaturing the many theoretical subtleties at work but they do underscore the point that social policy is at the heart of modern conceptions of the good society and is not an administrative add-on concerned merely with a bit of community management here or a bit of truancy there (Jones Finer & Nellis, 1998; Boutellier, 2001; Gilling, 2001). Two important points follow from this.

Firstly, while it is vitally important to investigate the links between crime, poverty, inequality and unemployment, such issues remain inevitably contestable and only the most blinkered positivist will insist that policy prescriptions follow unproblematically from statistics (Hagan & Peterson, 1995; *Journal of Quantitative Criminology*, 2001). Common sense intuits that as indicators such as poverty, inequality and unemployment rise so should levels of crime, and a fair amount of research suggests common sense is not far wrong (Cook, 1997; Currie, 1998; Witt *et al*, 1998; Kelly, 2000; Kramer, 2000; Vieraitis, 2000; Carmichael & Ward, 2001; Gould *et al*, 2002). Yet in his review of the literature Taylor (1997) makes the point that since political specificities always intervene then what matters is the 'quality' of the poverty, inequality and unemployment in question, e.g. whether poverty 'causes' crime depends upon a complex of political, sociocultural and psychosocial influences (Vold *et al*, 2002: 88–99). Therefore, we cannot say that the welfare state does or does not cause crime because there is no such thing as *the* welfare state but a diversity of political, sociocultural and psychosocial densities. So while it is useful to explore links and associations between crime and welfare (e.g. Beckett & Western, 2001) the qualitative (human) dimension always militates against the discovery of law-like regularities.

Secondly, both welfare and criminal policies constitute a policy regime that has been under-theorised in the comparative literature. Even so, criminologists seem to agree with their counterparts in social policy and political economics that an important realignment has taken place in recent decades (Young, 1999; Garland, 2001a; Esping-Andersen, 1999; Jessop, 2002). If we characterise the 'regime of solidarity' as a combination of state welfare and rehabilitative principles, and the 'regime of security' as a combination of workfare reform and punitiveness, then a shift from the former to the latter seems to have occurred in most developed countries in the 1980s or 1990s. So where the solidarity regime views the criminal as a lapsed citizen who nevertheless remains within the social interior, a temporary fracture in society's incorporative structures, the security regime treats citizens simultaneously as potential victims *and* criminals, as portals to a hazardous exterior that have to be forever monitored and resocialised through the ever-present possibility of exclusion and confinement. The former regime is integrative and mappable while the latter is disintegrative and modular.

This returns us to the governance debate. I suggested, at the end of the last section, how governance denotes a social world in which the more we try to 'preactivate' our environments through technologies of inspection, auditing, targeting and tabling then the more we are reacting half-blindly to the reactions of our former selves in a fog of simulacra. Criminology illustrates the point well. Techniques of governance offer to secure an insecure environment by measuring the performance of police officers, police forces, courts, prisons, local authorities and probation services so that consumers/taxpayers can see where their money is being spent and with what effect. Yet since fear of crime usually outstrips its actuality, since to be successful performance has to address the former as much as the latter, what is offered up for measurement is as much fiction as it is fact, e.g. a statistical construction through which realities are glimpsed briefly and infrequently, meaning that information received by consumers/taxpayers is as often a reflection and confirmation of their indelible anxieties. If crime levels rise then our worst expectations have been realised; but even if levels fall then the threshold of security grows and we only become more over-sensitive to imagined threats and possibilities, and so as fearful as before – what Bauman (2000c: 215) calls the 'self-propelling of fear'. Performance therefore becomes what it is: a show or spectacle. And since we have only an approximate idea of how much crime there really is, and a hazy idea of what works to reduce it, then techniques of governance cloud the picture still further.

It is into this dimness that ideological critiques stumble in an effort to make sense of what is there according to a particular set of descriptions and explanations. The recent shift from solidarity to security indicates that it is conservative narratives that have been winning the battle. And the cloudier the world appears then the greater the impulse to render it visible grows.

Surveillance

Theories of surveillance

Lyon (2001: 2) defines surveillance as,

> ...any collection and processing of personal data, whether identifiable or not, for the purposes of influencing or managing those whose data have been garnered.

Surveillance can imply protection and may operate as a form of care; or it can imply moral proscription where those surveilled are being subject to some form of social control. In one sense, then, every society is a surveillance society because social interaction inevitably involves processes of watching and monitoring. In small-scale societies these processes are more likely to be informal and interactive, occurring in and around ordinary familial and communal forms of association. As societies develop, however, formal systems of surveillance begin to appear that, abstracted from families and communities, initiate much more organised, remote practices. Of obvious importance here is the growth of the modern state and the converse appearance of a civil society in which actual or potential forces of disruption are thought to reside. In *Hamlet* Shakespeare depicts a court of suspicions and betrayals in which the old social bonds are being replaced by those based upon constant acts of spying and eavesdropping.

A surveillance society therefore implies the attempt to reintegrate social practices that have become dis-integrated. Yet analysts such as Giddens (1985), Lyon (1994, 2002, 2003) and Ericson and Haggerty (1997) also want to regard surveillance as being constitutive of the contemporary age. A surveillance society implies a normalisation in the collection of personal data: not only acts of watching but people *knowing* they are being watched routinely and, for the most part, accepting this as an inevitable part of the everyday. Yet by the last quarter of the twentieth century a kind of technological determinism was establishing itself – 'because we can do x then we ought to do it' – which, allied to the ubiquity of technology and present-day fears of crime and terrorism, makes it more important that we monitor and control the systems that seek to monitor and control us. While the surveillance society may be inescapable this does not mean that we cannot determine its specific ends or modes of operation.

First of all we might ask how surveillance can operate as a method. It is still common to imagine surveillance as a type of visualisation, not just of what *is* there but of what *might* be there in the future; the means by which a given territory can be mapped so that the territory itself becomes an object of effective intervention. Through the eleventh century Domesday Book William I was able to gather not only information on his new land but also a tool for the more efficient raising of taxation (Schama, 2000: 109–10). Today, visualisation occurs through street lighting, security cameras, road cameras (whether to detect speeding or to collect charges), sensors and satellites. Yet if we limit our definition to the visual we are missing an essential point: surveillance is not only seeing and being seen but acting and being acted upon. It is as much spatial as visual (Ball, 2000).

Urban space has long been designed as a form of surveillance apparatus (Soja, 1996: 235; Lyon, 2001: Ch. 4) and medieval cities were often rebuilt with this purpose in mind. In Paris, in the wake of the 1848 insurrections, the wide boulevards were intended to make it easier to detect signs of urban unrest and to move large numbers of troops through the streets (Berman, 1982: 150). More recently urban geographers have noted how pervasive spatial forms of micro-surveillance have become. In *City of Quartz* Davis (1990) recorded the many ways in which the built environment operates as a type of control in which social problems are exiled from view and 'problem people' are diverted away from the commodified spaces in which society preserves its self-image. Flusty (2001) has developed a wide spectrum of concepts to explain the new urban architecture, e.g. 'interdictory spaces' are those designed to cushion affluent areas from outside threats by making incursions into those areas visible, and so interceptable, from a remote distance (cf. Marx, 1995). And many have noted how the ghettoisation of affluent households in gated communities is only an extreme example of a wider trend towards the privatisation of public space where zones of inclusion and exclusion are maintained through a panoply of surveillance techniques (Bauman, 1998a).

In addition, computers and communication technologies now provide a means of advancing visual and spatial techniques to a digital level. Firstly, computerisation means that more information than ever before can be contained on databases and that the cross-matching of databases can rapidly occur. With CCTVs what matters is not so much the camera as the way in which the resulting pixels are processed since images can be analysed by facial, movement and gait-recognition technologies. Secondly, it is now practically impossible to live in developed societies without leaving a data trail in the form of credit card purchases and credit records. And while the Internet may feel like an anonymous form of virtual travel, ISP addresses and 'cookies' ensure that all but the most resourceful surfers can eventually be found, whether by state authorities or advertisers selling anything from pornography to insurance. Thirdly, mobile phones allow the operator of the phone to be located due to global positioning satellites. Finally, the body's surveillance capacity is expanding as DNA databases proliferate and biometric identification promises to become a primary method of identification, in banks and airports for instance (Fitzpatrick, 2002b). Due to computerisation Graham and Wood (2003) identify the emergence of what they call 'algorithmic surveillance' in which what matters is ultimately the mathematical codes through which data is processed.

What this does is to remind us that surveillance is first and foremost a form of classification and recording. What matters is less how the data is gathered and more the categories into which the information is sorted and the social uses to which it is put. At one extreme this cataloguing may reflect the actual attributes of the population being surveilled but, at another, it may be that the categories are designed for administrative and political convenience. What, then, are the normative stances which have been taken towards surveillance?

It is very easy to panic and interpret a surveillance society as a kind of 'virtual' police state, as being consistent with the subtle forms of disciplinary control around which some believe capitalist democracies to be based (Marcuse, 1964). Yet we should be wary of adopting too reductive an interpretation of surveillance (McGrath, 2004). Working class communities have often been the first to demand CCTVs as a way of controlling an environment essential to their history and so sense of identity. The electronic tagging of convicted rapists and children may make, respectively, rape victims and parents feel more secure. Surveillance may therefore offer a sense of security and so an improvement in quality of life (Ross, 2000). If surveillance enables a patient's medical history to be accessed quickly and accurately, hastening treatment that might otherwise be delayed, then perhaps the benefits outweigh the erosion of privacy. From a more radical perspective, forms of counter-surveillance can be deployed against both commercial firms and state authorities where, the more they grow technologically dependent, the easier it becomes to launch acts of subversion against what the state/market nexus prefers to keep hidden.

Yet there are others on both Right and Left who caution against too Panglossian an assessment. Conservatives tend to worry that surveillance represents an undesirable extension in the powers of the state, though they also welcome other aspects of surveillance where this can help to fight crime and so maintain social order. Etzioni, to take one example, supports the use of surveillance technologies where they are targeted against suspected criminals and where their use can demonstrably assist in the strengthening of society's common good, e.g. a willingness to be surveilled may be taken as a sign of trustworthiness. In contrast to 'individualists' Etzioni (1999: 213) says that it is an obsession with privacy that leads to greater state control of people's lives, whereas '...the best way to curtail the need for governmental control and intrusion is to have somewhat less privacy.'

Libertarians are less ambiguous, tending to view surveillance as a totally unwarranted intrusion into individual space. This is one of the reasons why libertarians have been at the forefront of resisting attempts by the governments to regulate cyberspace through the use of encryption chips and by requiring Internet Service Providers to become moral overseers (Jordan, 1999).

Liberals of one shade or another (Liberty, 1999) recognise the definite advantages of surveillance to individuals when it allows privacy and autonomy to be protected and even enhanced. This is the case where checking information already on record substitutes for repeated and more direct intrusions into people's lives. However, a liberal perspective also warns against surveillance when the implications for privacy and autonomy are less obvious. States and corporations easily succumb to a 'just-in-case' instinct: there are imaginable circumstances under which we might need such information in the future, therefore we'd better accumulate it now *just in case*. Also, surveillance can be sold to people as a means of speeding up procedures, e.g. a passport or credit card application, that would otherwise take longer, but means that a digital shadow of yourself is permanently inhabiting the informatic surroundings. ID cards are sold as a convenient appendage to the main items that we already use to identify ourselves but they can quickly become a sign of inequality and a source of discrimination and abuse. Liberals also worry that as surveillance of children expands the children who regard this as normal will grow into adults less capable of exhibiting the skills of independence and adaptation to unexpected circumstances.

Marxists and other Left radicals tend to regard surveillance as unwelcome, not because it represents some form of statist conspiracy against 'the individual' but because it operates in the interests of certain groups of individuals against others (Whitaker, 1999). Robins and Webster (1999: 92–110) attribute the growth in surveillance to the social management and control upon which capitalist development has depended. The advent of Taylorist 'scientific management' was vital: a closer monitoring of the workforce being the *sine qua non* of a leap in industrial productivity. So surveillance is the very *raison d'etre* of modern bureaucracies and corporations, whether in the search for social and political deviancy or whether for the purposes of capital accumulation. This is why the intrusion of surveillance techniques into more and more aspects of society is hardly surprising; so workplace surveillance, to take one example, is more pervasive than ever in the form of drugs testing, DNA testing, the monitoring of emails and Internet searches, and minicams (Fitzpatrick, 2002c).

Some researchers have also found that far from being neutral the technology functions according to the familiar structures of social power. Norris and Armstrong (1999) and Coleman and Sim (2000) found that CCTVs are there mainly to protect commercial and affluent areas and that camera operators routinely survey those they perceive, in line with stereotypical norms, as being socially excluded, disadvantaged and vulnerable. The crime-fighting effects of CCTVs are far from proven but at least provide a neat distraction from their actual role of assisting the police and quasi-police in controlling the populations they are advertised as defending (Fox, 2001).

Post-structuralists, by contrast, reintroduce a perspective of ambivalence into the debate. To regard governance and freedom as components of a zero sum game is naïve since each is activated and enhanced through the presence of the other. These 'components' are therefore much more closely integrated, while by no means being identical (M. Dean, 1999: 13), and so it therefore follows that surveillance should not be interpreted according to a discourse of invasion, violation and encroachment, one effect of which is to reduce surveillance practices to a single locus, e.g. the state or the corporation:

> ...the idea of a maximum security society is misleading. Rather than the tentacles of the state spreading across everyday life, the securitization of identity is dispersed and disorganized. And rather than totalising surveillance, it is better seen as conditional access to circuits of consumption and civility ... recurrent switch points to be passed in order to access the benefits of liberty. (Rose, 1999b: 243)

So while exclusionary practices may be a cause for concern these should not be confused with those of 'inclusionary surveillance'. Indeed, surveillance should be welcomed whenever it replaces the authoritarian forms of control and policing that the Left otherwise objects to.

The key to a post-structuralist analysis is obviously the panopticon (see Fitzpatrick, 2001a: 180), Foucault's metaphor for a system of carceral surveillance in which we are simultaneously the objects of the normative gaze that we direct towards others. The recent literature has added a host of amendments to Foucault's basic idea (see Boyne, 2000). For instance, Poster identifies a 'superpanopticon' in that, whereas Marxists regard surveillance as a form of action upon given subjects, Foucault directs our attention to the way in which subjectivity is itself fabricated through the operation of discursive categories and binary oppositions (see Poster & Aronowitz, 1997). It is not that surveillance is directed towards already-existing subjects, so much that surveillance 'hails' to the discursive categories those whom those categories come to embody.

Influenced more by Baudrillard, Bogard (1996) goes even further in suggesting that the panopticon is too modernist a system and has been overtaken by 'surveillant simulation' in which reality and its representations have long since imploded. Once surveillance became ubiquitous it ceased to be identifiable as its former self. So while 'surveillance' sought to penetrate the social surface, surveillant simulation is about the endless manufacture of depthless surfaces upon which codified streams of data flow. Bogard (1996: 181) therefore leaves us in a shadowy world from which the old concepts and distinctions do not vanish so much as become virtual (freedom vs. control, real vs. appearance, self vs. other, environment vs. action):

> Today, the gap separating the imaginary and the real is narrowing, but we shouldn't simply conclude from this that telematic systems aim to close it for good. More accurately, they aim to absorb it in simulation, to simulate the difference. The more resistance to closure, the more the system itself resists closure .... It feeds on it in order to reproduce it...

Marxists and post-structuralists obviously disagree about a great deal. For the former, post-structuralism ignores the importance of action and social structure by regarding power as an infinite modulation of kaleidoscopic fragments; for the latter, Marxism ignores the importance of discourse in its attempt to preserve static models of the social. Yet both theories agree that what is crucial to surveillance is *self*-surveillance, i.e. the way in which subjects police the boundaries of themselves. Analogous to the ways in which people living under dictatorships censor themselves, the effects of surveillance already pre-empt the systems of surveillance that circulate through and around us. Because of the traces that we and others have left before the imperative to surveil resides already within the social spaces through which we come to occupy ourselves. Processes of surveillance shape the world upon which they gaze and we are already enmeshed within the surveillance web: the web does not capture you, the web *is* you.

According to Ericson and Haggerty (1997: Ch. 2) this has led us to become the self-assessors of risk management, organising ourselves into various profiles of risk through the ways in which we respond to the circuits of social policing and surveillance. Policing a risk society is less about punitive deterrence as about people voluntarily offering knowledge of themselves to the databases of administration. By demonstrating that they are aware of, and are always seeking to manage, risks people prove themselves to be responsible, i.e. as not imposing unnecessary burdens upon others.

Surveillance and social policy

This leads us neatly on to a discussion of social policy. If surveillance is a process of making information visible and manipulable then state welfare has been at the forefront of this process. To some extent the adoption of a more paternalistic and benevolent agenda enabled governments to extend their data collection operations beyond what might otherwise have been achievable. Information flows more freely when it is voluntary and is more likely to be voluntary when the ultimate aims are popularly seen as benign. At the same time, of course, no welfare system can work effectively without policymakers possessing a considerable knowledge of the population. The allocation of educational capacity (schools, teachers, resources) depends upon knowing how many children people are giving birth to; planning health services requires some knowledge of people's habits and lifestyles; if social problems are to be tackled then detailed knowledge of material circumstances is needed – hence the development of empirical social science. Therefore the growth of modern surveillance techniques and the growth of the welfare state ran in parallel (Piven & Cloward, 1971), each being both cause and effect of the other: surveillance enabling welfare services to expand which, in turn, requires more and more information about the client population as those services take effect.

The nineteenth century therefore witnessed the initial stages of this dual expansion but the main impetus obviously came with the introduction of insurance benefits such as pensions. Indeed, in many countries like the UK an 'insurance number' or equivalent is still the main way governments keep track of their citizens. In the years after the Second World War the system of 'welfare surveillance' was well and truly advanced (Squires, 1990). Cradle-to-grave provision requires the tagging and monitoring of the employment, contributory, educational, marital and medical histories of its citizens, a bureaucratic and administrative machine that files, catalogues, indexes and processes you in hundreds of ways (Lyon, 1994: 94–6).

Here, then, we have a useful illustration of the twin care-and-control aspects of modern surveillance. Few deny that state welfare is a means of caring for those who would be imperfectly cared for otherwise. Equally, there can be few who imagine that state welfare does not also constitute a form of social control; indeed, social expenditure is frequently sold to electorates on the basis that it will help to restrain those who are dependent and/or undeserving. We therefore have to grapple with the kind of ambivalence that some of the above theories identify where it is neither a question of care *or* control because submitting yourself to the systems of surveillance is the condition of receiving care and attention from the state. This might imply that what exists is a hierarchy of control. While almost nobody fails to receive assistance from the state at some point during their lives, those wealthy enough to buy themselves out of the public sector are also thereby able to reduce the amount of state surveillance to which they are subject. Conversely, those on low incomes are much more likely to be the objects of care *as* control whether through the medium of social work (Jones, 2001), education or social security in particular. Think of the extent to which the benefits system surveils its clients through income-testing, means-testing, the scrutiny of lifestyles (e.g. the cohabitation rule) and of job search activities.

Such forms of social control can be justified in a number of ways: to prevent fraud or to help those who have lost the habits of work and independence. Yet Marxists and post-structuralists might both agree that the categories of desert and dependency do not precede surveillance as such. Instead, these categories and their human contents are the *effects* of state surveillance: you prove yourself to be deserving by accepting or even welcoming the gaze of surveillance, while those who in any way resist of challenge it are thereby identifying themselves as risky and problematic. Some aspects of benefit fraud might regarded as a *consequence* of surveillance, as an attempt to get back at an intrusive and ineffectual system. And once the category of deserving/ undeserving is widely taken to be representative of innate human character, rather than the administrative construction of a particular social regime, then even more surveillance of problem populations can be justified. A realisation that care, control and surveillance operate through one another is expressed by one of John Gilliom's (2001: 51) interviewees, Mary:

> All the time you are on welfare, yeah, you are in prison. Someone is watching like a guard. Someone is watching over you and you are hoping every day that you won't go up the creak, so to speak, and [that you will] get out alive in any way, shape or form. You know, 'Did I remember to say that a child moved in?' 'Did I remember to say that a child move out?' ... It's as close to prison that I can think of.

But does this mean that as state welfare has been rolled back that surveillance has declined also? That the poorest can now also 'buy themselves out'? According to Ericson and Haggerty (1997) we should conclude that the exact opposite has happened: that the relative withdrawal of the state has accompanied, and itself driven, the emergence of new sources of risk in a changing socioeconomic environment. For instance, as collectivised insurance has withered so people are expected to become more flexible and entrepreneurial in looking after themselves leading, under both conservative and social democratic governments, to a welfare system of 'supply-side activation' where producers and consumers must exhibit dynamic relationships and aspirations based upon the ideal of market-led independence.

Yet rather than just leaving people to get on with it many conservatives and social democrats have come to support what Mead calls the new paternalism (see Chapter 1). While the affluent are assumed to already possess the necessary capital to survive in this new environment the socially excluded have to be guided in the right direction. So as the direct control of the state is actually 'rolled forward' for those most dependent upon it, forms of 'remote control' and 'remote viewing' are also emphasised as never before (Fitzpatrick, 2003: Ch. 3): the state contracts more of itself out to quasi-state agencies, social and criminal policies converge, a new managerialism comes to prevail, greater use of selectivism means that information on both compliant and non-compliant individuals becomes more personalised, data-bases spread as the capacity to integrate them improves, and intervention becomes more pre-emptive, e.g. the greater use of school tests producing a population which regards compliance with externally-set criteria as normal.

Here, then, we have revisited the second theme anticipated earlier, where governance implies the paradoxical loosening and strengthening of power. Surveillance enables control to roll forward even as the most visible borders of sovereignty recede: the grip tightens as the arm extends. The journey towards hyper-individualisation, through a loosening of traditional bonds, strengthens the need to encircle the spaces and times of individuality, to offer it up to the imperatives of work and consumption. Surveillance terminals do not lead to an Orwellian or Benthamite centre since no centralised apparatus can be as efficient as the imaginary centres through which we constantly restabilise a destabilising world. Governance through freedom is really governance through the fragmentations upon which we depend for our sense of freedom and through the social narratives by which those fragments must be reconnected for our sense of security. Surveillance resides in the interstices which both link and separate these fragments, the means by which contemporary freedoms are narrated. And if freedom is surveillance-dependent then surveillance is equally freedom-dependent, meaning that we cannot evade surveillance-as-control without substantially reconfiguring what it means to be free. The pessimisms of many political radicals come from recognising the enormity of that task.

Conclusion

The literatures on, and implications of, what is called governance are vast and I indicated from the beginning of this chapter that the aim was to draw out the two features of contemporary society to which it seems to draw attention. The first of these concerns not just the indeterminacy of the social world but the extent to which our interventions and interactions make things less rather than more determinate: the more administrative systems become both the objects and subjects of cataloguing then the more our visual field is saturated with reflections of the cataloguing process itself. This point was illustrated by looking at crime and I concluded that the spectacle of performance is making the picture hazier than ever. The second feature concerns the paradoxical advance and retreat of systemic power, the governance at a distance that is facilitated by the growth of surveillance technologies and norms.

Both this chapter and the last have reviewed the extent to which the social field is inhabited by a series of openings and closures. We have seen that each of the six themes covered embodies a degree of ambiguity: each can be interpreted as both a closure and an opening, the meaning of which differs according to the political presumptions that are brought to bear. I now want to underline this point for a final time as we move into the more sociocultural aspects of recent debates.

9
Culture and Media

Culture
   Some theories of culture
   Cultures of welfare

Media
   Pluralism and criticalism
   Media and social policy
Concluding Thoughts

Culture

Culture is notoriously difficult to define since it is as self-referential a concept as they come (Eagleton, 2000). We use culture to shape culture: it is a tool that works on itself. Any definition is itself culturally configured and so endlessly contestable. The term has been used to encompass at least the following: values, belief-systems, norms, meanings, ways of life, social symbols, interpretative grids, codes and representations, histories, customs and conventions, language and discourse, aesthetics, ethics, religion, rituals, myths, social habits, assumptions and instincts, understandings, identities and divisions, popular attitudes and popular culture. Culture is we might say *the way we do things around here.*

One way for social policy researchers to think of culture is in terms of motivations and expressed values, permitting us to catch culture in our empirical net by examining attitude surveys (van Oorschot, 2002). Taylor-Gooby (2004) identifies a contradiction between welfare values (support for redistributive, interventionist state welfare) and market values (individualism, personal aspiration). He anticipates that this contradiction will sharpen in the future, as will the paradox that many people who value egalitarian aims are less willing to vote for them in the ballot box (see Chapter 7). Yet if culture also works 'behind our backs' then we cannot be content with such surface manifestations alone. There are also those who conceive of culture as so indelible that it appears entirely detached from post-WWII (British) welfare reforms (Baldock, 1999). I am going to adopt an approach that slides between these alternatives: to make culture workable while not losing sight of its elusiveness.

As a starting-point I will therefore define culture as *the constitution and representation of shared meanings in material objects and social practices.* The notion of shared meanings is absolutely central and captures the idea that referents are or are not evocative depending upon the complex of historical, national and social associations within which they resonate. Culture also has something to do with representation and self-image: the stories that we tell ourselves about ourselves; but it is at the same time a material practice that is woven in and around social relations.

This last point is a reminder that culture cannot be detached from ideological critique. On the face of it what could be more dissonant? The cultural seems vast, dynamic and intangible, whereas the ideological appears bounded, static and reductive by comparison. Yet if culture infuses and is infused by the material, and unless we are to neglect the importance of the political economy (I return to this point below), then we cannot avoid relating it to an ideological orientation. Though he is concerned specifically with popular culture Thompson (1990: 7) makes this very point. Ideology,

> ...is meaning in the service of power. Hence the study of ideology requires us to investigate the ways in which meaning is constructed and conveyed by symbolic forms of various kinds, from everyday linguistic utterances to complex images and texts; it requires us to investigate the social contexts within which symbolic forms are employed and deployed; and it calls upon us to ask whether, and if so how, the meaning mobilised by symbolic forms serves, in specific contexts, to establish and sustain relations of domination.

So culture is about power and power (if it is not to disappear into a Foucauldian maze – see Fitzpatrick, 2001a: 90) involves reference to asymmetry, hierarchy and domination.

Some theories of culture

Although it is easy to propose that culture and social policy are old relatives only now meeting for the first time they have in fact been communicating for ages. Commentators on the Right have long stressed the importance of culture, as an established order that ought to be defended or as an explanation of social problems in the form of cultural/moral breakdown (Fitzpatrick, 2001a: 92–4). Overall, the conservative take on culture tends to involve essentialism, hierarchy, homogeneity and naturalism (Scruton, 2001). Essentialism, because it is believed important to distinguish between the culturally normal and abnormal (or deviant); hierarchy, because social and cultural order is thought to depend upon distinguishing between the higher/superior and lower/inferior; homogenous, because cultural closure is assumed to provide the sources of identification and integration that diversity cannot provide; naturalistic, because for conservatives social culture can and should be read off from the natural order, e.g. in attributing gendered roles to inherent biological tendencies (see Chapter 6). Cultural conservatism therefore involves the insistence that welfare policies should be orientated to a moral system that reflects 'how things really are'.

Cultural conservatism has been attacked from the Left in a number of guises (Honderich, 2003). Marxists see it as a legitimation of *bourgeois* culture in which capitalist economics is defended by treating the cultural and the aesthetic as given and so obscuring their ultimate roots in society's material base. They criticise conservatives for treating culture as apolitical, as unrelated to structures of exploitation and alienation. Yet the Marxist base/superstructure model has problems of its own. For instance, even in its sophisticated versions it encourages a class analysis of cultural forms that may misread the circulation of other cultural repertoires, formulating an abstract structuralism that feeds the perception that the Left ignores questions of agency and individualism (see Chapter 3). Two leading alternatives to cultural conservatism and Marxism have therefore emerged: cultural materialism and postmodernism.

Cultural materialism is the analysis of signification in terms of the conditions of its production. It therefore agrees with Marxism that culture has to be related to the material yet wishes to grant culture a greater degree of specificity and autonomy.[1] The economic certainly contextualises culture but *the economic is itself contextualised by culture*. So we cannot read the material and the cultural off one another according to some kind of Rosetta Stone. The key influence here remains Williams (1961, 1981; and see Hall, below). Williams views cultural forms as overdetermined, as being saturated with a multiplicity of causes, so that a hegemonic formation is always in process, always spilling over the boundaries of its present self. Culture is therefore a battleground of domination rather than a superstructure per se. Despite this Gramscian influence, though, Williams also remains wedded to a rarified paradigm of literary criticism in which meaning is buried, uncovered and distributed, with little room for ambiguity or contradictoriness (Stevenson, 2002: 25). Postmodernists, and their fellow travellers, therefore allege that by staying too close to a productivist framework cultural materialists attribute too much stability and essentialism to meaning.

Fiske (1987) believes that material production in no way structures consumption; they are autonomous spheres that may interact but never according to some kind of inherent logic where the economic dominates 'in the last instance'. What this does is open up the possibility that consumers are themselves the producers of meaning; meanings that do not track along predetermined lines but can be perpetually re-signified. This image of the *active audience*, able to interpret and (if necessary) resist the stream of cultural commodities, is crucial to postmodernism (Featherstone, 1990). Its concern is with heterogeneity, fragmentation and decentredness so that rather than a 'puppet master' view of culture it sees multidimensional circuits of production and appropriation. Signification is never fixed and so meaning is always ambivalent, deriving from an indefinite stream of differences. There are no cultural depths awaiting discovery by the expert for culture is always ever a series of eclectic, intertextual constructions that run ahead of themselves, and so no foundations (material or otherwise) upon which culture can be said to stand. Culture is made everywhere by everyone; it goes 'all the way down': you are your culture and your culture is you.

For those such as Rorty (1989), then, postmodernism slides into communitarianism (Fitzpatrick, 2001a: 181–4) in that communal contexts require no justification beyond themselves: they are their own foundations. Taken to a logical conclusion this may imply that all cultural communities are valuable to some degree. Indeed, a thoroughgoing communitarianism wants to reverse the Marxist polarity and treat matter as a manifestation of culture. Along similar lines, Honneth (1995) insists that economic oppression has to be understood as an articulation of a deeper, cultural oppression that relates to hierarchies of status (see Chapter 2).

Of those who have criticised postmodernism (e.g. Callinicos, 1994; Anderson, 1998) Eagleton (1996) is perhaps *the* heir to the tradition of cultural materialism. Eagleton contends that postmodernists underestimate the fact and the value of cultural unity. While people are not the dupes of cultural producers (see the media section, below) the latter nevertheless shape the boundaries of cultural possibilities. The fact that you can establish your own webpage or watch some DVD films from different angles does not mean that the power of Microsoft, Fox or MGM is any less. So an understanding of political economics *is* crucial to an understanding of culture. Furthermore, postmodernism risks collapsing into a cultural separatism (see the later discussion of multiculturalism) where (a) there are no context-less points of reference, e.g. human rights, (b) all contexts are equally valued, even those involving repression, and (c) no context can intrude upon the space of another without being labelled imperialistic. So culture does not go all the way down, according to Eagleton, and the things postmodernists value – difference and dynamism – are not inherently worthwhile or ubiquitous.

Yet although Eagleton offers persuasive arguments against its communitarian tendencies there are more liberal and materialist versions that are fully aware of the distractions media cultures provide against the frequent horrors of contemporary society (Kellner, 1995: 42–9, 331–3). Postmodernism is also a potentially useful reminder that liberalism is itself an historicised tradition, rather than the universal language many liberals have alleged, albeit one that seeks connections across traditions in ways – freedom of speech and belief, political and legal equality – that not every tradition will welcome. Indeed, in arguing that we are capable of grasping truth by subjecting the cultural contexts within which we find ourselves to critical reflection, Eagleton (2003: 62–3, 103–9) is not a million miles away from Rorty's contention that our context-dependency allows us to see truth as pragmatic rather than as either absolute or relative.

So even if we reject it as an alternative we do not have to regard post-modernism as entirely alien to cultural materialism. In the later discussion of multiculturalism I will indicate what this might imply for social policy.

Cultures of welfare

How might a cultural analysis frame social policy? What follows is an attempt to scoop up some of the most recent debates but please note that the very fuzziness of the term means that analyses have spun off in multiple directions and no systematic research programme yet seems to be in evidence.

Clarke (2004: 34–40) identifies three types of analysis which enable a reengagement with the 'social' in social policy. Firstly, there is culture as a field of social difference and differentiation. Cultural differences of identity underpin a politics of multiculturalism, for instance, where distributions of social resources become politicised – we explore this below. Secondly, and as we saw above, cultural explanations of social problems compete for attention either alongside, or as an alternative to, agent-centred and structural explanations. Finally, he says, culture denotes the process through which social construction occurs. In particular through the production of, and conflict between, meanings and symbolic forms some perspectives eclipse others and so come to dominate and be identified with a given 'way of life'. The 'nation', to take one example, is a conjuncture of multiple processes, interests and practices that is stabilised around particular meanings, e.g. Britishness has so often been equated with Englishness. Yet since cultural domination occurs by making the temporary appear permanent this stabilisation is only ever contingent and may be broken open again through contestation. Some have analysed the contribution of welfare institutions to the post-imperialist tenor of British nationality and the extent to which this conjuncture can be destabilised (Lewis, 1998; Hughes & Lewis, 1998). Some have therefore identified 'cultures of memory' (Mozina, 2002; Stubbs, 2002) as being crucial to a nation's sense of itself and so to the organisation of its welfare services. Through collective archives of retrospection society constructs itself endlessly by reimagining its past.

Freeman *et al* (1999: 278–80) add a fourth area which involves listening to the biographies and voices of welfare citizens. Having been dominated by an impulse to legislate and control they contend that conceptions of subjectivity can be shifted towards a more interpretative pole where the intention is to facilitate democratic dialogue. The enduring paradox of liberal democracy is that because the legislative paradigm is still relevant – social administration can hardly be dismantled – dialogical diversity has to be governed and shaped while at the same time being left alone (Fitzpatrick, 2002a, 2002c). Civil society has to be noisy without being chaotic, creative without being anarchic. So a cultural analysis may at least offer alternative possibilities to the modes of governance, control and surveillance we explored in Chapter 8 and which represent a more restrictive and less trustful attempt to contain the uncontainable.

Finally, it is worth drawing attention to what might be called the 'normative ambiguity' of culture. If culture is 'the way we do things around here' then it exerts an atavistic force that always draws us back to the forms of social life that already prevail. The centrality of culture to conservative thought is explained by the latter's attempt to legitimate existing distributions of income, power and wealth. Does this mean that culture inevitably bears conservative and so regressive implications for social policy? Far from it. For if a culture is always incomplete, contradictory, fragile and contingent then it will always contain within itself the possibility of change, of counter-cultural challenges to the dominant order. The implications of a cultural analysis for social policy may be conservative, then again they may not.

If the above areas establish a broad framework for cultural analysis I now want to review four specific debates (two of them at some length) related to social policy.

Cultural Capital

I touched upon this in Chapter 3 but it is of obvious relevance here too.

For Bourdieu (1984) capital is the resource from which power is derived. Rather than reduce it to its economic variant we also need to recognise the importance of *cultural* capital also, i.e. the degree to which you can competently manipulate the cultural forms through which a given society defines itself. Education is crucial in this respect (Bourdieu & Passeron, 1990). But education means much more than the acquisition of qualifications. Instead, education enables bourgeois families to transmit privilege from one generation to another and this means inculcating in those students the automatic habits of intellectual taste, confidence and leadership. For instance, knowing the difference between 'higher' and 'lower' types of literature, fashion, food and wine is one means by which inequality is maintained. So in addition to the qualifications that money can buy the distribution of cultural capital is another means by which advantage can be inherited, no matter how apparently egalitarian and/or meritocratic the education system may be.

What cultural capital does is to inculcate people into the 'habitus', a classificatory grid of dispositions that permits apprehension and cognition, through which a particular perspective is normalised and universalised. For the working class this involves aspirations to possess what the higher classes will only relinquish once its symbolic status has dissipated. Society therefore reproduces itself through the relations between one form of capital and another and the ways in which they are mutually convertible. So while drawing attention to the importance of consumption Bourdieu is insistent that we do not lose sight of the economic.

Sullivan (2001) has criticised Bourdieu for relying upon a circular argument: cultural capital is assumed to determine education and yet education is treated as a proxy for cultural capital. However, through a more precise operationalisation of his ideas she finds that certain aspects of transmission from parent to child are important – cultural knowledge (e.g. of famous personalities) and linguistic ability – while others are much less so – musical habits or participation in formal cultural activities (gallery and theatre visits). So although cultural capital is a useful variable it does not account fully for class differentials and so for sociocultural reproduction (also Nash, 1999). A more diversified critique than that offered by Bourdieu may therefore be appropriate.

Welfare Regimes and Cultural Paths

The basics of Esping-Andersen's typology were explained in Chapter 5 so I will not repeat myself here, but we do need to appreciate the many debates his work has inspired if we are to understand the importance of culture to 'regime theory'.

Esping-Andersen has been influential partly because he provided a clear and systematic formulation of what others had been working towards for years (Higgins, 1981) and because of his methodology. Distinguishing between commodification and decommodification – where the former denotes dependence upon, and the latter independence from, markets – Esping-Andersen (1990: Ch. 2) constructs a scale which permits degrees of decommodification to be measured by bringing together data on replacement ratios, entitlement criteria and contribution records. His clusters are therefore founded upon a threefold distinction between those welfare states which are most commodified (liberalism) and most decommodified (social democracies) – with corporatism lying in-between. This work has given rise to a vast literature among which we might distinguish the following.

There are, firstly, those who have attempted to refine and/or extend Esping-Andersen's classifications. Castles and Mitchell (1992) denied that Australia was a liberal regime because while its welfare system is based heavily upon means-testing such benefits supplement a strong employment policy designed to keep pre-transfer wages high; Ferrara (1996) identified a 'southern model' of Mediterranean nations based upon the extended family and a male breadwinner model (see below). Other attempts have been made to identify a Latin model (*Social Policy & Administration*, 1997), an Eastern European model (Deacon, 2000) and an East Asian model (Goodman *et al*, 1998). The latter has been particularly utilised as a way of illustrating how the cultural differences of families and religion assist in producing economic success without the need to imitate the free market capitalism of America (Shin & Shaw, 2003). And in the Middle East certain organisations straddle the spheres of welfare, politics, international development and (sometimes) military action to an extent unfamiliar in the west (Jawad, 2002).

Among those who have made use of Esping-Andersen's typology Goodin *et al* (1999) have argued, as noted in Chapter 1, that social democracy trumps both corporatism and liberalism not only on the basis of its own principles but even on those of its rivals. In short, since it produces not only more equality but also more social cohesion than corporatist nations and greater liberty and efficiency than liberal ones, social democracy is superior no matter which criterion is applied. Hicks and Kenworthy (2003) distinguish between progressive liberal states, geared towards income redistribution and gender equality, and conservative liberal ones where employment performance suffers due to high taxes, benefits and regulation. What this does is to make liberalism more attractive and corporatism less so than in Esping-Andersen's original schema. And Jessop (2003: Ch. 2) has sought to integrate Esping-Andersen's classifications into an even more ambitious narrative that identifies a shift from one historic bloc to another. The Keynesian Welfare National State was characterised by full employment, demand management, corporatist bargaining, social rights and a mixed economy; this has now given way to a Schumpeterian Competition Postnational Regime based around market flexibility, global competition, supply-side reforms, welfare obligations (as a way of making social policy subordinate to economic policy) and privatisation. So while welfare clusters continue to exist the configuration of, say, social democracy in the new historic bloc has evolved beyond what it was in the old one.

Secondly, others have pursued more radical critiques of Esping-Andersen's approach. Of particular importance are those feminist scholars (Sainsbury, 1999) who have seen in his decommodification scale an implicit bias towards questions of production and so away from a concern with domestic reproduction. So while he recognises the family as important Esping-Andersen has been accused of downplaying the specificity of gender relations and the contributions of unpaid work and care work to social wealth and quality of life. An alternative attempt to identify 'gender regimes' has therefore been made. For Lewis (1992, 2001) these ought to be centred around the 'male breadwinner model' in which the man is the main wage-earner while the women largely stays at home. She then characterises Ireland and Britain as strong male breadwinner regimes and Sweden as a weak one. So for feminists the concept of decommodification should be either replaced or supplemented by that of 'familialisation', i.e. the extent to which the needs of women are subordinated to the needs of families through a series of public policies. Feminist critiques have themselves been subject to criticism and revision but have made an undoubted contribution to comparative research (Daly & Rake, 2003).

Finally, there are those who have sought to move away from the traditional concepts of regime theory.[2] Abrahamson (1999) accuses most welfare state typologies of focusing too heavily upon state-market relations, especially social insurance provision, and neglecting civil society institutions such as families and other associative networks. Rather than the broad brush strokes of ideal-typical models he advocates a far greater sensitivity to local context and so for the incorporation of differences rather than similarities into welfare modelling. Goodin and Rein (2001) draw a distinction between regimes and pillars. The former refers to the recipient's point of view, i.e. who gets what and why? The latter looks at the providers, i.e. who pays and who delivers? Comparative studies have collapsed the latter into the former, hence the popular association of liberalism with markets, corporatism with family and community, and social democracy with the state. But Goodin and Rein insist that regimes and pillars should be disentangled, enabling us to recognise how the two can combine in multiple ways. This implies a shift from static to dynamic models, i.e. to welfare 'blurs' rather than welfare clusters.

In addition to these critiques debates about globalisation have added another dimension. I have already dealt with globalisation in Fitzpatrick (2001a: 163–75) and in Chapter 4, but we also need to be aware of an older strand of regime theory whose reinvention it has inspired: the convergence thesis. In the 1950s it was fashionable to believe that welfare states developed in parallel with industrial modernisation so that economic development would drive all systems in the direction of the most advanced model, i.e. the British! Subsequent scholarship preferred to highlight differences between welfare states rather just than their similarities (Titmuss, 1974). Yet while most responses to Esping-Andersen have followed suit there are some who want to reinvent the convergence thesis, to see contemporary welfare states as collapsing into the market liberal model. For instance:

> ...from policies framed by a *universal* approach to *publicly delivered* benefits designed to *protect labor* [sic] against the vicissitudes of the market and firmly held as *social rights* to policies framed by a *selective* approach to *private delivery* of provisions designed to promote *labor force participation* and *individual responsibility* ... (Gilbert, 2002: 4; italics in original)

According to Gilbert the hegemony of the Scandinavian ideal has therefore given way to that of the Anglo-American 'enabling state' upon which welfare systems are gradually converging.

While the above trend is no doubt accurately described this kind of 'big picture' narrative risks equating particular changes with universal ones and so missing other, countervailing trends, e.g. Jessop (2003) also identifies historic trends but does not lose sight of key differences between regimes. Gilbert is himself ambivalent about recent developments. Both enthusiastic and worried about the effects of *laissez faire* markets he recommends the introduction of more family-friendly and public service policies. He apparently sees change as *possible* only up to the point at which he believes further change, i.e. 'back' towards the welfare state, to be *undesirable*. In particular, Gilbert passes over 'path dependent' explanations of social change.

Wilsford (1994) described path dependency as the means by which institutions and structures hem actors in by channelling them along established policy paths. It derives from the 'new institutionalist' school which analyses how the rules, conventions, habits and routines of organisations, i.e. their cultures, confine behaviour to particular tracks and explains why institutions (private and public) can be slow to reform (Rothstein & Steinmo, 2002). Yet path dependency can also be applied beyond institutions *per se* to a wider complex of conventions, practices and networks, to the dense webs of social signification and meaning (Geertz, 1973). What we can and do choose is significantly constrained by our heritage, i.e. the sum of previous choices, leading to a set of outcomes that may be sub-optimal. In Britain driving on the left seems irrational when most other countries drive on the right but it is an inherited practice (a culture) almost certainly impossible to alter. So path dependency is the insistence that 'history matters'. This does not mean that we are inevitably locked into a path due to some kind of systemic logic, just that deviation from a path is difficult and involves significant transition and opportunity costs.

Path dependency provides an answer to conservatives like Ohmae (1995) who see in the emergence of a borderless economy the death knell of welfare states (Yeates, 2001). For if history matters then globalisation is not simply going to hollow countries out. Institutions are so nationally embedded that global markets have to adapt to local characteristics and circumstances where any attempt to override local cultures will likely impel resistance by workers and consumers. Reiger and Leibfried (2003: 244–7) therefore observe that because history matters *politics* matters. More precisely, their methodology is one in which economics and politics are *culturally* framed by local particularities – which is not to imply that those frames are immutable. Put simply, cultural values and habits defy easy appropriation. So while those such as Paul Pierson (2001b) are aware of the challenges offered to social democratic welfare states by globalisation – see the description of Pierson's views in Chapter 4 – path dependency suggests that the former is more robust than its critics and some of its supporters imagine (Taylor-Gooby, 2001).

Therefore convergence theorists like Gilbert can be accused of over-generalising from the American experience. The research of Saint-Arnaud and Bernard (2003) underscores the extent to which convergence theorists miss the path dependent ways in which struggles over social inequality, as well as the interrelationships between state, market and family, produce important distinctions in the organisation of social policies. And even the industrialisation thesis of Wilensky (2002: 243–7) makes room for substantial, politically-determined differences among nineteen of the most developed welfare states.

Path dependency should by no means be accepted uncritically. Greener (2002b) criticises it for providing a passive theory of change, one in which actors must wait for the right conjunctural circumstances to break free from a given path and downplays the extent to which concerted action can work to create those very circumstances. He therefore calls for a more sophisticated rebalancing of structure and agency in explaining welfare developments. In Fitzpatrick (2003: 103–6) I have argued that path dependency over-homogenises at the level of the national, missing the extent to which national institutions and traditions are only ever the contingent, temporary effects of sub-national and trans-national struggles between competing groups, ideologies and cultures. So according to myself and Greener, path dependency gives too much prominence to cultural *constraints* and misses what I earlier termed culture's 'normative ambiguity'.

Nevertheless, path dependency is at least a reminder of the role played in social policies by cultures and because cultures are diverse then welfare states are likely to remain diverse also. More specifically, as Wilensky suggests, we need to avoid an analysis that either under- or over-differentiates. If our brush is too broad then we may over-generalise and so miss the significance of cultural specificities, but if it is too fine then we may lose ourselves in the details and be unable to design cross-national models or learn cross-national lessons. Changes in global capitalism can be identified but the impact of those changes are always going to be culturally particular. So the role played by culture demands a flexible approach to thinking and research (Chamberlayne *et al*, 1999). While we ought not to box welfare states into overlarge containers we should not rush to abandon containers altogether (Alcock & Craig, 2001). At any one time a degree of convergence and of divergence in policy developments is likely to be detectable. Its normative ambiguity also expresses the way in which culture both unifies and disperses.

Grids and Groups

Lockhart (2001) has applied the grid-group theory of Douglas (1978) and Wildavsky (1987, 1994) to social policy. This theory incorporates two dimensions of social explanation: the 'grid' axis refers to the degree to which someone does or does not accept external prescriptions, whether these be specific (an order) or backgrounded (rituals, customs); the 'group' axis refers to a person's desire for and experience of integration with others. Lockhart then derives four sectors from these dimensions. Individualists are those weak on both axes, these being people motivated by self-interest and a sense of themselves as the sovereign authors of their own fate; hierarchists are strong on both dimensions, that is they identify with a particular group while viewing social groups as arrayed in vertical layers of authority and sub-servience, superiority and inferiority. Between these extremes lie two further sectors. Fatalists are strong on grid but weak on group, i.e. a sense of constraint combines with low affiliation and so minimises the desire for collective identification and action; egalitarians are weak on grid but strong on group in that they resent external constraint and believe that it can be resisted through solidarity with others.

Lockhart characterises these sectors as the value clusters or, more grandly, as the 'cultural ontologies' that shape our perceptions and interpretations of the social environment: they are the 'subject positions' out of which our identities are formed. Few of us can be characterised in terms of one sector exclusively. Instead, they are the gravitational centres around which we circle as the trajectories of our lives and circumstances alter. Lockhart proposes that grid-group theory can fulfil the accounts left incomplete by rational choice and institutionalist models. The problem with rational choice models (Fitzpatrick, 2001a: 16–17) is that they treat preferences *ex nihilo*, as popping into existence from nowhere. They are concerned with the expression and ranking of preferences and values but not with *how* these came to be formed or why they evolve. The problem with institutionalist models (see above) is that although they may be sensitive to an institution's 'internal' culture they may be less so to the wider cultural fields which embed institutions historically and socially. Grid-group theory therefore draws attention to the processes of cultural socialisation that the above models neglect.

Hartley Dean (1999a: 18–20) has gone farther still, drawing upon grid-group theory but in conjunction with a greater range of other theories and with a more heuristic intent. Dean finds that when asked to consider issues of welfare, poverty, equality, rights and citizenship people draw upon a diverse range of moral repertoires and popular discourses in ways that are frequently unsystematic and contradictory. Dean illustrates the point that when culture is factored into social explanations the picture is far messier and less coherent than that which traditional social scientific models and taxonomies can accommodate.

Multiculturalism

Multiculturalism is both an acknowledgement of the fact of cultural plurality and a valuation of that pluralism. This apparently innocuous definition generates a vast range of questions and disagreements. What happens when one tradition or community conflicts with another? Must one of them give way? If so, on what grounds? Or can and should a synthesis between them be negotiated? But what happens when traditions and communities are incommensurable? Can they live side by side or are collisions inevitable? And how can we even recognise conflict in the first place? Is wearing a *burkha* a sign of culturally-embedded choice or of women's oppression or, somehow, both?

There are perhaps two ways of avoiding this debate, both of which involve abandoning multiculturalism. A 'perfectionist' (see Chapter 1) would insist that there is only one good life, one set of correct values and beliefs, so that multiculturalism is a misguided and possibly a dangerous dilution of the true way. The perfectionist therefore seeks a monocultural society. At the opposite extreme are those 'separatists' who believe that the fact of pluralism must be acknowledged but interaction between cultures must be kept to an absolute minimum to avoid the kind of disputes alluded to above. And while most postmodernists support cosmopolitan hybridity and cultural cross-fertilisation it is possible to imagine postmodernism shading into separatism on the grounds that because cultural differences should be valued then these are best maintained through a politics of non-intervention and non-contamination. As noted above, postmodernism shades into separatism when it views each and every form of cross-fertilisation as cultural imperialism.

The problem with perfectionism is that it overestimates the extent to which socialisation and the pursuit of the good and the true require familiarity with a disparate set of cultural contexts. The monocultural invites us to define identity very narrowly. Separatism meanwhile underestimates the extent to which cultures are already characterised by hybridity and sub-cultures of their own, preferring to see them as homogeneous entities. It might also mean that we could not intervene even in those cultures where torture and slavery are the norm.

Multiculturalism is, then, a particular problem of and for liberalism given the latter's adherence to universal values on the one hand but also to non-perfectionist procedures on the other.[3] Yet here we immediately run into a radical critique which says that liberalism is just another form of modernist imperialism where universal values are a Trojan Horse for specifically Western ways of thinking, living and acting. Western science sees itself as opening windows on to the laws of nature 'out there' in the real world but, according to its critics (Feyerabend, 1975), its mechanical, atomistic worldview represents only *one* way of understanding reality. Likewise, Bourdieu and Wacquant (1999: 42) condemn multiculturalist debates as the American-inspired attempt to present social exclusion as a problem of the 'ethnic other' rather than the effects of class warfare and state retrenchment. But assuming that a multiculturalist discourse is at least preferable to either the perfectionism or separatism criticised above I am going to assume that the questions listed earlier require some form of liberal response. But what we mean by liberalism is itself part of the multiculturalist problematic. Let's try to outline the following five important schools of thought in order to make sense of this, offering a brief critique of each.

Those such as Barry (2001) insist that multiculturalism is a superficial 'identity politics' which has nothing to offer liberalism, that the latter already makes room for difference and disagreement but within a robust framework that permits adjudication and reconciliation. Yet Barry's is an individualistic (albeit egalitarian) liberalism that dismisses the idea that we are constituted during our lives in and through the identities of cultural groupings. The later Rawls (1993) made some concessions to this criticism, believing that liberalism could not be founded upon comprehensive (metaphysical) foundations. He therefore describes a political community as *an overlapping consensus of reasonable doctrines* from which he derives a 'Law of Peoples' which would form the basis of international relations and permit liberal and nonliberal communities to come to agreement (Rawls, 1999). Yet here, too, we have what remains a substantially individualistic theory that treats the meaning of 'reasonableness' as relatively unproblematic and the cultural boundaries of liberalism as pre-determined.

If this kind of liberalism is procedurally 'thin' then Kymlicka (1995) offers a 'thick' alternative which acknowledges the density of culture. What is central to Kymlicka is autonomy since this allows him to move in two directions: towards a cultural specificity in which autonomy can assume many different forms and towards a liberal insistence that, underpinning this diversity, there must be a freedom of exit and redress for those who no longer wish to belong to a cultural community. As with Rawls, though, this arguably introduces a liberal principle that not all communities would wish to adopt. In the case of a religious order, for instance, what is important is a lifetime of commitment and devoutness rather than Kymlicka's emphasis upon autonomy and exit.

Communitarians therefore propose a much 'deeper' perspective than that proffered by liberalism *per se*, such that cultural identities are radically constitutive of who we are, how we interact and where we are going. In MacIntyre's (1981: 220–1) well known formulation we have to jettison concepts of the self that are abstracted from the particular social practices and narrative traditions out of which any coherent sense of self must be made. Yet while this treats cultural context more seriously it still leaves the problem of what to do when communities hold equally serious yet divergent and even conflictual views of what the good life involves. How does a communitarian commitment to the common good accommodate the fact that different cultures interpret this differently? Taylor (1994) bridges the gap through a 'politics of recognition' in which recognition of cultural diversity is what the common good is all about. MacIntyre's (1987: Chs 18–20) solution is to propose a discourse between traditions where those that prevail are those which can incorporate and gain from the strengths of alternative traditions. Yet while these could both be accepted as refinements of what contemporary liberals wish to say it is not clear why or whether they present alternatives to liberalism *per se* or easy solutions to the dilemmas of a multicultural society.

Postmodernists, too, bear an ambiguous relationship to liberalism. Young (1990) calls for a 'differentiated citizenship' in which social membership is tied to group membership so that individuals belong to the political community as group-specific participants rather than *qua* individuals. Citizenship

would therefore be layered with rights weighted towards the least advantaged cultural communities. However, in response to criticism that this
culturalist weighting is inadequate, because it involves displacing issues of
distribution, Young (2000: 102–8) came to accept a more familiar politics
where cultural *mis*recognition is attributed to struggles over scarce resources
(wealth, territory, jobs) so that questions of recognition, inclusion, democracy and redistribution are integral to one another (see Chapter 2 and
below).

Rorty also desires a postmodern liberalism. Rather than imagining that
multicultural problems can be resolved by finding general and indisputable
principles, Rorty (1991: 219–22) advocates a 'cosmopolitanism without
emancipation' where inter-communal tensions are resolved through a pragmatic emphasis upon mutual interests. No appeal to transcultural and ahis-
torical standards is going to prevent totalitarianism. Therefore we simply
have to learn from experience and relinquish the desire to dictate to others.
Yet Rorty's appeal to what is best in liberalism (the striving for progress; the
harm principle) is as much a product of the search for transcultural values as
what is worst in liberalism. If foundational principles have created difference-
blind institutions they have also led to a politics of social justice. So, like
MacIntyre Rorty invokes the very liberal universalism he otherwise disdains.

Finally, there are those who do not sit squarely in a single school of
thought. For instance, Parekh (2000: 109–13) criticises liberals for their
extra-cultural conception of the self and tendency to universalise what is particular to liberalism. He therefore argues that liberalism can achieve its objectives (tolerance, openness and freedom) by actually becoming less like itself;
by opening itself to otherness and becoming *more* abstract it can engage in a
truly human dialogue between cultures. However, Parekh's position relies
upon a restrictive notion of embeddedness. Because, he insists, only communal diversity is truly robust and wide-ranging multiculturalism is not concerned with differences and identities *per se* but only with those that are
culturally embedded. Yet there are surely degrees of embeddedness that
Parekh's preference for 'self-conscious, long-established and well-organised
communities' risks overlooking. Even if we accept the centrality of communal diversity the question of when a community becomes self-conscious,
long-established and well-organised is itself a question of struggle and contestation that cannot simply be deferred to the verdicts of the already established. By relying upon embeddedness Parekh perhaps underestimates the
scope and depth of cultural conflict, in which case his appeal to humanity
and generosity as *the* means of resolving multicultural disputes is naïve.

We seem to have reached an impasse. All of the above have something
going for them yet none is obviously superior. So what should we do?
Should we opt for one of the above and attempt to perfect it as much as
possible? The problem with this approach is that no theory can arguably
capture every aspect of cultural pluralism since it aims at the very closure that

pluralism exceeds. An alternative is to identify some kind of common denominator, a stage upon which all can stand even though everyone is bound to teeter off now and again.

For instance, they all agree on the importance of cross-cultural dialogue, even if they conceive this dialogue as ending in different places. For some the conversation must be threaded through a transcultural space, while for others any conversation must involve the admission that no such space is possible. Therefore, a discursive, open-ended, dialogical process which leaves such questions open is perhaps the best way of negotiating between these (Fitzpatrick, 2002a). Straddling the borders between the cultural and the transcultural is a means by which cultures can, through interaction, recognise their differences and similarities.

This means, secondly, that not every form of cultural difference is acceptable. While all cultures assess others according to certain criteria, entry into the democratic conversation depends upon the willingness to *be* assessed by those others. Such assessment is not necessarily the prelude to change but it is a means through which cultures can glimpse themselves in one another, of the commonality that underpins difference. For cultural materialists like Eagleton (2003: 164–7) this commonality is rooted in materiality, e.g. in struggles over resources and in the mortal needs of the physical body. Therefore the above theories all appear committed to fairer distributions of wealth, income, time and public goods, even though they may dispute the basis and scope of distributive justice.

Following on from this notion of a reciprocal conversation, multicultural societies are not required to tolerate those who would threaten it and so are entitled to maintain legal and military lines of defence. What happens when the gloves are off depends upon the rule of law, *realpolitik* and the principles of just war. Yet if liberal states have helped engineer a clash of civilisations (Huntington, 1995) other aspects of liberalism have offered a model of tolerance for others to follow. So although multiculturalism offers challenges to liberalism this does not mean the latter need be abandoned. Liberals have often been more effective than most in avoiding fundamentalism and finding accommodation between mainstream and minority communities.

We therefore have three elements: (a) an attempt to straddle the cultural and transcultural, (b) reference to the materiality of human life and needs, (c) the idea that a more self-aware liberalism offers a good (but not necessarily a perfect) framework for dialogue. Let's bring these points down to earth by looking at education.[4]

Multiculturalism impacts upon education debates at several points. Firstly, on teaching styles and curricula content. There are those who argue that multiculturalism is one instance of a trend that undermines education by needlessly diverting time, energy and resources towards issues of esteem and so away from questions of judgement and rigour (Phillips, 1998). This analysis accords with a conservative dislike for 'political correctness' and other fashions that are more concerned with intercultural respect than with grounding pupils in the basics (D'Souza, 1991). Secondly, there is the question of when and to what extent multiculturalism involves tolerating the intolerable. Enslin (2001) highlights the extent to which multicultural-ism can offend against the interests and rights of female pupils where the cultural differences being recognised are patriarchal and sexist (and Okin, 1999). She accuses multiculturalism of being a cover for the inability of liberal universalism to confront oppression. Finally, to what extent should the state facilitate and even underwrite cultural pluralism by, for instance, funding schools of different faiths? Don't such schools embody an exclu-sionary worldview with dividing lines between believers and non-believers? Does the state endorse pluralism by nurturing schools with a particular per-spective? If so, then does this not elevate religious faith above other types of belief, e.g. why not fund atheistic schools? Does it mean that sub-cultural factions should also be financed? Or can pluralism be best delivered through a curriculum which treats all belief-systems with respect but leaves individuals to make up their own minds by imparting the skills of critical reflection?

If we rely upon a single theory of multiculturalism then we might exclude as much as we include. A procedural individualism (Barry, Rawls) offers good grounds for teaching pupils the critical skills that they will need to decide between cultural alternatives and to value human rights. Yet, we noted above, this risks treating culture merely as an outer skin that can be painlessly shed. At the opposite extreme a postmodernist like Young might propose that because cultural difference is an important public good it should help determine the allocation of other public goods. Therefore, cultural respect has to be at the heart of the educational system. Yet too strong a focus upon group-specificity risks either locking the self into a cultural container or fracturing it internally along multiple lines of difference, where the self is conceived as a loose space of diverse containers.

By contrast, a perspective that embraces points (a)–(c) begins to suggest an alternative spin. The emphasis given to citizenship in many education systems is a more rigorous way of combining 'the basics' with a critical knowledge of social issues. Rather than regarding the esteem and identities of individuals and social groups as distinct from the learning process it can be a means by which children learn more effectively by being opened up to the needs and interests of others. This is to give citizenship studies more of a philosophical, dialogical or Socratic angle where citizenship and national identity are thought of not as rules to be obeyed but as social relations to be made and remade. This Socratic angle means always being willing to re-open the kind of questions for which culturalists and transculturalists believe that they, and only they, have the answers.

Secondly, Enslin is no doubt correct that group-sensitivity can detract from the concern with human rights. So when the identities of two disadvantaged groups collide it is tempting to appeal to a simple universalism. Yet this raises other problems, e.g. it may ignore forms of harm that are not immediately obvious. Enslin is indeed aware of this and calls for a '*critical* universalism' which is sensitive to the capabilities and functionings of individuals. But assuming that harm and oppression are related to the cultural and not only the material distribution of resources then we are entitled to revisit Fraser's distinction between those group-identities which command respect and those that do not because of their oppressive implications for others (see Chapter 2). Cultural and material distribution should therefore correct *all* oppressive practices rather than being aimed at some crude, group-blind equalisation; and rather than having to rely solely upon abstract principles we might identify oppression as that which the group performing an act would not wish reflected back on themselves. So Enslin's call is not too far away from May's (1999) support for a 'critical *multiculturalism*', i.e. a politics calling for social change rather than just recognition *per se*.

Finally, Parker-Jenkins (2002) makes the point that the great error in state funding is inconsistency, where some denominations are funded but not others – as happened with UK Muslim schools until 1998. Resolving that inconsistency by denying religious affiliation any state funding is sometimes attractive to secular humanists (like myself) but throws the baby of culture out with the bathwater of religion and might give the state less power to knit cultural communities together or to challenge faith-inspired forms of discrimination and intolerance.[5] Resolving it by funding every cultural identity that moves is to risk making purblind judgements, especially if we start chasing sub- and sub-sub-cultures down into an endless, fractal descent. One alternative is to ground all education outlets in a model which treats transcultural needs as foundational but accepts that, beyond an non-negotiable minimum, different moral systems and ethnic layers can give variable expression to those needs. The legal and funding systems would therefore create incentives and disincentives against exclusionary practices. A culturally-sensitive liberalism would arguably do this through a dialogue which, sensitive to particular contexts and occurring among different communities, is more likely to be effective than *a priori* modelling. The goose and the gander may receive the same sauce but are entitled to embellish it depending upon their different tastes.

Earlier I observed the irony of attempts to deal with cultural plurality generating as extensive a theoretical plurality. To expect a grand social theory to solve problems thrown up by the former is asking too much. Therefore, we perhaps need a more flexible approach that does not attempt to contain the uncontainable but accepts that its boundaries will *and should* continue to be breached. By emphasising the merits of cultural dialogue, material needs and resources, and a mature liberalism we gain some glimpse of what this might mean in a policy arena.

Media

In what follows we are going to concentrate upon the news media rather than mass communications *per se* for reasons of limited space. I am also avoiding the 'new media' (Internet and digital technology) since many of the relevant themes were addressed in Chapter 5.

Pluralism and criticalism

At the risk, as always, of simplification I am going to offer two main theories of the media (McQuail, 1994; Thompson, 1995).[6]

Pluralism dominates the image the British press has about itself, though it only became generally accepted within broadcasting from the 1950s. This is the idea that a diversity of media outlets reflects the openness of a free society and facilitates the flow of information and opinion upon which a liberal democracy depends. As the 'fourth estate' a free press constitutes the circuits of a free nation. So while some newspapers will certainly be owned by rich magnates there will also be room for radical opinions and newspapers that embody a different agenda.

According to Curran and Seaton (2003: Ch. 21) this broadly liberal theory sees the press as performing four roles. Firstly, it keeps the public informed of the significant events affecting their lives and so assists in the process of public education. Secondly, the press holds government and parliament to account, operating as a source of critique and opposition that counterbalances the state's tendency to centralise and conceal itself from public view. Thirdly, it is a stage upon which public debates can take place and the dialogue essential to democracy can occur. Finally, the press takes the temperature off public opinion and so captures changes to national identity over time.

There are, though, two dimensions to pluralism that need to be distinguished. Firstly, and most obviously, there is the *market* dimension of free speech and of competition between media outlets. If a free press is that which is independent of the state then it flourishes most effectively in a socioeconomic environment that is free from state interference. While at the extreme this dimension seems to recommend a libertarian free-for-all (and now a globalised one too) it is most often visible in the view held by newspapers that while the state may legitimately monitor the press, so that it can occasionally step in to prevent abuses of power, e.g. those coming from monopoly ownership, it should largely leave newspapers alone to regulate themselves.

Secondly, however, there is a *public good* dimension that resists the anything-goes tendencies of the market. In one respect this dimension articulates a public service ethos. In UK broadcasting that ethos continues to be associated with John Reith, first Managing Director of the BBC, in his belief that broadcasters should seek to educate their audience to observe higher moral and aesthetic standards than those embodied by the vulgar market. So widely held was this paternalist view that it took a long time for resistance to commercial television to break down (Weight, 2002: 240–54). Yet the clash between paternalists and anti-paternalists remains visible, certainly within broadcasting where the BBC is sometimes valued as a redoubt against the commercialised tendency to dumb-down, but also within newspapers over issues of social responsibility that flare up from time to time around the worst excesses of the tabloids. In short, paternalism has been incorporated into and rearticulated within a pluralist framework.

Pluralist theory can be criticised for a number of reasons. Most obviously, because the free market is not a level playing-field but a skewed one that provides an implicit advantage to those with the most resources and the greatest powers of mobilisation. While radical newspapers and magazines have occasionally flourished their longevity is incomparable to those sitting within the political mainstream. Moreover, rather than mirroring attitudes 'out there' in civil society newspapers and television news play a considerable role in shaping and 'mediating' public opinion through a process of filtering (Thompson, 1998). Filtering can occur either by amplifying some opinions and treating them as natural and/or by suppressing others and representing them as alien or just plain daft. In either case the media is dissimulative, obscuring the hand of editorial control in order to be regarded as a trustworthy, transparent screen. The media are not as independent of the state as they believe (the extent to which even broadsheets regurgitate government press releases is alarming) and so there is little need for state censorship when self-censorship is so prevalent. Finally, the distinction between information and entertainment has collapsed which, at its best, reflects a wider shift in politics and social relations but, at its worst, encourages a trivia-obsessed ignorance that can be marshalled for reactionary and even bigoted ends. In the end, then, pluralism may represent an ideal to strive for rather than a reality to be celebrated.

Does this mean we should prefer a criticalist theory of the media? Criticalists are those who interpret the media not as a transparent medium but as a set of conduits that reside within an ideological and hegemonic field. Newspapers and broadcast news programmes do not offer an objective, neutral perspective on 'the way things are' since they are an essential means through which the social world is constructed. The media is a construct that constructs. And in an environment of material and cultural domination the media has to be understood accordingly. As early as the 1920s commentators such as Lippmann and Niebuhr believed that in a mass society information overload and social disintegration could only be contained by a media that reduced complexity to a series of stereotypical and easily digestible simplicities, e.g. in the form of slogans and maxims that translate particular viewpoints into 'obvious' common sense (Lippmann, 1922).

Therefore, some criticalists detect authoritarian undercurrents within liberal democracies. According to the Frankfurt School (see Chapter 6), as an element of the culture industry the news media propagates the rationalistic ideology of American capitalism that saturates aesthetic traditions with commodified values and encourages a passive, atomised consumerism. By crushing human horizons onto a one-dimensional plane, philosophical critique and social change become less and less possible: the culture industry neutralises opposition by absorbing all points of resistance into itself, e.g. radical cinema, literature and music are quickly infused with the logic of the very system they set out to challenge. The culture industry negates negation. And as variety transmutes into versions of 'the same' so compliance and obedience are produced without the need for secret police and overt repression. The media identifies and demonises otherness, allowing the superiority of sameness to be endlessly reconfirmed:

> If the worker and his boss enjoy the same television programme ... if they all read the same newspaper, then this assimilation indicates not the disappearance of classes, but the extent to which the needs and satisfactions that serve the preservation of the Establishment are shared by the underlying population. (Marcuse, 1964: 8).

What the Frankfurt School does, unfortunately, is to collapse the consumption of media messages into their production, as if the latter determines the former. That the worker and his boss watch the same programme does not necessarily mean that they read it in the same way and it was this kind of flippancy which would eventually boost the popularity of postmodern critiques, as equally simplistic in their way (recall our earlier discussion of the active audience).

In the work of those such as Habermas and Chomsky we find a similar radicalism but combined with an insistence that social closure is never finalised. For Habermas (1989) the public sphere is the uncoerced home of public opinion in which sites of economic and political power are subjected to critique through interactive communication. In the coffee houses, clubs and newspapers of Enlightenment Europe the modern world achieved something approximating to the Athenian *agora* (the open spaces of the ancient *polis*): the means by which the bourgeoisie challenged aristocratic rule. Yet while rooted in a particular time and space the public sphere transcends its immediacy and expresses universal values and truths. However, the subsequent dominance of the bourgeoisie has brought with it a degradation of the public sphere; where the early media threw the light of publicity onto the nobility the mass media is less transparent, obscuring the operation of power and manipulating public opinion. Yet rather than have us remain trapped with an administrative machine Habermas leaves open the possibility of us reaching mutual understanding though communicative competence performed in a new public sphere (Habermas, 1987a: 390–1).

Chomsky (1989) has concerned himself specifically with the American press, viewing this as an adjunct of US foreign policy, manufacturing consent in order to make American acts of state terrorism appear nothing of the sort. Chomsky sees the state and press as telling a simple story. The world is divided into good and evil. We are good and so it follows that all those opposed to us are evil. Evil must therefore be contained and, if necessary, fought and eliminated. This 'wild west' story lies behind the last 60 years of US foreign policy in successive operations against communists, terrorists and insurgents. The press assists in making friendly dictatorships appear benign and hostile dictatorships appear malevolent. In the 1980s, for example, the Nicaraguan Sandanistas were successfully portrayed as terrorists while the Contras (heirs to the fascist regime the Sandanistas had overthrown) were 'freedom fighters'. Furthermore, when friendly autocrats turn unfriendly (as in the case of Noriega, Saddam Hussein and Osama Bin Laden) the press assists in masking the role originally played by American governments in creating these 'new Hitlers'. Consent is therefore manufactured by making American power synonymous with freedom and democracy. But, like Habermas, Chomsky still holds out the possibility of radical social change.

As well as representing a more optimistic politics such theorists signal an empirical turn away from the Frankfurt School's grand philosophising. The Glasgow University Media Group, for instance, exposes a bias in British television news in favour of dominant class interests (Philo, 1990). In industrial conflicts they have found that employees are regularly represented as militant while employers embody a vulnerable reasonableness, e.g. the former 'demand' while the latter 'make offers'; and the consequences of strikes are magnified while their causes are occluded. The news therefore reflects a middle-class worldview where market inequalities are natural, inevitable and desirable. This does not mean that other worldviews are entirely excluded but they are certainly shunted to the interpretative sidelines. The Glasgow Group has come in for a great deal of criticism (see Stevenson, 2002: 26–34) and the extent to which specific examples of bias can be generalised across the entire news media is unclear. Even so, the basic critique continues to be periodically confirmed, e.g. in television's portrayal of the 1984–85 UK miners' strike.

The influence of Stuart Hall (Rojek, 2002), another cultural materialist, has endured even more. For Hall the news media belongs to a wider discourse through which audiences are coded within a particular hegemonic formation. So, in the 1970s images of social breakdown were disseminated as a way of inducing moral panic and so of making authoritarian and populist conservatism more politically attractive (Hall *et al*, 1978). Street crime was subtly linked to issues of industrial unrest and (black) immigration so that they all appeared to be part of the same problem: the failure of post-war social democracy. The media is therefore an ideological agency, reproducing the power relations from which it is, nevertheless, institutionally separate. It does not brainwash or dupe but it does conjoin subjectivities to a particular construction of social reality, e.g. news does not create a fear of crime but it certainly diverts popular perceptions away from complex, structural explanations since these are harder to reduce to easily digestible segments and soundbites.

Criticalists, though, are perhaps less adept at suggesting realistic alternatives. Some degree of collective control is recommended so that the news media is detached from corporate interests but it is far from clear how this could be done. For Williams (1966) the media can be democratised by placing them under the control of public trusts which should be as decentralised and participatory as possible. Keane (1991: Chs 4 and 5) would relocate the media in civil society, distinct from both market and state, and encourage a plurality of outlets to flourish across a multiplicity of public spheres – in contrast to Habermas's (cf. 1987b) nostalgia for a single, integral public *sphere*. Curran (2002: 240–7) proposes a democratic media system consisting of a core – competing public service organisations composed of general interest channels designed for mass audiences – and peripheral sectors, including private and social market ones, that make space for dissenting and minority views. Yet while Curran can point to embryonic versions of his system even in this moderate 'third way' approach it is not clear how we are to get from here to there.

In sum, it may be that criticalist reforms would attempt to fulfil the promise of pluralist approaches rather than replacing them with something entirely alien.

Media and social policy

There are two key aspects to this relationship. Firstly, we have to understand how and why the media construct social problems and represent social policies in particular ways (Franklin, 1999a). Does public opinion transcend its media representations, which the latter can be said to articulate, or is public opinion little more than a function of the news media? Do the media fit a pluralist model of openness and neutrality or a criticalist model where the social world is constructed? Secondly, how does the media actually influence policy making? As the media and politics interpenetrate one another, so that a 'pre-media' politics becomes harder to identify, policies are usually now shaped, announced and revised through sensitivity to media environments (see Franklin, 1999b). 'Spin' becomes generalised as the distinction between policy substance and policy presentation becomes harder to discern. In what follows I am going to concentrate upon the first set of questions since the latter takes us into the realm of policy processes and so into another book for someone else to write.

Sotirovic (2000, 2003) attributes to the media the kind of cognitive distortions that we reviewed in Chapter 7, e.g. an overestimation of how much is spent on benefits. This means that while people are not parroting what they have seen in the media, the media does encourage the use of specific frames of meaning by the audience, i.e. it either expands or contracts the range of 'thinkable approaches' to social problems and policy solutions. Her research suggests that these media frames are even more important than ideology, social location and interpersonal relationships in influencing perceptions, though because frames are conflictual rather than homogeneous no one repertoire can be said to dominate. For example, by presenting news stories in a format that is more contextualised and complex than that offered by broadcast news, papers are more likely to work in support of welfare programmes; while television news has a habit of presenting poor people and criminals dramatically, as exceptional or abnormal, therefore directing attention to personal deficiencies rather than social ones. So to some extent the media may counteract the anti-welfare individualism of recent American governments.

Sotirovic's research, however, was conducted in the US where television news is driven by commercial imperatives and political timidity; nor does she review the ideological orientation of newspapers. From a European perspective, we can say with more confidence that *some* broadcast news programmes are more reliable than *some* newspapers. Yet while this indicates an even greater role for conflict within and between media frames, a greater sensitivity to ideological orientation suggests that this conflict may lean in a conservative direction nevertheless. Further research and reflection has illustrated what this might mean for social policy, as discussion of the following reveals: ethnicity, mental illness, social work and media representations of the poor (also Franklin 1999a).

Law (2002) found that there was a marked improvement in the media coverage of ethnicity between the 1980s and 90s. Where anti-racist discourse was once either ignored or mocked as a 'loony Left' agenda, it has become a predominant aspect of British news. However, this shift has occurred against a more enduring background where race is treated as biologically real, rather than a construct (Fitzpatrick, 2001a: 145–6), and presented according to implicit hierarchies of superiority and inferiority, with ethnic minorities being more frequently associated with crime, poverty and immigration. Recent improvements have therefore created an ambiguous product at best – and it should be noted that Law's research was conducted when the Stephen Lawrence case was at its height and before more recent panics about asylum seeking, terrorism and Islam.

The contributors to Philo (1996) argue that the media is dominated by negative representations of mental illness and distress. There is a tendency to associate such illness with 'madness'. This both treats the mentally ill as an alien, abnormal other and elides the extent to which many of us will experience some form of mental distress during our lives. Violence and danger is also a recurring theme despite the fact that most mental illness does not induce violence and when it does this tends to be of the self-harming sort. Even so, such images slot easily into a political culture where it sells to depict the world as threatening and risky (Eldridge, 1999) (see Chapter 8). Finally, mentally ill people are usually seen in a positive light when viewed as objects of pity. What each of these representations does is to help deny the mentally ill a voice in their condition and a say in their treatment. They open up a gap between those labelled normal and abnormal (Hannigan, 1999) so that social policies, such as community care, are infused with an ethos of security and public protection that holds this gap open and diverts both material and emotional resources away from those needing help.

Media attitudes towards social work demonstrate contradictory tendencies. On the one hand, it makes the news on those rare occasions when mistakes happen, e.g. when children are taken away from their parents by over-vigilant officials or when a child is harmed or killed having fallen through the cracks of the system (Aldridge, 1994; Ayre, 2001). Yet, on the other, the fine-tuning involved in steering a course between acting either too cautiously or not cautiously enough means that easy solutions are rarely proposed. Furthermore, Reid and Misener (2001) found that the UK press is noticeably less appreciative of social workers than that in the US, despite the fact that America is popularly conceived as a welfare laggard compared to Britain. They speculate that this is perhaps due to the sharp anti-welfare turn that occurred in Britain in the 1970s and 80s and the fact that, while America is a vast country that sometimes appears awash in crime, the UK is smaller (so crimes against children are more likely to receive a nationwide audience) and still likes to think of itself as a familial community.

Finally, from their research Bullock *et al* (2001) concluded that in the late 1990s depictions of the poor in the American media were generally sympathetic, focusing upon the difficulties faced by benefit recipients. This suggests that the media can assist antipoverty movements in influencing the political agenda. However, they also make the point that the late 1990s was a time of economic expansion when Clinton's dismantling of Roosevelt's 1935 welfare reforms was widely seen as successful (because the number of welfare recipients was falling). So even sympathetic portrayals may reflect an individualistic ethos of poverty-stricken heroes battling bravely against the odds, an image that comfortably avoids analyses of social structures, economic mismanagement, political struggles and class oppression. Moreover, Gilens (1999: 206–8) demonstrates the extent to which the US media associates the most residual, means-tested schemes with black people so that most people overestimate the numbers of black claimants; as a result the general reluctance to raise social expenditure on the poorest displays and perpetuates an implicit racism in American society.

In a British context Golding (1999) illustrates how post-1970s media obsessions with benefit scrounging and fraud have become so entrenched within the vocabulary of common sense that it is difficult to imagine them ever being fully dislodged. Along similar lines, according to Platt (1999: 113) the media (both Left and Right) veer away from complex narratives of homelessness – where a homeless person may be both culpable *and* deserving – in favour of a 'victim or villain' view of the world. This, too, involves reducing a dense and complex social problem to a simplistic storyline that can be easily swallowed. Liddiard (1999) concurs, noting how homelessness is easily pictured in stereotypical frameworks (rooflessness, begging, addiction). Advocates of welfare users, claimants and vulnerable groups may themselves promote stereotypical images as a way of eliciting public support through the media.

What does this suggest? Do the media primarily reflect social problems, policy solutions and public opinion, or construct them according to particular agendas? The pluralist model suggests that the media is largely a social mirror that enables policy-makers, practitioners, commentators and the lay public to clarify what is going on, and make appropriate decisions, but involves no more significant intervention than that. Therefore, and allowing for human fallibility, news stories reflect the reality of social problems and policies and if in their treatment of welfare they do tend towards the negative then there is no point in shooting the messenger. If the public experiences state welfare as something less than it needs, wants and feels it deserves then journalists have a duty to report this. The media's influence is ultimately minimal, e.g. they do not win elections for political parties.

The criticalist model insists that the media is less a mirror and more a portraitist that shapes and fashions perceptions and so reactions. Whereas it does not create social problems *ex nihilo* the media plays an active part in determining what is and is not defined as a problem, as well as the order in which problems are prioritised. As indicated above, this occurs through filtering and framing mechanisms in which public opinion is encouraged to resonate with some things and not others. This can be deliberate, i.e. done according to a political agenda (if schools are seen as out of control then it is easier to demand a change away from 'trendy teaching' and back to corporal punishment), or due to other factors, e.g. a human interest approach makes reports more interesting, albeit at the expense of deeper, more structural analyses. Though the media's influence is not always strong immediately – as in the case of elections – over the long-term it wields a considerable influence over political climates.

Another possibility is that the above distinctions (reflect/construct, pluralism/criticalism) are rather overdrawn because the relationship between media and welfare cannot be unambiguously one thing or another. If the pluralist model *per se* is rather naïve, and assuming that we do not want to regard (with the Frankfurt School) the media merely as the conduit of dominant ideas and values then, like Sotirovic, we are led to suspect that the media operates and is operated upon in terms of conflicting and ambivalent frames that nevertheless carry ideological implications. So while voices and viewpoints are not equally present, all may *potentially become* present depending upon the wider social context. There have always been and always will be those opposed to state welfare but enough evidence to suggest that such movements can be counterbalanced during propitious circumstances. For instance, Curran and Seaton (2003: 63–5) note how wartime rationing freed newspapers from reliance upon advertising and so encouraged the kind of radical outlets and opinions through which intellectual support for post-war reform could be mobilised. Therefore, the media audience not only reinterprets the message but is capable of mobilising alternative messages and of helping to bring those propitious circumstances into being. So if media representations of the social policy field are ambivalent at best and negative at worst this is not because the media is essentially this or that, but because of much broader socio-political developments during which progressives have recently lost influence.

An either/or analysis is dated and misleading, therefore. Problems, solutions and opinions neither precede the media nor trail them. The media is neither cause nor effect but enmeshed within a social loop in which it amplifies and influences the partial pictures it receives from elsewhere. This is another way of saying that rather than being either dupes or sovereign cultural producers we conspire in the distortions through which we are able to perceive, communicate and interact. Yet although the media is integral to the social field this does not mean that we are always internal to it, unable to achieve a critical distance (see Chapter 5). It is precisely the proliferation of ambivalent frames that makes critique necessary (since surely some frames can be identified as more accurate than others) and possible (since critique proceeds through a comparison of contrasting perspectives). This is what enables us to regard the social/media field as leaning in a conservative direction while being susceptible to progressive challenge and occasional reformation. So in the recent political environment, what is remarkable is not that people dislike state welfare *because* of the media but that they continue to support it *despite* much of the media.

Concluding Thoughts

This long chapter has attempted to track a diverse array of debates and research that are ongoing in the field of cultural and media studies. As with many of the subjects reviewed in this book we have seen the relevance of social policy and welfare systems to them, but also noted how difficult it is to apply a single theoretical framework or imagine a research programme inclusive enough to do all the work that needs to be done. A pessimistic conclusion would therefore be that many of the above debates will continue at the margins of welfare studies with cultural and media issues making relatively few impacts upon the discipline's mainstream. Yet the huge amount of thought and analysis that is occurring also suggests that alternative spaces dwell beyond the orthodoxies that often dominate discussions in politics and mainstream media outlets. What they impact they make, whether upon academic work or policy-making, is therefore indeterminate, depending greatly where we want our societies to take us.

I have therefore felt justified in continuing with the ideological theme of this book and its predecessor, for it is in applying an ideological orientation that we can identify what is important: the agreements and disagreements, the similarities and differences, the points in society at which stability is required and achievements need to be consolidated, but also those where further change is possible and certainly desirable. The social field is never fully open, nor never fully closed.

Conclusion

Rather than a standard summary of previous chapters I want to conclude by drawing your attention to the main themes of the book and their implications for social policy.

As anticipated in the Introduction, the distinction between matter and culture has been one recurring theme. Sometimes this has been fairly prominent (as in Chapters 2 and 9) and sometimes less so. In Chapter 7, for example, I explored three areas that could be said to lie at the interface of matter and culture. Our psychologies, emotions and bodies are variously matter-dependent yet also framed within sociocultural contexts. And in Chapter 8 I observed that crime and surveillance are not only questions about the manipulation of bodies in space, e.g. via incarceration, but also of how people perceive themselves and others, and why they desire certain mediums of interaction, e.g. of security rather than solidarity. There are two aspects to these kinds of matter/culture distinctions that I now want to say a bit more about: the ontological and the political.

The ontological debate occupies those who do and do not believe that self and society can be explained ultimately in materialist terms. There are many different types of materialist explanation, and this book never intended to review them all, but in Chapter 6 I did draw attention to debates among geneticists regarding the role played by genes in human affairs. I proposed that while the differences between genetic and organic Darwinists are really degrees of emphasis, the former offer a less rounded account since they wish ultimately to describe our contemporary social environment in the language of genes. Culture is portrayed as being held on a leash with the 'meme' as the links in the chain. Yet it is perfectly possible to attribute human evolution to the evolution of genetic matter while distinguishing between the early stages of human development, when the leash was stronger, and the later stages, when it begins to unravel. The organic Darwinists are therefore more subtle in their belief that our sociocultural environments require explanations that recognise the distinctness of their structures, regularities, conventions and self-images. This view is consistent with the kind of cultural materialism defended in Chapter 9 where culture and nature are regarded as mutually irreducible (Eagleton, 2000).

But nor should we swing to the opposing extreme and view everything as cultural. This is a view that can be attributed to some (but not necessarily all) postmodernists and communitarians. In Chapter 9 I reviewed the ideas of those such as Rorty for whom cultural context is everything. The basic argument seems to be that nothing can exist without being named because it is naming that makes something present to us; even the most imaginary object, being or event must signify at some level. Reality may or may not *precede* language but it cannot be apprehended by us unless it is appropriated by and named *from within* language. And since culture is that through which naming is performed then everything must be saturated with cultural signification. The problem is that this is to treat matter as, at best, a moment of culture or, at worst, as a cultural effect or epiphenomenon. If the world is filled with nothing but culture, if there are no material determinants, then we are left without a foothold or a means of perceiving the whole. And if we are always inside, because there is no outside to attain (see Chapter 5), then any representation of it is ultimately as worthwhile as any other.

If, then, our task ought to involve a more rigorous balancing out of the material and cultural then this leads us towards the political aspect of the distinction. The Left has straddled both sides. Historical materialism is the most obvious expression of a materialist critique, where the cultural is one of a number of elements within the superstructure. Yet others on the Left have made culture more central. Some have appropriated religious themes in their call for human solidarity, and others (some strong constructionists) have thought that cultural change is the key to reconfiguring the social world. The Right have also jumped back and forth across the fence. For instance, some have adopted a strain of Hobbesian materialism where life is interpreted as the blind interaction of matter in motion, leading to a pessimistic view of human nature and society such that strong constraints are required to prevent the worst features of human being from breaking free. But culture has also been important for the Right, whether thought of as a set of behaviours, values and motivations, or as a hierarchy of higher and lower forms that reflects the aristocratic ordering of humanity.

Recent debates have also sought ways of relating matter and culture together, though where this is taking us is uncertain. In Chapter 2 I noted the insistence of Honneth and Young that the cultural and material are so entwined that we perhaps need a new vocabulary capable of overcoming dichotomised approaches. For Fraser, by contrast, we need a vocabulary which is capable of speaking in different languages depending upon the type of analysis needed at any one time. In social policy contemporary theoretical debates might be characterised as another series of endeavours to relate culture and matter together more satisfactorily than in the past, followed by inevitable disagreements between the protagonists over which is the most persuasive.

Among conservatives Murray is one of those who has zigzagged in this direction. As we saw in Chapter 1 he has attempted to incorporate rational choice arguments, focusing upon the decisions people deliberately make to the monetary incentives and disincentives available to them, with other arguments that draw attention to what he sees as cultural, pre-rational dependencies. Murray's success (or otherwise) in weaving these strands together is less important than his attempt to do so. In Chapter 3 I mentioned those who believe that conservatives are ahead of the game in this respect, that the Left has been too obsessed with structural explanations and with the redistribution of income and wealth, necessitating greater attention in the future to questions of agency (behaviour, values, motivations) and, by implication, culture. Redistribution should therefore involve both material and cultural reform. In Chapters 3 and 4 I explored various reasons why this narrative might mislead, not least of which is because it relies upon a one-sided reading of what the Left has been and is still trying to do. In addition to the above it is therefore possible to identify a series of new radicalist ideas that agree on the importance of balancing the material and cultural, even if (as Chapter 2 acknowledged) they do not presently add up to as coherent a programme as that of their opponents.

If the theoretical agenda for social policy therefore consists of debates over how best to balance the material and cultural (born of the unshakable, if not always fair, sense that past debates have been inadequate in this respect) then we have some decisions to make. What kind of balance is appropriate, both ontologically and politically, and what kind of policy reforms would it inspire? This returns us to the book's second theme, as discussed in the Introduction. An ideological approach is not the only method that can be applied (and I am still willing to be persuaded that it is not the best one), but it remains a useful means of making sense of a vast range of ideas, critiques and frameworks. The agenda for this century is therefore the same as the traditional one, yet is also profoundly original. It consists of tracking the movements of old adversaries across new battlegrounds, of acknowledging that new maps are always drawn as improvements of old maps, that even social earthquakes do not destroy landscapes entirely, and of realising that the future is written not just by the winners of political struggles but by *all* the participants.

This book ends, and starts, at that realisation.

Notes

Introduction

1. In Chapter 6 I argue why it is social circumstances to which we should give most attention, rather than genetic ones.

Chapter 1

1. Although this outrage at what it perceives as cultural nihilism may of course be a feigned means of perpetuating the political war on other frontiers.
2. Or what we will simply call 'conservatism' for convenience. Note that this terminology differs from what was used in *Welfare Theory*.
3. But note that I will nowhere be discussing the far Right.
4. I am not going to discuss Christian Democracy (van Kersbergen, 1995) because this links to the social conservatism already sketched in Fitzpatrick (2001a: 126–7).
5. This has become the 'big idea' of the American Right. Its intellectual godfathers are Leo Strauss and Irving Kristol. The latter is married to Gertrude Himmelfarb and their son, William Kristol, has a considerable influence upon recent Republican thinking, including its foreign policy.
6. Note that some conservatives take liberalism to mean a kind of Left-leaning social democracy while for others, like Strauss, it denotes the whole tradition of individualistic rights and liberties.
7. D'Souza (2000: 128, 233) is another erstwhile neoconservative which we can see if we combine 'most people who are well off today weren't born to their money; they earned it' with 'poor people are far more likely than rich people to perpetrate certain social atrocities.'

Chapter 2

1. See various arguments in the next chapter also.
2. In fact, I am sure this is true of all principles but let that pass.
3. Though the idea originated in the 1930s (Fitzpatrick, 1999a: 137–50).
4. And see the discussion of stakeholding in the next chapter.

5. Alternatively, it could require a complete redistribution of talents, or internal goods, but this hints at the kind of bodily and psychological reengineering that the Right regard as the inevitable consequence of egalitarianism.

6. I will make occasional use of this metaphor of the 'cut', since it occurs within the literature. It is misleading, however, in implying that there is a determinate line at which choice succeeds circumstance. In truth this 'line' is very fuzzy and we ought to talk of how circumstance and choice meld and shade into one another. In balancing them this would mean weighing probabilities rather than quantifying certainties, a difference that might bear considerable implications for redistributive policies.

7. For simplicity's sake I am ignoring the philanthropic role played by tobacco companies in all of this.

8. For conservatives similar logical absurdities derive from any attempt to maximise the position of the least well-off and so are used to condemn the Left in general.

9. This of course begs the question of what an egalitarian system of law would look like, especially during the transition to a more equal state of affairs. I assume it would be proceduralist, constitutionally-grounded and non-arbitrary while possessing a greater remit vis-à-vis property rights.

10. You can blame these on myself and not Parfit.

11. One reason why Arneson prefers priority to sufficiency is because the latter defines 'enough' with reference to subjectivist feelings of well-being.

12. Following the lead of Rawls (1993) John Gray insists that ontological liberalism (the search for ultimate foundations) must give way to political liberalism (the search for a liveable consensus) in the face of a liberal tradition which conflates the two, though he also seems to be rather attached to Christianity.

13. I should note that I prefer a cultural/material distinction to Fraser's for a cultural/economic one. This is because I think we need to attend to environmentalist, technological and genetic debates that while allied to 'the economic' cannot be fully contained within it. This begs the question of how to relate the material to the economic, and both to the cultural. See the conclusions to this chapter and the book for how I play my get-out-of-jail card.

Chapter 3

1. And, yes, I am aware that some workfare schemes are more benign and developmental.

2. We will have more to say about risks in the next chapter.

3. Note that this is a philosophical take on the subject. For a sociological angle, see Fitzpatrick (2001a: 103–114).

4. And note that while some interesting work on this issue has been published within the social movement literature it is better dealt with in the relevant sections of future editions of *Welfare Theory*, as indicated above in the introductory chapter.

Chapter 4

1. Note that I will talk of insecurity rather than risk because the latter is associated with a particular debate that has been reviewed in Fitzpatrick (2001a: 187–9) and

because I think we need a wider frame of reference. However, some aspects of this debate are inevitably touched upon in what follows.

2. Though my argument is not that this trajectory is deterministic and inevitable.

3. For a lengthier treatment of globalisation see Fitzpatrick (2001a: 163–75).

4. While job tenure may not have declined in recent years as sharply as alarmists originally predicted the growth of job insecurity is not necessarily based upon delusions since the growth in unemployment, short-term contracts, 'permatemps', overwork and the ideology of flexibility (where employers are often defined as disposable commodities) is real enough.

Chapter 5

1. Note that this chapter leads on from many of the themes in Fitzpatrick (2001a: Ch. 9).

2. To my knowledge Bauman has not given any extended discussion to information and ICTs but we can certainly infer his general position from what he says elsewhere.

3. I am ignoring the question of how and to what extent interstate forms of governance are altering the configurations of regimes.

4. I have been advised that devolution within the UK means I am over-simplifying.

Chapter 6

1. Of course, this begs the question as to whether social constructionist arguments can be characterised as 'blank state' ones in the first place.

2. We might also note some of the offensive remarks of James Watson, co-discoverer of the double helix, to the effect that mothers should have the right to terminate foetuses if a predisposition for homosexuality could be shown (cited in Kerr & Shakespeare, 2002: 99).

3. It may also mean that the demand for counselling could rise leading to difficult decisions on who is to pay for this and when.

Chapter 7

1. A game the disadvantaged also play by identifying those at an even lower altitude than themselves: the hierarchy of desert is still maintained by constructing groups who are subordinate, i.e. less worthy, to oneself.

2. Though 'reason' may also be substituted by 'faith' in this quotation, especially given Hume's atheism.

3. Though the very language of codes, programmes and systems indicates that the genetic body is also a metaphorical body which is precisely why some are critical of genetic Darwinism: that it confuses metaphor for nature.

4. The last point captures the ways in which the body becomes both software and hardware for various technologies, such as genetic modification and ICTs that, in

turn, assume the 'fuzzy' qualities of adaptability and reprogrammability that have been associated with humans (Featherstone & Burrows, 1995).
5. As a familiar example think of how people learn to swim or to drive by disciplining their bodies to perform in a certain way without the conscious mind having to give much direction.

Chapter 8

1. Though many years ago I remember walking down a street and seeing a poster which proclaimed that 'violence against women was violence against the working class'.

Chapter 9

1. Given twentieth century developments in Marxist theory there is in truth no fixed line dividing Marxist critiques from those of cultural materialism.
2. In addition to the following see the argument about decommodification towards the end of Chapter 1.
3. Note that by liberalism I here mean the philosophical attachment to pluralism and toleration, and not support for *laissez faire* economics.
4. Though multiculturalism bears implications for a much wider range of welfare systems, obviously.
5. The question I am not addressing here concerns religious discrimination. Is there religious discrimination distinct from racial or ethnic discrimination? Would legislating for it be one step to a blasphemy law? Upon what basis might liberal multiculturalists defend cultural pluralism while allowing religious belief – essential to some people's sense of identity – to be challanged?
6. I am leaving functionalist theories largely to one side as they no longer appear to be influential, though see Luhmann's (2000) systems theoretical approach.

References

Abrahamson, P. (1999) 'The Welfare Modelling Business', *Social Policy and Administration*, 33(4): 394–415.

Ackerman, B. & Alstott, A. (1999) *The Stakeholder Society*, Yale: Yale University Press.

Adam, B. (1990) *Time and Social Theory*, Cambridge: Polity.

Adam, B. (1996) *Timewatch*, Cambridge: Polity.

Adam, B. (1998) 'Values in the Cultural Timespaces of Science', in Lash, S., Quick, A. & Roberts, R. (eds) *Time and Value*, Oxford: Blackwell.

Adams, J. (1995) *Risk*, London: UCL Press.

Alcock, P. & Craig, G. (eds) (2001) *International Social Policy*, London: Palgrave.

Alcock, P., Glennerster, H., Oakley, A. & Sinfield, A. (eds) (2001) *Welfare and Wellbeing: Richard Titmuss's Contribution to Social Policy*, Bristol: Policy Press.

Aldridge, M. (1994) *Making Social Work News*, London: Routledge.

Alldred, P. (1999) 'Not Making a Virtue of a Necessity: Nancy Fraser on Postsocialist Politics', in Jordan, T. & Lent, A. (eds) *Storming the Millennium*, London: Lawrence & Wishart.

Althusser, L. (1969) *For Marx*, London: Allen Lane.

Anderson, P. (1998) *The Origins of Postmodernity*, London: Verso.

Anderson, E. (1999) 'What is the Point of Equality?', *Ethics*, 109(2): 287–337.

Andrews, D. (1997) 'Gen-Etiquette: Genetic Information, Family Relationships, and Adoption', in Rothstein, M. (ed.) *Genetic Secrets*, New Haven & London: Yale University Press.

Andrews, L. (2001) *Future Perfect*, New York: Columbia University Press.

Andrews, L. & Nelkin, D. (2001) *Body Bazaar*, New York: Crown Publishers.

Archer, M. (1995) *Culture and Agency*, London: Routledge.

Arneson, R. (1989) 'Equality and Equal Opportunity for Welfare', *Philosophical Studies*, 56: 77–93.

Arneson, R. (2002) 'Why Justice Requires Transfers to Offset Income and Wealth Inequalities', *Philosophy & Social Policy*, 19(1): 172–200.

Association of British Insurers (1997) *Policy Statement on Life Insurance and Genetics*, London: ABI.

Augoustinos, M. & Reynolds, K. (2001) *Understanding Prejudice, Racism and Social Conflict*, London: Sage.

Axelrod, R. (1984) *The Evolution of Cooperation*, New York: Basic Books.

Ayre, P. (2001) 'Child Protection and the Media: Lessons from the Last Three Decades', *British Journal of Social Work*, 31(6): 887–901.

Bacchi, C. & Beasley, C. (2002) 'Citizen Bodies: Is Embodied Citizenship a Contradiction in Terms?', *Critical Social Policy*, 22(2): 324–352.

Baldock, J. (1999) 'Culture: The Missing Variable in Understanding Social Policy?', *Social Policy & Administration*, 33(4): 458–73.

Ball, M. (2000) 'The visual availability and local organisation of public surveillance systems: the promotion of social order in public space', *Sociological Research Online*, Vol. 5, No. 1.

Bane, M. & Ellwood, D. (1996) *Welfare Realities*, Cambridge, MA: Harvard University Press.

Barbalet, J. M. (1998) *Emotion, Social Theory and Social Structure*, Cambridge: Cambridge University Press.

Barbalet, J. M. (ed.) (2002) *Emotions and Sociology*, Oxford: Blackwell.

Barro, R. (1997) *Getting it Right*, Massachusetts, CA: MIT Press.

Barry, B. (2001) *Culture and Equality*, Cambridge: Polity.

Barry, N. (2003) 'Some Feasible Alternatives to Conventional Capitalism', *Social Philosophy & Policy*, 20(1): 178–203.

Bauman, Z. (1997) *Postmodernity and Its Discontents*, Cambridge: Polity.

Bauman, Z. (1998a) *Work, Consumerism and the New Poor*, Milton Keynes: Open University Press.

Bauman, Z. (1998b) *Globalization*, Cambridge: Polity.

Bauman, Z. (1999) *In Search of Politics*, Cambridge: Polity.

Bauman, Z. (2000a) *Liquid Modernity*, Cambridge: Polity.

Bauman, Z. (2000b) *Community*, Cambridge: Polity.

Bauman, Z. (2000c) 'Social Issues of Law and Order', *British Journal of Criminology*, 40: 205–21.

Beck, U. (1992) *Risk Society*, London: Sage.

Beck, U. (1995) *Ecological Politics in an Age of Risk*, Cambridge: Polity.

Beck, U. (2000) *The Brave New World of Work*, Cambridge: Polity.

Beck, U., Giddens, T. & Lash, S. (1994) *Reflexive Modernisation*, Cambridge: Polity.

Beck, U. & Beck-Gernsheim, E. (2002) *Individualisation*, London: Sage.

Beckett, K. & Western, B. (2001) 'Governing Social Marginality', *Punishment and Society*, 3(1): 43–60.

Benhabib, S. (1992) *Situating the Self*, Cambridge: Polity.

Beresford, P. (2002) 'Thinking about "Mental Health": Towards a Social Model', *Journal of Mental Health*, 11(6): 581–584.

Berman, M. (1982) *All That Is Solid Melts Into Air*, London: Verso.

Berry, J. (2001) 'A Psychology of Immigration', *Journal of Social Issues*, 57(3): 615–31.

Blackman, L. & Walkerdine, V. (2001) *Mass Hysteria*, London: Palgrave.

Blackmore, S. (1999) *The Meme Machine*, Oxford: Oxford University Press.

Blair, T. (1994) *Speech to the Labour Party Annual Conference*.

Blair, T. (2002) 'My Vision for Britain', *The Observer*, November 10.

BMA (1998) *Human Genetics*, Oxford: Oxford University Press.

Bobbio, N. (1996) *Left and Right*, Cambridge: Polity.

Bogard, W. (1996) *The Simulation of Surveillance*, London: Sage.

Boron, A. (2005) *'Empire' and Imperialism*, London: Zed Books.

Bourdieu, P. (1984) *Distinction*, London: Routledge.

Bourdieu, P. & Passeron, J-C. (1990) *Reproduction in Society, Education and Culture*, 2nd ed., London: Sage.

Bourdieu, P. & Wacquant, L. (1999) 'On the Cunning of Imperialist Reason', *Theory, Culture & Society*, 16(1): 41–58.

Boutellier, H. (2001) 'The Convergence of Social Policy and Criminal Justice', *European Journal on Criminal Policy and Research*, 9: 361–80.

Bowles, S. & Gintis, H. (1998) *Recasting Egalitarianism*, London: Verso.

Bowring, F. (2003) *Science, Seeds and Cyborgs*, London: Verso.

Boyne, R. (2000) 'Post-Panopticism', *Economy and Society*, 29(2): 285–307.

Braithwaite, J. (1989) *Crime, Shame and Reintegration*, Cambridge: Cambridge University Press.

Broberg, G. & Roll-Hansen, N. (1996) *Eugenics and the Welfare State*, Michigan: Michigan State University Press.

Brown, R. (2000) *Group Processes*, 2nd ed., Oxford: Blackwell.

Brown, P. & Lauder, H. (2001) *Capitalism and Social Progress*, London: Palgrave.

Buchanan, A., Brock, D., Daniels, N. & Wikler, D. (2000) *From Chance to Choice*, Cambridge: Cambridge University Press.

Bullock, H. E., Fraser, K. & Williams, W. R. (2001) 'Media Images of the Poor', *Journal of Social Issues*, 57(2): 229–246.

Burbules, N. C. & Callister, T. A. (1999) 'The Risky Promises and Promising Risks of New Information Technologies for Education', *Bulletin of Science, Technology and Society*, 19(2): 105–12.

Burke, E. (1968) *Reflections on the Revolution in France*, Middlesex: Penguin.

Burleigh, M. (2000) *The Third Reich*, London: Pan.

Burns, D., Williams, C. & Windebank, J. (2003) *Community Self Help*, London: Palgrave.

Butler, J. (1990) *Gender Trouble*, London: Routledge.

Callinicos, A. (1994) *Against Postmodernism*, New York: St. Martin's Press.

Callinicos, A. (2000) *Equality*, Cambridge: Polity.

Carlen, P. (ed.) (2002) *Women and Punishment*, Cullompton: Willan Publishing.

Carmichael, F. & Ward, R. (2001) 'Male Unemployment and Crime in England and Wales', *Economics Letters*, 73: 111–5.

Carens, J. (2003) 'An Interpretation and Defence of the Socialist Principle of Distribution', *Social Philosophy & Policy*, 20(1): 145–77.

Carrington, K. (2002) 'Feminism and Critical Criminology: Confronting Genealogies', in Carrington, K. & Hogg, R. (eds) *Critical Criminology*, Cullompton: Willan Publishing.

Carrington, K. & Hogg, R. (eds) (2002) *Critical Criminology*, Cullompton: Willan Publishing.

Castells, M. (1996) *The Rise of the Network Society*, Oxford: Blackwell.

Castells, M. (1997) *The Power of Identity*, Oxford: Blackwell.

Castells, M. (1998) *The End of Millennium*, Oxford: Blackwell.

Castells, M. (2000) 'The Contours of the Network Society', *Foresight*, 2(2): 151–57.

Castells, M. (2001) *The Internet Galaxy*, Oxford: Oxford University Press.

Castells, M. & Himanen, P. (2002) *The Information Society and the Welfare State*, Oxford: Oxford University Press.

Castles, F. and Mitchell, D. (1992) *Three Worlds of Welfare or Four?*, Discussion Paper, Australian National University.

Chamberlayne, P., Cooper, A., Freeman, R. & Rustin, M. (eds) (1999) *Welfare and Culture in Europe*, London: Jessica Kingsley Publishers.

Choi, Y-B. (2002) 'Misunderstanding Distribution', *Social Philosophy and Policy*, 19(1): 110–39.

Chomsky, N. (1989) *Necessary Illusions*, London: Pluto Press.

Christie, N. (2000) *Crime Control as Industry*, 3rd ed., London: Routledge.

Clarke, J. (2004) *Changing Welfare, Changing States*, London: Sage.

Clarke, J., Gewirtz, S. & McLaughlin, E. (eds) (2000) *New Managerialism, New Welfare*, London: Sage.

Clarke, J. & Newman, J. (1997) *The Managerial State*, London: Sage.

Cohen, G. A. (1995) *Self-Ownership, Freedom and Equality*, Cambridge: Cambridge University Press.

Cohen, G. A. (2000) *If You're an Egalitarian, How Come You're So Rich?*, Cambridge, Mass: Harvard University Press.

Cohen, S. (1985) *Visions of Social Control*, Cambridge: Polity Press.

Coleman, R. & Sim, J. (2000) '"You'll Never Walk Alone": CCTV Surveillance, Order and Neo-Liberal Rule in Liverpool City Centre', *British Journal of Sociology*, 51(4): 623–640.

Commission on Social Justice (1994) *Social Justice*, London: Vintage.

Cook, D. (1989) *Rich Law, Poor Law*, Milton Keynes: Open University Press.

Cook, D. (1997) *Poverty, Crime and Punishment*, London: CPAG.

Cronin, H. (1991) *The Ant and the Peacock*, Cambridge: Cambridge University Press.

Cullen, R. (2003) 'The Digital Divide: a Global and National Call to Action', *The Electronic Library*, 21(3): 247–257.

Culpitt, I. (1999) *Social Policy and Risk*, London: Sage.

Curran, J. (2002) *Media and Power*, London: Routledge.

Curran, J. & Seaton, J. (2003) *Power Without Responsibility*, 6th ed., London: Routledge.

Currie, E. (1998) *Crime and Punishment in America*, New York: Metropolitan Books.

D'Souza, D. (1991) *Liberal Education*, New York: Vintage Books.

D'Souza, D. (2000) *The Virtue of Prosperity*, New York: Free Press.

Dagger, R. (1997) *Civic Virtues*, Oxford: Oxford University Press.

Daly, M. (2003) 'Governance and Social Policy', *Journal of Social Policy*, 32(1): 113–28.

Daly, M. & Rake, K. (2003) *Gender and the Welfare State*, Cambridge: Polity.

Davis, M. (1990) *City of Quartz*, London: Verso.

Davis, M. (1998) *Ecology of Fear*, New York: Metropolitan Books.

Dawkins, R. (1976) *The Selfish Gene*, Oxford: Oxford University Press.

Dawkins, R. (1982) *The Extended Phenotype*, Oxford: W. H. Freeman.

Dawkins, R. (1996) *Climbing Mount Improbable*, Middlesex: Penguin.

Dawkins, R. (1999) 'Foreword', in Burley, J. (ed.) *The Genetic Revolution and Human Rights*, Oxford: Oxford University Press.

Deacon, A. (2002) *Perspectives on Welfare*, Milton Keynes: Open University Press.

Deacon, A. & Mann, K. (1999) 'Agency, Modernity and Social Policy', *Journal of Social Policy*, 28(3): 413–35.

Deacon, B. (2000) 'Eastern European Welfare States: The Impact of the Politics of Globalization', *Journal of European Social Policy*, 10(2): 146–161.

Dean, H. (1999a) *Poverty, Riches and Social Citizenship*, London: Macmillan.

Dean, H. (1999b) 'Bodily Metaphors and Conceptions of Social Justice', in Ellis, K. & Dean, H. (1999) *Social Policy and the Body*, London: Macmillan.

Dean, H. & Taylor-Gooby, P. (1992) *Dependency Culture*, Hemel Hempstead: Harvester Wheatsheaf.

Dean, M. (1999) *Governmentality*, London: Sage.

Dean, M. (2002) 'Liberal Government and Authoritarianism', *Economy & Society*, 31(1): 37–61.

Dean, M. (2003) *Governing Society*, London: Sage.

Dennett, D. (1996) *Darwin's Dangerous Idea*, Middlesex: Penguin.

Dennis, N. (ed.) (1997) *Zero-Tolerance*, London: IEA.

Derrida, J. (1994) *Spectres of Marx*, London: Verso.

Detmer, D. (2000) 'Counterpoint. Your Privacy or Your Health', *International Journal for Quality in Health Care*, 12(1): 1–3.

Dobson, A. (2003) *Citizenship and the Environment*, Oxford: Oxford University Press.

Douglas, M. & Wildavsky, A. (1983) *Risk and Culture*, California: University of California Press.

Douglas, M. (1978) *Cultural Bias*, London: Royal Anthropological Society.

Dowding, K., De Wispelaere, J. & White, S. (2003) 'Stakeholding – a New Paradigm in Social Policy?', in Dowding, K., De Wispelaere, J. & White, S. (eds) *The Ethics of Stakeholding*, London: Palgrave.

Downing, K. (2001) 'Information Technology, Education and Health Care', *Educational Studies*, 27(3): 229–235.

Dreyfus, H. (2001) *On the Internet*, London: Routledge.

Driver, S. & Martell, L. (2002) *Blair's Britain*, Cambridge: Polity.

Drury, S. (1997) *Leo Strauss and the American Right*, Basingstoke: Macmillan.

Duckitt, J. (2000) 'Culture, Personality and Prejudice', in Renshon, S. & Duckitt, J. (eds) *Political Psychology*, London: Macmillan.

Durham. M. (2000) *The Christian Right*, Manchester: Manchester University Press.

Duster, T. (1990) *Backdoor to Eugenics*, London: Routledge.

Dutton, B. (1996) *Information and Communication Technologies*, Oxford: Oxford University Press.

Dworkin, R. (2000) *Sovereign Virtue*, Cambridge, MA: Harvard University Press.

Dwyer, P. (2000) *Welfare Rights and Responsibilities*, Bristol: Policy Press.

Dyer-Witheford, N. (1999) *Cyber-Marx*, Urbana and Chicago: University of Illinois Press.

Eagleton, T. (1996) *The Illusions of Postmodernism*, Oxford: Blackwell.

Eagleton, T. (2000) *The Idea of Culture*, Oxford: Blackwell.

Eagleton, T. (2003) *After Theory*, London: Allen Lane.

Eatwell, R. & O'Sullivan, N. (eds) (1989) *The Nature of the Right*, London: Pinter.

Edwards, R. & Glover, J. (eds) (2001) *Risk and Citizenship*, London: Routledge.

Eldridge, J. (1999) 'Risk, Society and the Media: Now You See It, Now You Don't', in Philo, G. (ed.) *Message Received*, London: Longman.

Ellis, K. & Dean, H. (eds) (1999) *Social Policy and the Body*, London: Macmillan.

Ellison, N. (2000) 'Proactive and Defensive Engagement: Social Citizenship in a Changing Public Sphere', *Sociological Research Online*, 5(3).

Elster, J. (1985) *Making Sense of Marx*, Cambridge: Cambridge University Press.

Elster, J. (1999a) *Alchemies of the Mind*, Cambridge: Cambridge University Press.

Elster, J. (1999b) *Strong Feelings*, Cambridge, MA: MIT Press.

End Child Poverty (2003) *Child Poverty and Education*, briefing paper, London: End Child Poverty Group.

Enslin, P. (2001) 'Multicultural Education, Gender and Social Justice: Liberal Feminist Misgivings', *International Journal of Educational Research*, 35(3): 281–92.

Ericson, R. & Haggerty, K. (1997) *Policing the Risk Society*, Oxford: Clarendon.

Esping-Andersen, G. (1990) *The Three Worlds of Welfare Capitalism*, London: Sage.

Esping-Andersen, G. (1999) *Social Foundations of Post-Industrial Economies*, Cambridge: Cambridge University Press.

Esping-Andersen, G. (2000) 'Notes and Issues: Interview on Postindustrialism and the future of the Welfare State', *Work, Employment & Society*, 14(4): 757–69.

Esping-Andersen, G. (2002) *Why We Need a New Welfare State*, Oxford: Oxford University Press.

Etzioni, A. (1994) *The Politics of Community*, London: Fontana.

Etzioni, A. (1999) *The Limits of Privacy*, New York: Basic Books.

Evans, M. & Cerny, P. (2003) 'Globalisation and Social Policy', in Ellison, N. & Pierson, C. (eds) *Developments in Social Policy 2*, London: Palgrave.

Fairclough, N. (1999) *New Labour, New Language*, London: Routledge.

Faludi, S. (1992) *Backlash*, London: Vintage.

Faludi, S. (1999) *Stiffed*, London: Vintage.

Featherstone, M. (1990) *Consumer Culture and Postmodernism*, London: Sage.

Featherstone, M. (2002) 'Book review of *Empire*', *Sociological Review*, 50(2): 300–303.

Featherstone, M., Hepworth, M. & Turner, B. (eds) (1991) *The Body*, London: Sage.

Featherstone, M. & Burrows, R. (eds) (1995) *Cyberspace/Cyberbodies/Cyberpunk*, London: Sage.

Feeley, M. & Simon, J. (1994) 'Actuarial Justice: the Emerging New Criminal Law', in D. Nelken (ed.) *The Futures of Criminology*, London: Sage.

Ferrara, M. (1996) 'The "Southern" Model of Welfare in Social Europe', *Journal of European Social Policy*, 6(1): 17–37.

Feyerabend, P. (1975) *Against Method*, London: Verso.

Field, F. (1996) *Making Welfare Work*, London: Institute of Community Studies.

Field, F. (1998) *Stakeholder Welfare*, London: IEA.

Field, F. (2003) *Neighbours from Hell*, London: Politico's.

Fieschi, M. (2002) 'Information Technology is Changing the Way Society Sees Health Care Delivery', *International Journal of Medical Informatics*, 66(1): 85–93.

Finlayson, A. (2003) *Making Sense of New Labour*, London: Lawrence & Wishart.

Fiske, J. (1987) *Understanding Popular Culture*, London: Routledge.

Fitzpatrick, T. (1999a) *Freedom and Security*, London: Macmillan.

Fitzpatrick, T. (1999b) 'Social Policy for Cyborgs', *Body and Society*, 5(1): 93–116.

Fitzpatrick, T. (2000) 'Critical Cyber Policy: Network Technologies, Massless Citizens, Virtual Rights', *Critical Social Policy*, 20(3): 375–407.

Fitzpatrick, T. (2001a) *Welfare Theory*, Basingstoke: Palgrave.

Fitzpatrick, T. (2001b) 'New Agendas for Criminology and Social Policy: Globalisation and the Post-Social Security State', *Social Policy & Administration*, 35(2): 212–29.

Fitzpatrick, T. (2001c) 'Before the Cradle: Social Biopolicy, Genetics & Regulated Eugenics', *Journal of Social Policy*, 30(4): 589–612.

Fitzpatrick, T. (2002a) 'The Two Paradoxes of Welfare Democracy', *International Journal of Social Welfare*, 11(2): 159–69.

Fitzpatrick, T. (2002b) 'Critical Theory, Information Society and Surveillance Technologies', *Information, Communication and Society*, 5(3): 357–78.

Fitzpatrick, T. (2002c) 'In Search of a Welfare Democracy', *Social Policy and Society*, 1(1): 11–20.

Fitzpatrick, T. (2003) *After the New Social Democracy*, Manchester: Manchester University Press.

Fitzpatrick, T. (2004a) 'Social Policy and Time', *Time and Society* (forthcoming).

Fitzpatrick, T. (2004b) 'Time, Liberal Justice and UK Social Policies', *Economy & Society* (forthcoming).

Fitzpatrick, T. (2005) 'The Fourth Attempt to Construct a Politics of Welfare Obligations', *Policy & Politics*, 33(1).

Fitzpatrick, T. & Cahill, M. (2002) 'The New Environment of Welfare', in Fitzpatrick, T. & Cahill, M. (eds) *Environment and Welfare*, London: Palgrave.

Flusty, S. (2001) 'The Banality of Interdiction: Surveillance, Control and the Displacement of Diversity', *International Journal of Urban and Regional Research*, 25(3): 658–664.

Foucault, M. (1975) *Discipline and Punish*, Middlesex: Penguin.

Foucault, M. (1977) *The History of Sexuality: Volume 1*, London: Allen Lane.

Fox, R. (2001) 'Someone to Watch Over Us: Back to the Panopticon?', *Criminal Justice*, 1(3): 251–276.

Frank, T. (2001) *One Market Under God*, London: Secker & Warburg.

Franklin, B. (ed.) (1999a) *Social Policy, the Media and Misrepresentation*, London: Routledge.

Franklin, B. (1999b) 'Soft Soaping the Public? The Government and Media Promotion of Social Policy', in Franklin, B. (ed.) *Social Policy, the Media and Misrepresentation*, London: Routledge.

Fraser, N. (1989) *Unruly Practices*, Cambridge: Polity.

Fraser, N. (1997) *Justice Interruptus*, London: Routledge.

Fraser, N. (2001) 'Recognition Without Ethics?', *Theory, Culture and Society*, 18(2–3): 21–42.

Fraser, N. & Honneth, A. (2003) *Redistribution or Recognition?*, London: Verso.

Freeden, M. (1996) *Ideologies and Political Theory*, Oxford: Oxford University Press.

Freeman, R., Chamberlayne, P., Cooper, A. & Rustin, M. (1999) 'Conclusion: a New Culture of Welfare', in Chamberlayne, P., Cooper, A., Freeman, R. & Rustin, M. (eds) *Welfare and Culture in Europe*, London: Jessica Kingsley Publishers.

Friedman, T. (1998) *The Lexus and the Olive Tree*, New York: Doubleday.

Froggett, L. (2002) *Love, Hate and Welfare*, Bristol: Policy Press.

Fukayama, F. (1995) *Trust*, New York: Free Press.

Fukayama, F. (2002) *Our Posthuman Future*, London: Profile Books.

Furedi, F. (2002) *Culture of Fear*, London: Continuum.

Galston, W. (2002) *Liberal Pluralism*, Cambridge: Cambridge University Press.

Garland, D. (1985) *Punishment and Welfare*, Gower: Aldershot.

Garland, D. (1990) *Punishment and Modern Society*, Clarendon: Oxford.

Garland, D. (2001a) *The Culture of Control*, Oxford: Oxford University Press.

Garland, D. (2001b) 'Introduction: the Meaning of Mass Imprisonment', *Punishment and Society*, 3(1): 5–8.

Gauthier, D. (1986) *Morals by Agreement*, Oxford: Oxford University Press.

Geertz, C. (1973) *The Interpretation of Culture*, New York: Basic Books.

Geras, N. (1998) *The Contract of Mutual Indifference*, London: Verso.

Gershuny, J. (2000) *Changing Times*, Oxford: Oxford University Press.

Giddens, T. (1985) *The Nation-State and Violence*, 2 vols, Cambridge: Polity Press.

Giddens, T. (1991) *Modernity and Self-Identity*, Cambridge: Polity.

Giddens, T. (1994) *Beyond Left and Right*, Cambridge: Polity.

Giddens, T. (1998) *The Third Way*, Cambridge: Polity.

Giddens, T. (2000) *The Third Way and Its Critics*, Cambridge: Polity.

Giddens, T. (ed.) (2001) *The Global Third Way Debate*, Cambridge: Polity.

Giddens, T. (2002) *Where Now for New Labour?*, London: Fabian Society.

Gilbert, N. (2002) *Transformation of the Welfare State*, Oxford: Oxford University Press.

Gilens, M. (1999) *Why Americans Hate Welfare*, Chicago: Chicago University Press.

Gilleard, C. & Higgs, P. (1998) 'Ageing and the Limiting Conditions of the Body', *Sociological Research Online*, 3(4).

Gilligan, C. (1982) *In A Different Voice*, Cambridge, MA: Harvard University Press.

Gilling, D. (2001) 'Community Safety and Social Policy', *European Journal on Criminal Policy and Research*, 9: 381–400.

Gilliom, J. (2001) *Overseers of the Poor*, Chicago: University of Chicago Press.

Gingrich, N. & Armey, D. (1995) *Restoring the Dream*, New York: Times Books.

Glover, J. (1999) 'Eugenics and Human Rights', in Burley, J. (ed.) *The Genetic Revolution and Human Rights*, Oxford: Oxford University Press.

Glover, J. (2001) 'Future People, Disability, and Screening', in Harris, J. (ed.) *Bioethics*, Oxford: Oxford University Press.

Goffman, E. (1969) *The Presentation of Self in Everyday Life*, Middlesex: Penguin.

Golding, P. (1999) 'Thinking the Unthinkable: Welfare Reform and the Media', in Franklin, B. (ed.) *Social Policy, the Media and Misrepresentation*, London: Routledge.

Goodin, R. (2002) 'Structures of Mutual Obligation', *Journal of Social Policy*, 31(4): 579–96.

Goodin, R., Headey, B., Muffels, R. & Dervin, H-J. (1999) *The Real Worlds of Welfare Capitalism*, Cambridge: Cambridge University Press.

Goodin, R. & Rein, M. (2001) 'Regimes or Pillars: Alternative Welfare State Logics and Dynamics', *Public Administration*, 79(4): 769–801.

Goodman, R., White, R. & Kwon, H-J. (eds) (1998) *The East Asian Welfare Model*, London: Routledge.

Gould, E., Weinberg, B. & Mustard, D. (2002) 'Crime Rates and Local Labor Market Opportunities in the United States: 1979–97', *The Review of Economics and Statistics*, 84(1): 45–61.

Gould, S. (1997) *The Mismeasure of Man*, 2nd edition, London: Penguin.

Gould, S. (2000) 'More Things in Heaven and Earth', in Rose, H. & Rose, S. (eds) *Alas, Poor Darwin*, London: Jonathon Cape.

Gould, S. & Lewontin, R. (1979) 'The Spandrels of San Marco', *Proceedings of the Royal Society B*, 205: 581–98.

Graham, S. & Wood, D. (2003) 'Digitizing Surveillance', *Critical Social Policy*, 23(2): 227–48.

Gramsci, A. (1971) *Selections from Prison Notebooks*, London: Lawrence & Wishart.

Gray, C. (2001) *Cyborg Citizen*, London: Routledge.

Gray, J. (1992) *The Moral Foundations of Market Institutions*, London: IEA.

Gray, J. (1993) *Beyond the New Right*, London: Routledge.

Gray, J. (1996) *After Social Democracy*, London: Demos.

Gray, J. (2000) *Two Faces of Liberalism*, London: New Press.

Green, D. (1995) *Community Without Politics*, London: IEA.

Greener, I. (2002a) 'Agency, Social Theory and Social Policy', *Critical Social Policy*, 22(4): 688–706.

Greener, I. (2002b) 'Theorising Path-Dependency: How Does History Come to Matter in Organisations?', *Management Decision*, 40(6): 614–619.

Gutmann, A. & Thompson, D. (1996) *Democracy and Disagreement*, Cambridge, Mass: Harvard University Press.

Habermas, J. (1987a) *The Theory of Communicative Action*, 2 vols, Cambridge: Polity.

Habermas, J. (1987b) *The Philosophical Discourse of Modernity*, Cambridge: Polity.

Habermas, J. (1989) *The Structural Transformation of the Public Sphere*, Cambridge, MA: MIT Press.

Habermas, J. (2003) *The Future of Human Nature*, Cambridge: Polity.

Hagan, J. & Peterson, R. (eds) (1995) *Crime and Inequality*, Stanford: Stanford University Press.

Hall, S., Critcher, C., Jefferson, T., Clarke, J. & Roberts, B. (1978) *Policing the Crisis*, London: Macmillan.

Halpern, D. (2001) 'Moral Values, Social Trust and Inequality', *British Journal of Criminology*, 41(2): 236–251.

Hameed, K. (2003) 'The Application of Mobile Computing and Technology to Health Care Services', *Telematics and Informatics*, 20(2): 99–106.

Hamel, P., Lustiger-Thaler, H., Pieterse, J. & Roseneil, S. (eds) (2001) *Globalisation and Social Movements*, London: Palgrave.

Hannigan, B. (1999) 'Mental Health Care in the Community: an Analysis of Contemporary Public Attitudes Towards, and Public Representations of, Mental Illness', *Journal of Mental Health*, 8(5): 431–440.

Haraway, D. (1991) *Simians, Cyborgs and Women*, London: Routledge.

Hardt, M. & Negri, A. (2000) *Empire*, Cambridge, MA: Harvard University Press.

Harlow, E. & Webb, S. (2003) *Information and Communication Technologies in the Welfare Services*, London: Jessica Kingsley.

Harris, J. (1998) *Clones, Genes and Immortality*, Oxford: Oxford University Press.

Harris, J. (2002) 'Liberation in Reproduction', in Institute of Ideas (eds) *Designer Babies*, London: Institute of Ideas.

Haworth, A. (1994) *Anti-Libertarianism*, London: Routledge.

Hayek, F. (1982) *Law Legislation and Liberty*, London: Routledge.

Held, D. & McGrew, A. (2002) *Globalization/Anti-Globalization*, Cambridge: Polity.

Hellawell, S. (2001) *Beyond Access*, London: Fabian Society.

Henman, P. & Adler, M. (2001) 'Information Technology and Transformations in Social Security Policy and Administration', *International Social Security Review*, 54(4): 23–47.

Henman, P. & Adler, M. (2003) 'Information Technology and the Governance of Social Security', *Critical Social Policy*, 23(2): 139–64.

Henwood, F., Miller, N., Senker, P. & Wyatt, S. (2000) *Technology and In/equality*, London: Routledge.

Herrnstein, R. & Murray, C. (1994) *The Bell Curve*, New York: Free Press.

Hertz, N. (2000) *The Silent Takeover*, London: William Heinemann.

Hibbitt K., Jones P. & Meegan R. (2001) 'Tackling Social Exclusion: The Role of Social Capital in Urban Regeneration on Merseyside', *European Planning Studies*, 9(2): 141–161.

Hicks, A. & Kenworthy, L. (2003) 'Varieties of Welfare Capitalism', *Socio-Economic Review*, 1(1): 27–61.

Higgins, J. (1981) *States of Welfare*, London: Macmillan.

Himmelfarb, G. (1995) *The Demoralisation of Society*, New York: Alfred A. Knopf.

Hitchens, P. (2003) *A Brief History of Crime*, London: Atlantic Books.

HMSO (1999) *Modernising Government*, Cm 4310, London: HMSO.

Hochschild, A. (1983) *The Managed Heart*, California: University of California Press.

Hoggett, P. (2000) *Emotional Life and the Politics of Welfare*, London: Macmillan.

Hoggett, P. (2001) 'Agency, Rationality and Social Policy', *Journal of Social Policy*, 30(1): 37–56.

Hoggett, P. & Thompson, S. (2002) 'Toward a Democracy of the Emotions', *Constellations*, 9(1): 106–26.

Holloway, J. (2002) *Change the World Without Taking Power*, London: Pluto Press.

Hombach, B. (2000) *The Politics of the New Centre*, Cambridge: Polity.

Honderich, T. (2002) *After the Terror*, Edinburgh: Edinburgh University Press.

Honderich, T. (2003) *Conservatism*, 2nd edition, Boulder: Westview Press.

Honneth, A. (1995) *The Struggle for Recognition*, Cambridge: Polity.

Honneth, A. (2001) 'Recognition of Redistribution? Changing Perspectives on the Moral Order of Society', *Theory, Culture and Society*, 18(2–3): 43–55.

Howarth, D. (2000) *Discourse*, Milton Keynes: Open University Press.

Howson, A. & Inglis D. (2001) 'The Body in Sociology: Tension Inside and Outside Sociological Thought', *The Sociological Review*, 49(3): 297–317.

Hubbard, R. & Wald, E. (1998) *Exploding the Gene Myth*, Boston: Beacon Press.

Huber, E. & Stephens, J. (2001) *Development and Crisis of the Welfare State*, Chicago: University of Chicago Press.

Hudson, J. (2003) 'E-galitarianism? The Information Society and New Labour's Repositioning of Welfare', *Critical Social Policy*, 23(2): 268–90.

Hughes, G. & Lewis, G. (eds) (1998) *Unsettling Welfare*, London: Routledge.

Hume, D. (1969) *A Treatise on Human Nature*, Middlesex: Penguin.

Huntington, S. (1995) *The Clash of Civilisations and the Remaking of World Order*, London: Simon & Schuster.

Hutton, W. (1995) *The State We're In*, London: Vintage.

Hutton, W. (2002) *The World We're In*, London: Little, Brown.

Jawad, R. (2002) 'A Profile of Social Welfare in Lebanon: Assessing the Implications for Social Development Policy', *Global Social Policy*, 2(3): 319–342.

Jessop, B. (2002) *The Future of the Welfare State*, Cambridge: Polity.

Jessop, B. (2003) *The Future of the Capitalist State*, Cambridge: Polity.

Jones Finer, C. & Nellis, M. (eds) (1998) *Crime and Social Exclusion*, Oxford: Blackwell.

Jones, C. (2001) 'Voices From the Front Line: State Social Workers and New Labour', *British Journal of Social Work*, 31(4): 547–562.

Jones, C. & Novak, T. (1999) *Poverty, Welfare and the Disciplinary State*, London: Routledge.

Jones, J. (1996) *The Psychology of Racism and Prejudice*, New York: McGraw Hill.

Jones, S. (1994) *The Language of the Genes*, London: Flamingo.

Jordan, B. (1996) *A Theory of Poverty and Social Exclusion*, Cambridge: Polity.

Jordan, B. with Jordan, C. (2000) *Tough Love as Social Policy*, London: Sage.

Jordan, T. (1999) *Cyberpower*, London: Routledge.

Journal of Quantitative Criminology (2001) special edition on unemployment and crime.

Journal of Social Issues (2000) *The Impact of Welfare Reform*, edited by Zuckerman, D. & Kalil, A., Oxford: Blackwell.

Kahn, R. & Juster, F. (2002) 'Well-Being: Concepts and Measures', *Journal of Social Issues*, 58(4): 627–44.

Kant, I. (2001) *Basic Writings of Kant*, edited by Allen Wood, New York: The Modern Library.

Kaplan, J. (2000) *The Limits and Lies of Human Genetic Research*, London: Routledge.

Kass, N. (1997) 'The Implications of Genetic Testing for Health and Life Insurance', in Rothstein, M. (ed.) *Genetic Secrets*, New Haven & London: Yale University Press.

Keane, J. (1991) *The Media and Democracy*, Cambridge: Polity.

Kekes, J. (1998) *A Case for Conservatism*, New York: Cornell University Press.

Kellner, D. (1995) *Media and Culture*, London: Routledge.

Kellner, D. (1999) 'New Technologies, the Welfare State, and the Prospects for Democratization', in Calabrese, A. & Burgelman, J-C. (eds) *Communication, Citizenship, and Social Policy*, Lanham, Md.: Rowman and Littlefield.

Kellner, D. (2000) 'New Technologies/New Literacies: reconstructing education for the new millennium', *Teaching Education*, 11(3): 245–65.

Kelly, S. E. (2002) '"New" Genetics Meets the Old Underclass: Findings from a Study of Genetic Outreach Services in Rural Kentucky', *Critical Public Health*, 12(2): 169–186.

Kelly, G., Kelley, D. and Gamble, A. (eds) (1997) *Stakeholder Capitalism*, London: Macmillan.

Kelly, M. (2000) 'Inequality and Crime', *The Review of Economics and Statistics*, 82(4): 530–9.

Kemper, T. (1978) *A Social Interactional Theory of the Emotions*, London: John Wiley.

Kemshall, H. (2002) *Risk, Social Policy and Welfare*, Buckingham: Open University Press.

Kerr, A. & Shakespeare, T. (2002) *Genetic Politics*, Cheltenham: New Clarion Press.

Kevles, D. (1985) *In the Name of Eugenics*, Cambridge, Mass.: Harvard University Press.

King, D. (1999) *In the Name of Liberalism*, Oxford: Oxford University Press.

Kitcher, P. (1996) *The Lives to Come*, New York: Touchstone.

Klein, M. (1932) *The Psychoanalysis of Children*, London: Hogarth Press.

Klein, N. (2000) *No Logo*, London: Flamingo.

Klein, N. (2002) *Windows and Fences*, London: Flamingo.

Kramer, R. (2000) 'Poverty, Inequality and Youth Violence', *Annals of the American Academy of Politics and Social Science*, 567(1): 123–39.

Kristol, I. (1995) *Neoconservatism*, New York: Free Press.

Kumlin, S. (2002) 'Institutions – Experiences – Preferences: How Welfare State Design Affects Political Trust and Ideology', in Rothstein, B. & Steinmo, S. (eds) *Restructuring the Welfare State*, London: Palgrave.

Kutchins, H. (2001) 'Neither Alms Nor a Friend: The Tragedy of Compassionate Conservatism', *Social Justice*, 28(1): 14–34.

Kymlicka, W. (1995) *The Rights of Minority Cultures*, Oxford: Clarendon.

Kymlicka, W. (2002) *Contemporary Political Philosophy*, 2nd edition, Oxford: Oxford University Press.

Laclau, E. (1990) *Reflections on the Revolution of Our Time*, London: Verso.

Laclau, E. (ed.) (1994) *The Making of Political Identities*, London: Verso.

Laclau, E. (1996) *Emancipation(s)*, London: Verso.

Laclau, E. & Mouffe, C. (1985) *Hegemony and Socialist Strategy*, London: Verso.

Lash, S. (1999) *Another Modernity, A Different Rationality*, Oxford: Blackwell.

Lash, S. (2002) *Critique of Information*, London: Sage.

Lavalette, M. & Mooney, G. (eds) (2000) *Class Struggle and Social Welfare*, London: Routledge.

Lavalette, M. & Mooney, G. (2002) *Rethinking Welfare*, London: Sage.

Law, I. (2002) *Race in the News*, London: Palgrave.

LeGrand, J. (2003) *Motivation, Agency & Public Policy*, Oxford: Oxford University Press.

Leadbetter, C. (1999) *Living on Thin Air*, London: Viking.

Leadbetter, C. (2004) 'Personalisation Through Participation', London: Demos.

Legrain, P. (2002) *Open World*, London: Abacus.

Leisering, L. & Leibfried, S. (1999) *Time and Poverty in Western Welfare States*, Cambridge: Cambridge University Press.

Lenaghan, J. (1998) *Brave New NHS?*, London: IPPR.

Leonard, P. (2003) *Promoting Welfare?*, Bristol: Policy Press.

Levitas, R. (1998) *The Inclusive Society?*, London: Macmillan.

Lewis, G. (ed.) (1998) *Forming Nation, Framing Welfare*, London: Routledge.

Lewis, J. (1992) 'Gender and the Development of Welfare Regimes', *Journal of European Social Policy*, 2(3): 159–73.

Lewis, J. (2001) 'The Decline of the Male Breadwinner Model: Implications for Work and Care', *Social Politics*, 8(2): 152–69.

Lewontin, R. (2000) *It Ain't Necessarily So*, London: Granta Books.

Liberty (eds) (1999) *Liberating Cyberspace*, London: Pluto Press.

Liddiard, M. (1999) 'Homelessness: The Media, Public Attitudes and Policy Making', in Hutson, S. & Clapham, D. (eds) *Homelessness*, London: Cassell.

Ling, T. (1998) *The British State Since 1945*, Cambridge: Polity.

Lippmann, W. (1922) *Public Opinion*, London: Transaction Publishers.

Lister, R. (ed.) (1996) *Charles Murray and The Underclass*, London: Civitas.

Lister, R. (1997) 'Social Inclusion and Exclusion', Kelly, G., Kelley, D. and Gamble, A. (eds) (1997) *Stakeholder Capitalism*, London: Macmillan.

Lister, R. (2001) 'Towards a Citizens' Welfare State: the 3+2 "R's" of Welfare Reform', *Theory, Culture and Society*, 18(2–3): 91–111.

Lister, R. (2003a) *Citizenship: Feminist Perspectives*, 2nd ed., London: Macmillan.

Lister, R. (2003b) '(Re)conceptualising Poverty', paper presented to the SPA annual conference.

Lockhart, C. (2001) *Protecting the Elderly*, Pennsylvania: Penn State Press.

Long, C. (ed.) (1999) *Genetic Testing*, Washington DC: The AEI Press.

Lopez, J. (2003) *Society and Its Metaphors*, London: Continuum.

Luhmann, N. (2000) *The Reality of the Mass Media*, Cambridge: Polity.

Lyon, D. (1994) *The Electronic Eye*, Cambridge: Polity Press.

Lyon, D. (2001) *Surveillance Society*, Buckingham: Open University Press.

Lyon, D. (2002) 'Everyday Surveillance: Personal Data and Social Classifications', *Information, Communication and Society*, 5(2): 242–57.

Lyon, D. (ed.) (2003) *Surveillance as Social Sorting*, London: Routledge.

MacIntyre, A. (1981) *After Virtue*, London: Duckworth.

MacIntyre, A. (1987) *Whose Virtue?, Which Rationality?*, London: Duckworth.

Macpherson, C. B. (1977) *The Life and Times of Liberal Democracy*, Oxford: Oxford Paperbacks.

Maguire, M., Morgan, R. & Reiner, R. (eds) (2002) *The Oxford Handbook of Criminology*, 3rd ed., Oxford: Oxford University Press.

Marcuse, H. (1964) *One-Dimensional Man*, London: Routledge & Kegan Paul.

Marshall, G. (1997) *Repositioning Class*, London: Sage.

Marshall, G., Swift, A. & Roberts, S. (1997) *Against the Odds*, Oxford: Clarendon Press.

Marshall, T. H. & Bottomore, T. (1992) *Citizenship & Social Class*, London: Pluto.

Martin, P. & Frost, R. (2003) 'Regulating the Commercial Testing of Genetic Testing in the UK: Problems, Possibilities and Policy', *Critical Social Policy*, 23(2): 186–207.

Marx, G. (1995), The Engineering of Social Control: the Search for the Silver Bullet', in J. Hagan and R. Patersen (eds) *Crime and Inequality*, Stanford: Stanford University Press.

Mathews, R. & Young, J. (2003) *The New Politics of Crime and Punishment*, Cullompton: Willan Publishing.

Mathiesen, T. (1974) *The Politics of Abolition*, London: Martin Robinson.

Mauer, M. (2001) 'The Causes and Consequences of Prison Growth in the USA', *Punishment and Society*, 3(1): 9–20.

May, S. (ed.) (1999) *Critical Multiculturalism*, London: Falmer Press.

McCormick, J. (1997) 'Mapping the Stakeholder Society', Kelly, G., Kelley, D. and Gamble, A. (eds) (1997) *Stakeholder Capitalism*, London: Macmillan.

McGleenan, T. & Wiesing, U. (1999) 'Policy Options for Health and Life Insurance in the Era of Genetic Testing', in McGleenan, T., Wiesing, U. & Ewald, F. (eds) *Genetics and Insurance*, Oxford: Bios Scientific Publishers Ltd.

McGrath, J. (2004) *Loving Big Brother*, London: Routledge.

McKibben, B. (1989) *The End of Nature*, New York: Random House.

McLaughlin, E., Fergusson, R., Hughes, G. & Westmarland, L. (eds) (2003) *Restorative Justice*, Buckinghamshire: Open University Press.

McNay, L. (1993) *Foucault: A Critical Introduction*, Cambridge: Polity.

McQuail, D. (1994) *McQuail's Mass Communication Theory*, London: Sage.

Mead, L. (1986) *Beyond Entitlement*, New York: Free Press.

Mead, L. (ed.) (1997) *The New Paternalism*, Washington: Brookings Institute.

Merleau-Ponty, M. (1962) *The Phenomenology of Perception*, London: Routledge.

Meštrović, S. (1997) *Post-Emotional Society*, London: Sage.

Midgely, M. (1995) *Beasts and Men*, London: Routledge.

Midgley, M. (2000) 'Why Memes?', in Rose, H. & Rose, S. (eds) *Alas, Poor Darwin*, London: Jonathon Cape.

Miller, D. (1989) *Market, State & Community*, Oxford: Clarendon.

Miller, D. (1999) *Principles of Social Justice*, Cambridge, Mass: Harvard University Press.

Mishra, R. (1999) *Globalisation and the Welfare State*, Aldershot: Edward Elgar.

Misztal, B. (1996) *Trust in Modern Societies*, Cambridge: Polity.

Monbiot, G. (2000) *Captive State*, London: Pan.

Monbiot, G. (2003) *The Age of Consent*, London: Flamingo.

Mooney, J. (2000) *Gender, Violence and the Social Order*, London: Macmillan.

Morris, C. & Ripstein, A. (eds) (2001) *Practical Rationality and Preference*, Cambridge: Cambridge University Press.

Mouffe, C. (ed.) (1992) *Dimensions of Radical Democracy*, London: Verso.

Mouffe, C. (1993) *The Return of the Political*, London: Verso.

Mouffe, C. (2000) *The Democratic Paradox*, London: Verso.

Mozina, M. (2002) 'Can we Remember Differently? A Case Study of the New Culture of Memory in Voluntary Organisations', *International Journal of Social Welfare*, 11(4): 310–320.

Mulgan, G. (1998) *Connexity*, Cambridge, MA: Harvard Business School Press.

Murray, C. (1984) *Losing Ground*, New York: Basic Books.

Murray, C. (1990) *The Emerging British Underclass*, London: IEA.

Murray, C. (1997) *Does Prison Work?*, London: IEA.

Murray, C. (2000) 'Genetics of the Right', *Prospect* (April edition): 28–31.

Murray, C., Philips, M. & Green, D. (2001) *Underclass Plus Ten*, London: Civitas.

Narveson, J. (1998) 'Egalitarianism: Partial, Counterproductive and Baseless', in Mason, A. (ed.) *Ideals of Equality*, Oxford: Blackwell.

Narveson, J. (2001) *The Libertarian Idea*, Peterborough, Canada: Broadview Press.

Nash, R. (1999) 'Bourdieu, "Habitus", and Educational Research: Is It All Worth the Candle?' *British Journal of Sociology of Education*, 20(2): 175–187.

Nelkin, D. (1999) 'Behavioural Genetics and Dismantling the Welfare State', in Carson, R. & Rothstein, M. (eds) *Behavioural Genetics*, Baltimore: John Hopkins University Press.

Nettleton, S. & Burrows, R. (2003) 'E-Scaped Medicine? Information, Reflexivity and Health', *Critical Social Policy*, 23(2): 165–85.

Nettleton, S. & Watson, J. (eds) (1998) *The Body in Everyday Life*, London: Routledge.

Newman, J. (2001) *Modernising Governance*, London: Sage.

Newton, K. (2001) 'Trust, Social Capital, Civil Society, and Democracy', *International Political Science Review*, 22(2): 201–214.

Nixon, P. & Keeble, L. (2001) 'New Communication Technologies – Connected Welfare: New Media and Social Policy', in Sykes, R., Ellison, N. & Bochel, C. (eds) *Social Policy Review 13*, Bristol: Policy Press.

Noddings, N. (2002) *Starting at Home*, California: University of California Press.

Norris, C. & Armstrong, G. (1999) *The Maximum Surveillance Society*, Oxford: Berg.

Norris, P. (2001) *Digital Divide*, Cambridge: Cambridge University Press.

Novas, C. & Rose, N. (2000) 'Genetic Risk and the Birth of the Somatic Individual', *Economy & Society*, 29(4): 485–513.

Nove, A. (1991) *Economics of Feasible Socialism*, 2nd edition, London: Allen & Unwin.

Nozick, R. (1974) *Anarchy, State and Utopia*, Oxford: Blackwell.

Nozick, R. (1989) *The Examined Life*, New York: Touchstone.

Nuffield Council on Bioethics (1999) *Genetic Screening*, London: Nuffield Foundation.

O'Hear, A. (1997) *Beyond Evolution*, Oxford: Oxford University Press.

O'Hear, A. (1999) *After Progress*, New York: Bloomsbury.

O'Malley, P., Weir, L. & Shearing, C. (1997) 'Governmentality, Criticism, Politics', *Economy and Society*, 26(4): 501–17.

Oakeshott, M. (1962) *Rationalism in Politics and Other Essays*, London & New York: Methuen & Co.

Ohmae, K. (1995) *The End of the Nation State*, London: HarperCollins.

Okin, S. M. (1999) *Is Multiculturalism Bad for Women?*, Princeton: Princeton University Press.

Olasky, M. (2000) *Compassionate Conservatism*, New York: Free Press.

Ollman, B., Lawler, J. & Ticktin, H. (1998) *Market Socialism*, London: Routledge.

Osbourne, D. & Gaebler, T. (1992) *Reinventing Government*, Reading, MA: Addison-Wesley.

Page, R. (1996) *Altruism and the British Welfare State*, Aldershot: Avebury.

Pantazis, C. (2000a) 'Tackling Inequalities in Crime and Social Harm', in Pantazis, C. & Gordon, D. (eds) *Tackling Inequalities*, Bristol: Policy Press.

Pantazis, C. (2000b) '"Fear of Crime", Vulnerability and Poverty', *British Journal of Criminology*, 40: 414–36.

Parekh, B. (2000) *Rethinking Multiculturalism*, London: Palgrave.

Parenti, C. (1999) *Lockdown America*, London: Verso.

Parfit, D. (2001) 'Equality or Priority?', in Harris, J. (ed.) *Bioethics*, Oxford: Oxford University Press.

Park, A. (2003) *British Social Attitudes*, London: National Centre for Social Research.

Parker, I. (1997) *Psychoanalytic Culture*, London: Sage.

Parker-Jenkins, M. (2002) 'Equal Access to State Funding: the Case of Muslim Schools in Britain', *Race, Ethnicity and Education*, 5(3): 273–89.

PAT 15 (2000) *Closing the Digital Divide*, London: Dept. for Trade and Industry.

Patel, K. & Rushefsky, M. (2002) *Health Care Policy in an Age of New Technologies*, Armonk: M. E. Sharpe.

Peterson, C., Maier, S. F. & Seligman, M. (1993) *Learned Helplessness*, Oxford: Oxford University Press.

Pettit, P. (1997) *Republicanism*, Oxford: Oxford University Press.

Phillips, A. (1999) *Which Equalities Matter?*, Cambridge: Polity.

Phillips, M. (1998) *All Must Have Prizes*, New York: Time Warner.

Philo, G. (1990) *Seeing and Believing*, London: Routledge.

Philo, G. (ed.) (1996) *Media and Mental Distress*, London: Longman.

Pierson, C. (1995) *Socialism After Communism*, Cambridge: Polity.

Pierson, C. (2001) *Hard Choices*, Cambridge: Polity.

Pierson, P. (ed.) (2001a) *The New Politics of the Welfare State*, Cambridge: Cambridge University Press.

Pierson, P. (2001b) 'Post-Industrial Pressures on the Mature Welfare States', in Pierson, P. (ed.) *The New Politics of the Welfare State*, Cambridge: Cambridge University Press.

Pilbeam, B. (2001) 'Conservatism and Postmodernism: Consanguineous Relations or "Different" Voices?', *Journal of Political Ideologies*, 6(1): 33–54.

Pilnick, A. (2002) *Genetics and Society*, London: Sage.

Pinker, S. (1995) *The Language Instinct*, Middlesex: Penguin.

Pinker, S. (2002) *The Blank Slate*, Middlesex: Penguin Books.

Piven, F. F. & Cloward, R. (1971) *Regulating the Poor*, New York: Random House.

Pizzey, P., Shackleton, J. & Urwin, P. (2000) *Women or Men: Who are the Victims?*, London: Civitas.

Platt, S. (1999) 'Home Truths: Media Representations of Homelessness', in Franklin, B. (ed.) *Social Policy, the Media and Misrepresentation*, London: Routledge.

Pokorski, R. (1997) 'Insurance Underwriting in the Genetic Era', *American Journal of Human Genetics*, 60: 205–16.

Polanyi, K. (1944) *The Great Transformation*, Boston: Beacon Press.

Poster, M. & Aronowitz, S. (eds) (1997) *The Information Subject*, London: Routledge.

Powell, M. & Hewitt, M. (2002) *Welfare State and Welfare Change*, Milton Keynes: Open University Press.

Pratt, J. (2002) 'Critical Criminology and the Punitive Society: Some New "Visions of Social Control"', in Carrington, K. & Hogg, R. (eds) *Critical Criminology*, Cullompton: Willan Publishing.

Purdue, D. (2001) 'Neighbourhood Governance: Leadership, Trust and Social Capital', *Urban Studies*, 38(12): 2211–2224.

Putnam, H. (1999) 'Cloning People', in Burley, J. (ed.) *The Genetic Revolution and Human Rights*, Oxford: Oxford University Press.

Putnam, R. (2000) *Bowling Alone*, New York: Simon & Schuster.

Radcliffe Richards, J. (2000) *Human Nature After Darwin*, London: Routledge.

Rafter, N. H. (ed.) (2000) *Encyclopedia of Women and Crime*, Phoenix, Arizona: Oryx Press.

Rawls, J. (1993) *Political Liberalism*, New York: Columbia University Press.

Rawls, J. (1999) *Collected Papers*, edited by Samuel Freeman, Cambridge, MA: Harvard University Press.

Rawls, J. (2001) *Justice as Fairness*, Cambridge, MA: Harvard University Press.

Reid, W. J. & Misener, E. (2001) 'Social Work in the Press: a Cross-National Study', *International Journal of Social Welfare*, 10(3): 194–201.

Reiger, E. & Leibfried, S. (2003) *Limits to Globalisation*, Cambridge: Polity.

Reilly, P. (1999) 'Genetic Discrimination', in Long, C. (ed.) *Genetic Testing and the Use of Information*, Washington: The AEI Press.

Reiman, J. (1998) *The Rich Get Richer and the Poor Get Prison*, 5th ed., London: Allyn & Bacon.

Rhodes, R. (1996) *Understanding Governance*, Milton Keynes: Open University Press.

Richardson, E. H. & Turner, B. S. (2001) 'Sexual, Intimate or Reproductive Citizenship?', *Citizenship Studies*, 5(3): 329–338.

Ridley, M. (1996) *The Origins of Virtue*, Middlesex: Penguin.

Ridley, M. (1999) *Genome*, London: Fourth Estate.

Ridley, M. (2003) *Nature vs. Nurture*, London: Fourth Estate.

Rifkin, J. (1998) *The Biotech Century*, London: Orion Books.

Rifkin, J. (2000) *The Age of Access*, Middlesex: Penguin.

Robins, K. & Webster, F. (1999) *Times of the Technoculture*, London: Routledge.

Roche, M. (1992) *Rethinking Citizenship*, Cambridge: Polity.

Rodger, J. (2000) *From a Welfare State to a Welfare Society*, London: Macmillan.

Rodger, J. (2003) 'Social Solidarity, Welfare and Post-Emotionalism', *Journal of Social Policy*, 32(3): 403–22.

Roemer, J. (1982) *A General Theory of Exploitation and Class*, Cambridge, MA: Harvard University Press.

Roemer, J. (1994) *A Future for Socialism*, London: Verso.

Roemer, J. (1996) *Theories of Distributive Justice*, Cambridge, MA: Harvard University Press.

Roemer, J. (1998) *Equality of Opportunity*, Cambridge, MA: Harvard University Press.

Rojek, C. (2002) *Stuart Hall*, Cambridge: Polity.

Room, G. (2000) 'Commodification and Decommodification: A Developmental Critique', *Policy and Politics*, 28(3): 331–51.

Rorty, R. (1989) *Contingency, Irony and Solidarity*, Cambridge: Cambridge University Press.

Rorty, R. (1991) *Objectivity, Relativism and Truth*, Cambridge: Cambridge University Press.

Rorty, R. (1998) *Philosophy and Social Hope*, Middlesex: Penguin.

Rose, H. & Rose, S. (eds) (2000) *Alas, Poor Darwin*, London: Jonathon Cape.

Rose, N. (1996) 'The Death of the Social?', *Economy and Society*, 25(3): 327–56.

Rose, N. (1999a) *Governing the Soul*, 2nd edition, London: Free Association Books.

Rose, N. (1999b) *Powers of Freedom*, Cambridge: Cambridge University Press.

Rose, S. (1997) *Lifelines*, Middlesex: Penguin.

Ross, A. (2000) *The Celebration Chronicles*, London: Verso.

Rothstein, B. (1998) *Just Institutions Matter*, Cambridge: Cambridge University Press.

Rothstein, B. (2000) 'Trust, Social Dilemmas and Collective Memories', *Journal of Theoretical Politics*, 12(4): 477–501.

Rothstein, B. (2003) 'Social Capital, Economic Growth and Quality of Government: The Causal Mechanism', *New Political Economy*, 8(1): 49–71.

Rothstein, B. & Steinmo, S. (eds) (2002) *Restructuring the Welfare State*, London: Palgrave.

Ruggeiro, V. South, N. & Taylor, I. (eds) (1998) *The New European Criminology*, London: Routledge.

Runciman, G. (1966) *Relative Deprivation and Social Justice*, Middlesex: Penguin.

Sacks, J. (2000) *The Politics of Hope*, London: Vintage.

Sainsbury, D. (ed.) (1999) *Gender and Welfare State Regimes*, Oxford: Oxford University Press.

Saint-Arnaud, S. & Bernard, P. (2003) 'Convergence or Resilience? A Hierarchical Cluster Analysis of the Welfare Regimes in Advanced Countries', *Current Sociology*, 51(5): 499–527.

Savage, M. (2000) *Class Analysis and Social Transformation*, Milton Keynes: Open University Press.

Schama, S. (2000) *A History of Britain*, 1st vol., London: BBC Books.

Scheepers, P., Grotenhuis, M. & Gelissen, J. (2002) 'Welfare States and Dimensions of Social Capital', *European Societies*, 4(2): 185–207.

Schiller, H. (1996) *Information Inequality*, London: Routledge.

Schmidtz, D. (2002) 'Equal respect and Equal Shares', *Philosophy & Social Policy*, 19(1): 244–74.

Schumpeter, J. (1992) *Capitalism, Socialism and Democracy*, London: Routledge.

Schwartz, B. (2004) *The Paradox of Choice*, London: HarperCollins.

Scruton, R. (2001) *The Meaning of Conservatism*, 2nd ed., London: Palgrave.

Segal, L. (1999) *Why Feminism?*, Cambridge: Polity.

Selwyn, N. (2002) '"E-stablishing" an Inclusive Society? Technology, Social Exclusion and UK Government Policy Making', *Journal of Social Policy*, 31(1): 1–20.

Selwyn, N., Gorard, S. & Williams, S. (2001) 'Digital Divide or Digital Opportunity?', *Educational Policy*, 15(2): 258–77.

Sennett, R. (2003) *Respect*, London: Allen Lane.

Sevenhuijsen, S. (1998) *Citizenship and the Ethics of Care*, London: Routledge.

Shapiro, D. (2002) 'Egalitarianism and Welfare-State Redistribution', *Social Philosophy and Policy*, 19(1): 1–35.

Shilling, C. (2003) *The Body and Social Theory*, 2nd ed., London: Sage.

Shilling, C. (2004) *The Body in Culture, Technology and Society*, London: Sage.

Shin, C-S. & Shaw, I. (2003) 'Social Policy in South Korea: Cultural and Structural Factors in the Emergence of Welfare', *Social Policy and Administration*, 37(4): 328–341.

Shiva, V. (2000a) *Tomorrow's Biodiversity*, London: Thames & Hudson.

Shiva, V. (2000b) *Stolen Harvest*, London: Zed Books.

Sidanius, J. & Pratto, F. (1999) *Social Dominance*, Cambridge: Cambridge University Press.

Silver, L. (1998) *Remaking Eden*, London: Weidenfeld & Nicolson.

Singer, P. (1998) 'The Darwin Lecture: A Darwinian Left?', The Times Higher Education Supplement Internet Service, http://rfe.wustl.edu/NewsMedia/TimHigEduSup.html

Smith, A. (1998) *Laclau and Mouffe*, London: Routledge.

Smith, S. & Kulynch, J. (2002) 'It May Be Social, but Why Is It Capital? The Social Construction of Social Capital and the Politics of Language', *Politics & Society*, 30(1): 149–186.

Sober, E. & Wilson, D. (1998) *Unto Others*, Harvard, MA: Harvard University Press.

Social Policy & Administration (1997) special issue on Latin America.

Soja, E. (1996) *Thirdspace*, Oxford: Blackwell.

Sotirovic, M. (2000) 'Effects of Media Use on Audience Framing and Support for Welfare', *Mass Communication and Society*, 3(2): 269–296.

Sotirovic, M. (2003) 'How Individuals Explain Social Problems: The Influences of Media Use', *Journal of Communication*, 53(1): 22–137.

Spinoza, B. (1986) *Ethics*, London: Everyman.

Squires, P. (1990) *Anti-Social Policy*, Hemel Hempstead: Harvester Wheatsheaf.

Standing, G. (2002) *Beyond the New Paternalism*, London: Verso.

Stanko, E. (1990) *Everyday Violence*, London: Pandora.

Steiner, H. (1994) *An Essay on Rights*, Oxford: Blackwell.

Sterelny, K. (2001) *Dawkins vs. Gould*, Cambridge: Icon Books.

Stevenson, N. (2002) *Understanding Media Cultures*, 2nd ed., London: Sage.

Stiglitz, J. (2002) *Globalization and Its Discontents*, London: Allen Lane.

Stock, G. (2002) *Redesigning Humans*, London: Profile Books.

Stoney, C. & Winstanley, D. (2001) 'Stakeholding: Confusion or Utopia? Mapping the Conceptual Terrain', *Journal of Management Studies*, 38(5): 603–26.

Strauss, L. (1968) *Liberalism, Ancient and Modern*, New York: Basic Books.

Stubbs, P. (2002) 'Globalisation, Memory and Welfare Regimes in Transition: Towards an Anthropology of Transnational Policy Transfers', *International Journal of Social Welfare*, 11(4): 321–330.

Sullivan, A. (2001) 'Cultural Capital and Educational Attainment', *Sociology*, 35(4): 893–912.

Suzuki, D. & Knudtson, P. (1990) *Genethics*, Cambridge, MA: Harvard University Press.

Svallfors, S. (2002) 'Political Trust and Support for the Welfare State', in Rothstein, B. & Steinmo, S. (eds) *Restructuring the Welfare State*, London: Palgrave.

Svallfors, S. & Taylor-Gooby, P. (2002) *The End Of The Welfare State?*, London: Routledge.

Tawney, R. H. (1931) *Equality*, London: George Allen & Unwin.

Taylor, C. (1994) *Multiculturalism*, Princeton: Princeton University Press.

Taylor, I. (1997) 'The Political Economy of Crime', in Maguire, K., Morgan, R. & Reiner, R. (eds) *The Oxford Handbook of Criminology*, 2nd ed., Oxford: Oxford University Press.

Taylor, I. (1999) *Crime in Context*, Cambridge: Polity.

Taylor, I., Walton, P. & Young, J. (1973) *The New Criminology*, London: Routledge.

Taylor, I., Walton, P. & Young, J. (eds) (1975) *Critical Criminology*, London: Routledge.

Taylor-Gooby, P. (1997) 'In Defence of Second-Best Theory: State, Class and Capital in Social Policy', *Journal of Social Policy*, 26(2): 171–92.

Taylor-Gooby, P. (ed.) (2000) *Risk, Trust and Welfare*, London: Macmillan.

Taylor-Gooby, P. (ed.) (2001) *Welfare States Under Pressure*, London: Sage.

Taylor-Gooby, P. (2004) 'Open Markets and Welfare Values', *European Societies*, 6(1): 29–48.

Taylor-Gooby, P., Hastie, C. & Bromley, C. (2003) 'Querulous Citizens: Welfare Knowledge and the Limits to Welfare Reform', *Social Policy and Administration*, 37(1): 1–20.

Temkin, L. S. (1993) *Inequality*, Oxford: Oxford University Press.

Thompson, J. B. (1990) *Ideology and Modern Culture*, Cambridge: Polity.

Thompson, J. B. (1995) *Media and Modernity*, Cambridge: Polity Press.

Thompson, K. (1998) *Moral Panics*, London: Routledge.

Thomson, M. (1998) *The Problem of Mental Deficiency*, Oxford: Oxford University Press.

Thorngate, W. (2001) 'The Social Psychology of Policy Analysis', *Journal of Comparative Policy Analysis*, 3: 85–112.

Tierney, J. (1996) *Criminology*, Hemel Hemspead: Prentice Hall/Harvester Wheatsheaf.

Titmuss, R. (1970) *The Gift Relationship*, London: Allen & Unwin.

Titmuss, R. (1974) *Social Policy*, London: Routledge.

Tokar, B. (ed.) (2001) *Redesigning Life*, London: Zed Books.

Torfing, J. (1999) *New Theories of Discourse*, Oxford: Blackwell.

Tronto, J. (1993) *Moral Boundaries*, London & New York: Routledge.

Turner, B. (1992) *Regulating Bodies*, London: Routledge.

Turner, B. (1996) *The Body and Society*, 2nd ed., London: Sage.

Twigg, J. (2000) *Bathing*, London: Routledge.

Twigg, J. (2002) 'The Body in Social Policy: Mapping a Territory', *Journal of Social Policy*, 31(3): 421–40.

Vallentyne, P. (2000) 'Introduction' in Vallentyne, P. & Steiner, H. (eds) *Left-Libertarianism and Its Critics*, London: Palgrave.

Vallentyne, P. & Steiner, H. (eds) (2000) *Left-Libertarianism and Its Critics*, London: Palgrave.

van Kersbergen, K. (1995) *Social Capitalism*, London: Routledge.

van Loon, J. (2000) 'Virtual Risks in an Age of Cybernetic Reproduction', in Adam, B., Beck, U. & van Loon, J. (eds) *The Risk Society and Beyond*, London: Sage.

Van Oorschot, W. (2000) 'Who Should Get What, and Why?', *Policy & Politics*, 28(1): 33–49.

van Oorschot, W. (2002) 'Individual Motives for Contributing to Welfare Benefits in the Netherlands', *Policy and Politics*, 30(1): 31–46.

van Oorschot, W. (2003) 'Different Welfare States, Different Social Commitments?', paper presented to the conference Institutions and Inequalities, Helsinki, 20–24 September.

van Parijs, P. (1995) *Real Freedom for All*, Oxford: Oxford University Press.

Veit Wilson, J. (1998) *Setting Adequacy Standards*, Bristol: Policy Press.

Vieraitis, L. M. (2000) 'Income Inequality, Poverty and Violent Crime: A Review of the Empirical Evidence', *Social Pathology*, 6(1): 24–45.

Vold, G., Bernard, T. & Snipes, J. (2002) *Theoretical Criminology*, 5th ed., Oxford: Oxford University Press.

Wacquant, L. (2001) 'Deadly Symbiosis: When Ghetto and Prison Meet and Merge', *Punishment and Society*, 3(1): 95–134.

Wacquant, L. (2003) *Urban Outcasts*, Oxford: Blackwell.

Walker, D. (2002) *In Praise of Centralism*, working paper, Catalyst.

Walker, R. with Howard, M. (2000) *The Making of a Welfare Class?*, Bristol: Policy Press.

Walton, P. & Young, J. (eds) (1998) *The New Criminology Revisited*, London: Macmillan.

Weber, L. & Carter, A. (2003) *The Social Construction of Trust*, New York: Kluwer Academic.

Webster, F. (1995) *Theories of the Information Society*, London: Routledge.

Weight, R. (2002) *Patriots*, London: Palgrave.

Wellman, B. & Haythornthwaite, C. (eds) (2001) *The Internet in Everyday Life*, Oxford: Blackwell.

Westergaard, J. (1995) *Who Gets What?*, Cambridge: Polity.

Western, B. & Beckett, K. (1999) 'How Unregulated is the US Labor Market?', *American Journal of Sociology*, 104(4): 1030–60.

Wetherell, M. & Potter, J. (1992) *Mapping the Language of Racism*, Hemel Hempstead: Harvester Wheatsheaf.

Whitaker, R. (1999) *The End of Privacy*, New York: The New Press.

White, S. (2001) 'The Ambiguities of the Third Way', in White, S. (ed.) *New Labour*, London: Palgrave.

White, S. (2003) *The Civic Minimum*, Oxford: Oxford University Press.

Whitehead, S. (2002) *Men and Masculinities*, Cambridge: Polity.

Wildavsky, A. (1987) 'Choosing Preferences by Constructing Institutions', *American Political Science Review*, 81: 3–21.

Wildavsky, A. (1994) 'Why Self-Interest Means Less Outside of a Social Context', *Journal of Theoretical Politics*, 6: 131–59.

Wilensky, H. (2002) *Rich Democracies*, California: University of California Press.

Wilkinson, R. (1996) *Unhealthy Societies*, London: Routledge.

Williams, F. (1999) 'Good Enough Principles for Welfare', *Journal of Social Policy*, 28(4): 667–87.

Williams, F. (2001) 'In and Beyond New Labour: Towards a Political Ethics of Care', *Critical Social Policy*, 21(4): 467–93.

Williams, R. (1961) *The Long Revolution*, London: Chatto & Windus.

Williams, R. (1966) *Communications*, London: Chatto & Windus.

Williams, R. (1981) *Culture*, London: Fontana.

Williams, S. (2001) *Emotions and Social Theory*, London: Sage.

Wilsford, D. (1994) 'Path Dependency', *Journal of Public Policy*, 14(3): 251–83.

Wilson, E. O. (1975) *Sociobiology*, Cambridge, MA: Harvard University Press.

Wilson, E. O. (1978) *On Human Nature*, Cambridge, MA: Harvard University Press.

Wilson, E. O. (1998) *Consilience*, London: Abacus.

Wilson, J. Q. & Herrnstein, R. (1985) *Crime and Human Nature*, New York: Simon & Schuster.

Wilson, J. Q. (1975) *Thinking About Crime*, New York: Vintage Books.

Wilson, J. Q. (1993) *The Moral Sense*, New York: Free Press.

Wilson, W. J. (1997) *When Work Disappears*, New York: Alfred Knopf.

Witt, R., Clarke, A. & Fielding, N. (1998) 'Crime, Earnings Inequality and Unemployment in England and Wales', *Applied Economics Letters*, 5: 256–7.

Wright, E. O. (1994) *Interrogating Inequality*, London: Verso.

Yeates, N. (2001) *Globalization and Social Policy*, London: Sage.

Yergin, D. & Stanislaw, J. (1998) *The Commanding Heights*, New York: Touchstone Books.

Young, I. M. (1990) *Justice and the Politics of Difference*, Princeton, NJ: Princeton University Press.

Young, I. M. (2000) *Inclusion and Democracy*, Oxford: Oxford University Press.

Young, J. & Mathews, R. (2003) 'New Labour, Crime Control and Social Exclusion', in Mathews, R. & Young, J. (2003) *The New Politics of Crime and Punishment*, Cullompton: Willan Publishing.

Young, J. (1999) *The Exclusive Society*, London: Sage.

Zigler, E., Finn-Stevenson, M. & Hall, N. (2002) *The First Three Years and Beyond*, New Haven: Yale University Press.

Index